UNCHARTED WATERS

THE LIFE & LOVES
OF EMILY FAHRMANN,
AN AUSTRIAN LANDLADY'S
DAUGHTER

EDITHA MARIA FLOSSMANN

ISBN 978-0-9958625-0-0

The author thanks Norma Hill and Dawn Renaud for all their help.

Note to reader:

The ultimate goal of writing my memoir was for cathartic reasons, to find inner peace from the turmoils and challenges of my 'uncharted' life. I hope to reveal some of the psychological dynamics of Emily Fahrmann's family in order to promote an in-depth understanding not only for herself, but for all those concerned, whose names and places I have changed for privacy reasons, as well as to protect the innocent and the guilty. I hope never to offend anyone, rather it is a labor of love in an attempt to enlighten those I dearly miss and love, and to help others who have faced similar circumstances.

Contents

Introduction

2003: OKANAGAN VALLEY, BC; REFLECTIONS AT MOTHER'S GRAVE SITE

It is early autumn. I have enjoyed three glorious hours cycling around the hills of this beautiful community, and I eventually find my way to the cemetery overlooking Lake Okanagan. I soak up the warm rays of the late afternoon sun amidst those who have already departed from this world, including my mother, Margarete Del Fabbrosi, nee Wilflingsider/Fahrmann, laid to rest May 21, 1997. I force myself to say something as I stand beside her grave site. *"Hallo Mutti. Ich bin wieder hier. Das ist Emily, dein kleiner Wonnepfropfen."* – "Hello Mother. I'm here again. This is Emily, your 'chubby cherub.' I've been living here for almost seven years now. See you soon. Bye for now." I leave the cemetery with a mellow, bittersweet feeling. It is nice to walk away without criticism ringing in my ear.

A gentle wind makes happy sounds as it wafts through the trees and caresses my cheeks. The golden leaves glitter everywhere. The air is rich with the scent of fallen leaves and fruit. My negative thinking soon melts away and I am moved to thank the Lord for these precious moments. I also ask for forgiveness, because I am not able to fully appreciate what this country has offered me so far. My disability pension guarantees I will always have a roof over my head and never starve, yet I am full of regrets. I pray for help in my search for more suitable accommodations in this area (*no, not in the cemetery–somewhere brighter, and on a higher elevation*). I am tempted to ask God to take me away now, if paradise is anything like this. I cycle back to my apartment. I place an advertisement in the newspaper: "Lady Writer and Cyclist, in late 50's, needs large bright suite on higher elevation. Small pet. References. Tel. #..."

~/~

It is late autumn now, and I have spent most of the day in bed as if heavily sedated with drugs. That dreaded Seasonal Affective Disorder (SAD), aka Mr. Sad, is lurking around the corner again, prepared to remind me how persistently and relentlessly he has affected my mind, body, and soul, during the dreary months of November, December, January and February (and sometimes in March.) If I were a bird, I would fly south. If I were a bear, I would hibernate. But I am human, and it seems I must suffer here, right to the end of my journey on this planet. Since my depression is at its worst in the morning, I would settle for a half-life of afternoons and evenings, eliminating mornings entirely, if I had a choice.

We desperately need a change of atmosphere from an Octoberfest event, and my friend and I decide to check out a dance at the Legion. As soon as I step into its hall, all thoughts of discrimination seem to have vanished. I have often experienced squirmy feelings at German gatherings, but this time I am fully cognizant of my inner response. It is that of a misplaced child from Europe with a persecution complex. I resent harboring such a confusing heritage. *The people who caused World War II, and its repercussions, are my people. How could I be so torn between sides? Why do I still feel so embarrassed and ashamed? Is this how they feel too?*

~/~

It happens to be at a Valentine's dance in February of 2005, when my ex-boyfriend, with his irresistible charm and charisma, suddenly walks over the dance floor toward me as if nothing had ever happened, and asks me for a dance. We have already broken up twice since we met two years ago, but I can resist neither his ardent words, nor the most gorgeous bouquet of pink carnations, which would remain unusually fresh and vibrant during our reacquaintance.

Soon, we visit his daughter in Vancouver, and by November, we bask in the sun of Mazatlan, Mexico. Mr. Sad is likely tormenting other poor souls in the northern hemisphere, but he has certainly lost his grip on me for the time being.

~/~

I am experiencing the long-awaited sunlight signaling winter's gray days coming to an end. The sun's rays are beginning to flood my apartment in late afternoon. I must schedule my activities so I can be there and catch the magical extended moment of light diffusing in all directions, coloring and highlighting everything in the room with a lively radiance. When my personal space suddenly bursts with life for me, short-lived as it may be, it is the highlight of my day. This is my reward for exercising patience, for when the spell breaks with the setting of the sun I feel encouraged knowing there will be more uplifting afternoon hours, and I am compelled to thank God for his tender mercies. There is a limit to his mercies however, as the advertisement which I placed last fall has long gone unanswered.

~/~

It is a chilly day, and I decide to visit Mother at the cemetery before first snowfall to convey an issue long weighing on my conscience. I say, "Hello Mutti. I hope you don't mind if we go on a new topic. I remember so well how you so joyously celebrated Austrian music, culture, and folklore with me – such precious and happy moments. But I would like you to know, as much as I have cherished those moments, I have had to stifle my inherent joy and pride of being of Austrian descent. Did you know that? I believe it's about something called 'collective guilt.' It might surprise you that I still tend to cringe and feel apologetic whenever I reveal my nationality, particularly to veterans, male or female, who happened to be connected to the allied forces of World War II. Thanks for listening, Mother. It's one more thing off my chest."

~/~

Soon, I come across a book, titled *Tearing the Silence: On Being*

German in America, by Ursula Hegi, and I am swept into a fascinating world of immigrants like myself. In her book, she depicts sixteen Post-World War II German immigrants, who speak out about the legacy of grief and shame which still haunts them. I am mesmerized by their honesty, and relate instantly to the stigma of being born at a certain time and in a certain country. I instantly know her stories are going to serve as stepping stones to reveal my own history.

"Where there is ruin, there is hope for a treasure"
– Rumi

Mother, age 13, 1928; (below) age 15, 1929, a special orphan at the convent in Kitzbuhel, Austria.

My parents on their wedding day in 1939, and (below) with my sister Hanne, when Father home on leave in 1942.

Mother with Hanne, and with the five orphaned children she cared for during the war.

A romantic weekend in the Alps, and the result of their reunion is me.

Hanne holding me at six months; (below) 8 months later.

Hanne and Emily (in the stroller) with Mother, shortly after her hysterectomy in 1948, and (below), one year later, recovered.

Chapter 1

1946: Reinbach-Freistadt, my Birth Town in Austria

I experienced the universal repercussions of World War II within my mother's womb, of that I am certain. My mother had been under considerable pressure to abort me, because she and my father had divorced shortly before my birth. Another fatherless mouth to feed in a war-ravaged and occupied country was not a good idea. Besides, rumors had spread I had to be illegitimate, since they had been apart for most of the war years. In 1940, two years after their marriage, Mother had given birth to my sister Hannelore (Hanne) who had been spared any doubtful squabbles with regard to her legitimacy, but whenever the subject of my legitimacy came up, it was very important for Mother to defend it fervently, and to emphatically assure me Father had formally acknowledged me in a notarized document as his legitimate child. Mother was considered illegitimate because she had been born out of wedlock (1915). She was taken away from her mother, sent to foster parents for six years, when she was finally permitted to return to her newly married mother, and then find herself motherless once more, seven years later, at age thirteen, and sent to a convent. Those seven years with her mother would prove to be the best in her childhood, and that is why I loved it so much when Mother told me that I reminded her of her mother, because she portrayed my grandmother as very kind, loving and popular woman, with the voice of an angel.

Divorce, as a Roman Catholic, or having an illegitimate child was scandalous at that time. Mother would have gotten herself into a serious triple scenario if she had also aborted me. It really made no difference to me who my father was, nor that he was with Mother nine months prior to my birth. It may as well have been a Russian soldier, or the father of the five German foster children she tended to during the war years. However, the concept of having different fathers pleased my sister, since she liked to refer to Father explicitly as *her* father, and she told me he would leave his inheritance solely to *her*. It hurt me deeply to feel invalidated.

I understand why Hanne needed to cling to the idea that Father was exclusively hers. For the first six years of her life, until I was born, she had been the baby of a family of five foster children. She also had Father in her life, but her world had suddenly collapsed when the widowed foster siblings' father, as well as our own father had returned to be with their families at the end of the war. Hanne had been torn away from the only family she had ever known, only to witness Mother and Father's traumatic divorce thereafter (in Reinbach), and to be alienated from extended family on both sides (due to the scandal), and to suddenly be expected to care for a brand-new infant–me.

I was born on June 2, 1946, in Reinbach, near Freistadt, Upper Austria. My mother had already been traumatized from atrocities she had witnessed during the war, and she was distraught having to start all over, from scratch, as it were. She had already been deeply scarred from her own unfortunate childhood, but she liked to tell me she would not have managed very well without me. It seems I gave her a reason to carry on. She told me I was a very quiet and good-natured baby, fussing only if hungry or needing a change. Apparently my large head was a bit of a problem at birth, which I take as a compliment as intelligence housed in above average brain mass. Thirty-six years later, a psychiatrist in Calgary pointed out, "You were just another mouth to feed." I had never perceived myself in such a depressing way. I thought of myself as a peace offering, replacing everything Mother had just lost. I saw myself as a perfectly wonderful consolation prize. A gift of God!

~/~

Shortly after my birth, we had moved from Reinbach (a hamlet nearby) to Freistadt, where we occupied a unit in a barrack (a large simple structure with four or six independent units, originally built to accommodate military personnel), at #87 Salzgasse Street. Mother soon had a hysterectomy while she was hospitalized for a nervous breakdown. I was allowed to stay on the sick babies' ward on condition I didn't disturb the others. I passed with flying colors, except the time I got a little creative on the wall after sitting on my potty for too long. I can vaguely remember being carried around by doctors and staff, and I clearly remember the anticipation I felt when we approached Mother's ward. I had to be restrained from trying to dive down to be with my mommy too quickly, lest I were to cause injury to her wound. She breast-fed me for a long time. That was a good thing, and it was free to boot. It embarrassed me a bit knowing that at the age of two, I was still searching for her generous breasts. She was very well endowed.

~/~

Mother was a highly qualified, convent-educated nanny, and had always put her charges outside to sleep for fresh air all year round, including a doctor's baby boy she had taken care of until she married Father, and she put her own babies outside to sleep too. Mother came back from doing errands one day, to find my hands poking out from under my blankets, white and frozen solid. I am thankful she told me about the incident, because thirty years later, I was able to connect it to its probable cause when I was diagnosed with Raynaud's Syndrome.

I vaguely remember walking along a chestnut tree-lined avenue leading through the city tower and into the medieval city center, the *Hauptplatz* of Freistadt, while holding on to my sister's hand as she dropped me off at kindergarten. I looked up into the sky, in hopes of spotting a stork flying over us with a baby swaddled under its beak, and I clearly remember as Mother's boyfriend, who boarded at the back of our barrack, one day trying to carry me off to kindergarten as I protested angrily, kicking and screaming in his arms.

I was playing doctor and nurse under a shady tree with another toddler one day just as Hannelore whipped by on her way home from school to see me sprinkle sand into the toddler's belly button. *"Aber das sage Ich sofort der Mutter."* – "I am going to tell Mother about this!" she snapped. I was afraid of a spanking, but I wasn't reprimanded.

One day, Mother took me to the storage area at the back of our barrack where I saw little cubicles, all stacked-up with baby rabbits huddling together. She protected me from the gruesome thought of their ultimate demise because I did not see them very often while they were growing up, but we probably ate rabbit stew, and were dressed up warmly from head to toe, in luxurious white rabbit fur.

I spent Christmas in the hospital in the latter part of December of 1949. I had broken my left arm while sliding down a hill on my backside. It was on a school day, and no one had been around the little hill on which the older kids normally tobogganed. Mother had heard my screams from the barrack's kitchen window, and pulled me to the hospital on a sled. By then, she was irate too.

I screamed louder at the X-ray machine than I did for my broken arm, but there were nice daddy-figures I tried to charm out of my hospital crib. It was like *deja vu*, because the hospital had already been home to me when Mother had her hysterectomy, and I was told how much I had been missed at home over Christmas, especially by my sister (of all people). According to Mother, Hanne cried, *"Aber Emily is net da."* – "But Emily isn't here." However, the hospital was more fun than the days I had spent in our barrack by myself, or heaven forbid, having to stay with the neighbors down the hallway, which I hated. Their place was not clean like ours. They had earwigs crawling in and around clothing piled up on a couch, and I refused to go there. I preferred to stay at home alone. I guess I was somewhat fussy. I would not even accept food someone had already taken a bite of. I found the smell of anything made of plastic, such as plastic aprons or plastic tablecloths, offensive, and I did not appreciate a cheaply manufactured four-inch doll with flimsy clothes manufactured in a foreign country.

I remember Mother and a neighbor from down the barrack's

hallway glancing in on me with great approval for having voluntarily stood in a corner for time out after having inadvertently torn a page in a book. I remember sitting on a medieval Gothic pew beside Mother, with a *Groschen* – a penny, held tightly in my hand. I found it hard to let go when the collection pouch, made of purple satin, and attached to a long pole, came around. We tried to be good Roman Catholics.

Some neighbors, even a doctor, cautioned Mother not to leave me by myself so much. "She is too cute. She could easily be abducted" – *"Auf die mussen Sie einmal aufpassen."* – "Make sure you look after her." She had nicknamed me *Wonnepfropfen* – dumpling of joy, or sunshine, or chubby cherub, so I perceived myself as a special gift of God very early in life. The doctor's warning turned into a prophecy however, and Mother and Hannelore must have felt very bad for the secret they were compelled to keep from me for a very long time.

When Mother came home at the end of the day, there was much joy and excitement in the air over all the things she produced out of her backpack. Her *rucksack* was packed with staples such as eggs, bacon and bread and butter, and I was lavishly praised for having been so good, which made my long day's wait worthwhile. I took great pride in having been brave at home alone, while my sister was at school and stayed out with her friends. When I was old enough to understand Mother's accounts of her travels from farm to farm to barter her fine sewing, beautiful rabbit furs, and three-piece crucifix sets in exchange for food, I came to admire her very much for her industriousness. I thought we were way more fortunate than other children, whose parents didn't seem to care nearly as much as Mother did, all by herself. She was larger than life to me. She had to be the best mother in the world, because she said so, and I was simply in awe of her. I developed a superiority complex based on her accomplishments. She even remodeled used army uniforms into stylish and colorfully embroidered ladies' suits. I felt like nothing would ever go wrong as long as I loved and obeyed her unconditionally.

The best example of Mother's pluck and humor would be her story about hiking to farms to barter bootleg, after having bartered religious crucifix sets of the Holy Trinity. The farmer jokingly, yet affectionately greeted her with, *"Aber so was, einmal kommt sie mit den heiligen Geist, and jetzt kommt sie mit den Teufel"* – "Would you believe it? Last time she brought the Holy Spirit and here she is selling the devil himself." She also told us of her skirmishes with Russian soldiers when she got too close to a forested section of the Czechoslovakian border. *"Sie haben mich fast geschossen mit meinen verrenkten Bein,"* – "They almost shot me while I was trying to escape with my sprained leg."

Mother liked to start her stories with *"Fruher"*– "before," referring to her memories before the war, as if the present was too painful to discuss. Her sad and sometimes scary stories made me wish with all my heart I could take her back to the five children she had fostered during the war (before I was born), or take her back to her favorite cousin Kaethe in Frankfurt/Oder in Communist East Germany, or even take her back to the nuns in beautiful Kitzbuhel where she had been treated as a special orphan. I wished I were in an orphanage myself. I pictured myself polishing the children's shoes, and leaving them outside their rooms to find first thing in the morning. I fantasized about Mother's favorite people, places, and events, and I made them into my own reality. I couldn't get enough of her stories and fairy tales. I loved the way she told them to me, and how she explained parables and Christian values. I thought I was in heaven compared to all the stories I had heard about more unfortunate children. I felt lucky indeed.

As a four-year old, I found myself on a school stage beside a piano, singing *"Ticke Tacke Tingeling"*, which is an animated cuckoo clock song I had picked up at home from Hannelore's grade three class. The idea was to show them how it really should be sung. Many mothers have dreams for their children. My stage debut might lead to fame and fortune. I didn't turn out to be like Shirley Temple, Annette Funicello, or an academic genius, the role models Mother encouraged me to emulate. Only God knew the trials and tribulations that I would have to endure yet to find a balance between my personal limits and Mother's expectations. My stage debut had not led to fame and fortune, but sixty-seven years later, I would be pleasantly surprised to find myself confidently playing an instrument in front of an audience as a proud member of the newly established ukulele club.

When it came to children and some adults as well, Mother tended to treat them as if orphans, like herself, needy of tender loving care. She liked to rescue people, whether they needed it or not, but of the more affluent children from normal families, she liked to make examples of them for us to emulate, giving us the impression we were quite inferior.

I was too young to remember a short visit from Father at that time, when he had apparently noted, *"Das werden die reinsten Engel."* – *"These girls are turning into perfect angels."* Mother tried hard to make us look spotlessly clean, and use good manners. Mother had intentions of making angels out of us indeed, and I think she was fairly successful, from all accounts.

On a brief stay in a hospital near Linz, all three of us, conveniently, efficiently, and economically, had our tonsils removed simultaneously. I remember being anesthetized on a nurse's lap, and being asked to count (forward or backward) as far as I could. Mother told me that as soon as I had come around again, I immediately screamed for something to drink. In baby talk, it was *"Muelchie, Teelie, Cafeeli!"* – *"Milk, Tea, Coffee!"* My crying out in a hospital would remain as my last public vocal solo, after having sung the little cuckoo clock song in kindergarten not long ago, because I had heard that I would not be able to sing again without my tonsils intact. Hanne most likely believed that she had lost her singing voice permanently as well, because I never heard her sing, not even in church, where she criticized my attempt to carry a tune.

I was six years younger than Hanne, so I had to stay inside after supper and longingly watch from the bedroom window while I heard her having fun playing ball with her friends. Mother would give me a *"Zuckerl"* – "a candy" to pacify me, but as much as I tried, I couldn't settle down until we were in bed all together, and give thanks, sing, and say our prayers, turn over on our right sides, and go to sleep.

~/~

From the time I left the crib, I slept between Mother and my sister. While their proximity kept me extra warm in the winter, it wasn't so great, because I eventually landed on the crack between the two single beds that had been pushed together, and I had to keep perfectly still lest I awake either. However, we were safe and sound, with hot bricks wrapped in towels, keeping our feet warm. I couldn't wait until Mother finally joined us after she had made her preparations for the next day, and filled the vacant space beside me at last, so I could cuddle up to her warm body, and commence with our nightly routine. We started with repetitive prayers, *Vater Unser* and *Jesukindlein komm zu Mir* – The Lord's Prayer, and Jesus, Come to me, then we followed with singing (a mix of gospel and folk songs) with Mother's soprano in the lead, and our shy voices as her back up. Our performance must have reverberated throughout the four double units of our barrack, and we had, no doubt, earned the occupants' respect if not of all the neighbors' across the street as well. I think Hanne slept on the very edge of her side of the bed, and I was hardly ever aware she was actually near us. She never cuddled up to us. Before we said *"Gute Nacht"* – "Good Night", Mother reminded us to turn to our right sides, as not to breathe on each other, as well as for heart-smart reasons, claiming that the position was easier on the heart.

Our faith had been firmly established. So were my sleeping habits. My freedom to change positions and adjust blankets and pillows, without worrying about waking anyone, to this day, is a luxury I don't take for granted.

Hannelore and I attended a summer camp for underprivileged children the year before we left Freistadt. I was too young to join the rest of the children on their daily hikes into the mountains. I was three, the youngest there, but I enjoyed a freshly peeled apple slice handed to me by a kitchen aide working outside on a picnic table. I wandered around the vacated campsite until they came marching back, all in a row. For our afternoon naps, we rested on dozens of cots, all pushed together, trying hard to be quiet.

In Braunau, on Mattigstrasse, 1952.

Mother looking pretty good, considering she just had all her teeth extracted and was waiting for new dentures, 1953.

Chapter 2

1950: BRAUNAU, AUSTRIA; MATTIGSTRASSE

I remember dozing on Mother's lap throughout the night, while her musician boyfriend drove us (and our possessions stowed in the back of the truck) from Freistadt to Braunau-am-Inn. Mother had taken him up on his offer to move us to Braunau, hoping to use its strategic location on the border of Germany as a gateway back to Wasserburg-am-Inn where she had fostered the motherless family of five during the war years. We found ourselves relocated into a modest addition built onto a small house on a gravel road called Mattigstrasse.

~/~

The only barrier to Wasserburg-am-Inn from Braunau was German customs at the other side of the river Inn, which Mother was not aware of, had been closed to migrants since the end of the war. But I have reasons to suspect a reunion with the German family was not feasible in any case.

In a touching poem of gratitude written in 1945 to "Fahrmann Mutti" (as they had affectionately referred to my mother) by the father of the five children she had fostered, Mr. Alois Bauer gently reminded her that since the war was over, her duties lay with her husband Raymund (our father), with my sister Hannelore, and with an expected baby (me), back in their native Austria, even though they would not know if their apartment was still intact.

Zur dankbaren Erinnerung an die
Großtat, unserer Hofmann Tante wäh-
rend des Krieges 1941-45 in Wasserburg

O' treues goldenes Mutterherz,
du warst uns Sorgenbrecherin im ärgsten Schmerz,
du half'st überwinden all das Leid,
das durch den Tod einer Mutter uns zugeteilt.

Fünf Waisen hast du mit Liebe bedacht
und mit rührendster Sorgfalt treu bewacht-
du kanntest weder Eigennutz noch Gewinn
dein Tat ist heilig, rein deutscher Sinn.

Ob' gleich auch, quälender Schmerz
dein Herz oft bedrückt,
es ist die Sorge um deinen Liebsten,
der dich einst mate beglückt,
er kämpft treu für die Heimat
und du, stehst in der Tat nicht zurück.

Aus Dankbarkeit gewidmet von

Wasserburg a. Inn, den 16. 2. 45   Alois Bauer
Ich war bis Ost. 1945 dort !

This is the original letter of gratitude from Mr. Alois Bauer.
Whenever I read this tribute, it is a reminder that Mother was
one of the thousands of unsung heroes who bravely held up
the fort while their men were at war.

In Gratitude for the Courageous Deed
of our Fahrmann Auntie
during WWII 1941–1945

Oh faithful golden mother's heart
You came to rescue in our grief
Three boys, two girls
To comfort pain, so bereaved
It was our mother, you did substitute.

Five orphans, embraced in love
Bestowed with touching concern
In selfless measure without gain, non compensate
Your deed was holy, pure, German ideal

Though your heart ached with tortuous pain
It is the care for your loved ones
That fills you with joy
He fought with valor for the homeland
And you, his wife, did not fail.

Gratefully dedicated by Alois Bauer
Wasserburg am Inn. 16/2 1945

~/~

Hannelore continued making a beeline for the door and some-times out of the window to escape Mother's persistent demands, obviously not giving a hoot about the threats or the beatings she risked by abandoning me for her friends, and any opportunity gave her automatic license to escape from her dreaded care giving duty as a big sister. Once, when she had darted back inside, I heard real and unusual passion in her voice, *"Ich mochte so gerne ein Pferd haben!"* – "Oh, I'd love to have a horse!" When we were much older, I also heard her say, "I was aware Mother was mental-ly ill, so I just carried on with my own life." When I asked her if she had ever witnessed my being abused, she retorted, "Well, I would never let that happen to me!" I just could not accept the fact that my sister plainly and simply resented me and my needy loneliness. Or perhaps it was the whole situation she resented.

Whenever Mother's musician boyfriend showed up, I was so elated that I'd screech with excitement. I felt like an adorable little girl as soon as I saw his big smile and heard his enthusiastic *"Hallo meine kleine Emily"* – "Hello my little Emily", like a long-lost father would, when he had just found his way home. Then he tickled me. And sometimes he tickled me until I cried and begged for mercy. But Mother was confident that I was happy and in good care, and left us in our playful merriment and took advantage of an opportunity to do something really productive, such as explore a new bartering business. My fun and laughter suddenly stopped during that visit. I have no recollection of the rest of that day.

The following morning, Mother, verbally irate, took me by the hand, and briskly walked me up to the neighboring farm. I knew this man must have done something very bad to have so severely upset her. I knew it had to do with me because her eyes and fingers pointed toward me while she was expressing her anger. To witness her rage directed at someone else on my behalf and stand up on my behalf had made me feel rather special. The landlady gave Mother permission to search through his closet for the iron he had borrowed from her, and then Mother took me and the iron back home, and that day, Hannelore most likely stayed out as long as possible to avoid Mother's wrath.

After that incident, I was haunted with horrendous nightmares throughout my childhood, and most of my memories of grade one and two are gone, as if a section of a vivid film of memories had been cut off. During one of those episodes, Mother lifted me up into her arms and asked me to explain what was happening. *"Was ist denn los, Schatzi?"* – "What is the matter, sweetie?" Not able to explain verbally, I made a fist with her hand and tried to shove it down my throat to demonstrate a suffocating feeling. In the attacks, I spiraled upwards, squelched into a tight ball, through a tubular tunnel, as if propelled at a seemingly supersonic speed towards a distant light. I dreaded being swept away with a force of such magnitude that just could not be controlled. Rumors had spread around the community about my screaming attacks, and some kids on the street asked me what had happened. I almost felt like a celebrity with all the unusual attention I was getting. The attacks mercifully drifted away during my adolescence.

Mother showed me how to find my way to kindergarten in downtown Braunau. Hanne must have been in grade five, and her new school was located in another direction, a bit closer to home. One cold and rainy morning, Mother tied a coin into my handkerchief and told me to catch the commuter bus on top of the hill. I had a lot of trouble untying my hankie in front of the bus driver, and he helped me untie it. The air was stuffy, the bus was filled with standing-room-only dejected looking workers, and I never took the bus downtown again.

~/~

To get to kindergarten, I walked up the hill to the main road, turned left past the local tavern, went along a country road, past some wheat fields lined with red poppies and dotted with blue cornflowers, past railway tracks, a chestnut tree-lined avenue, a residential community, some cobble-stoned sidewalks, shops, a cloister, and an old folks' home. When I reached the huge city center, I saw the majestic St. Stephan's church towering on the other side, a medieval drawbridge to the left, and a huge bridge to the right. There were so many interesting things to see and stop for, that I hardly ever arrived where I was supposed to be – at kindergarten. I had an independent spirit. The poppies and cornflowers in the wheat field, the fallen chestnuts, and the inner-city park behind the ancient church were laden with gorgeous spring flowers. *Schneeglokchen* – snowdrops, in particular, made my heart sing. I liked to cross the bridge over the mighty River Inn, towards the German town of Simbach, and walk as far as the border guard station. I usually devoured my bun and apple in a nice spot under a shady tree way before lunchtime. That proved far more interesting than boring old kindergarten.

One of my favorite haunts was the *"Kapuzinerkirche"* – "The

Kapuziner Church", the home of some very nice nuns, and of some very poor old people. At Christmas time, the foyer of the nunnery had an ornate display of mechanically animated characters set in a charming miniature village. I dropped in and admired it every day on my way to kindergarten. Mother had already taken me up the narrow and winding stone staircase to visit the nuns and see if they had any handouts. So I availed myself to do the same whenever possible, because they were always nice, and sometimes they gave me a handkerchief, *ein Zuckerl* – a candy, or something little from a very special drawer. I was still in no hurry to get to kindergarten, so l walked up the empty church's center aisle, knelt in front of the altar with my arms wide open, and prayed and sang just like I had seen people doing on Sunday mornings. I was unaware of the amused and chuckling nuns who had seen me from the back balcony, until news of it got back to Mother, who was puzzled but never scolded me over my truancy.

Coming back from kindergarten was not as interesting though, as the sun was setting, and I tended to straggle. What was the hurry anyway? I must have been later than usual one day, when I spotted my sister cycling toward me. As she came closer, I heard her sobbing. Mother had sent her out to search for me. They must have panicked at the thought of me being kidnapped, or worse. She looked so relieved to have found me, and I felt wanted as she pedaled me back home. I felt so blessed. I had knelt at the altar and worshiped God early in the morning, and I had enjoyed God's beautiful creations all day.

Those feelings could change in an instant when Mother wanted to put me in my place. She resorted to repeating something Hannelore would have tattled against me: *"Was Hannelore sagte ist wahr. Warte nur, was Du mit der noch erlebst."* – "Hannelore was right by saying I was going to experience nothing but trouble with you."

At one point, Hanne's friend slapped me on the cheek because I tried to join in a game of tag, but I felt loved anyway as I walked home to mommy, crying. It must have been my Heavenly Father having pity on me. In defense of Hanne, I found her grade six class picture, in which my very blond sister looked quite stressed, even traumatized. No doubt, she had hardships of her own I didn't know about.

I clearly remember a lovely bed-time ritual, in which Mother had me write a little note to my special friends the angels, fold it up, and slide it into a crack in the windowsill for them to find during the night, hopefully answered by the morning. When I found it gone, or acknowledged with another note, I became a true believer in the communion with the angels. The joy and awe inspiring feeling I experienced from that wonderful ritual helped me take everything else that was happening in stride. Later in life, I would learn that angels are glorious spirit persons, intelligent and powerful, and that their ranks include seraphs and cherubs, and that the Bible mentions angels more than 250 times.

When I had tucked my beloved doll under its covers, and got tired of experimenting with Mother's sewing supplies, I imagined angels all around me, unless too many hours had passed waiting for Mother and Hanne, and the minute hand on the clock wouldn't move fast enough anymore. And when the clock seemed to come to a standstill (although the dials were still moving), an agonizing pain of loneliness would set in. I listened to its ticking while I looked out of the window, patiently waiting, with an awareness of a long day gone by as dusk was approaching like a heavy fog, and no one had arrived yet. Fortunately, the landlord I feared so much never forced his way into our suite, but he might have been lurking around the outhouse, so I waited to use the facilities until Mother and sister came home. I also visualized a farm-wives' tale going around about big rats suddenly jumping up from its hole, and I looked forward for my special bed time ritual with the angels to re- encourage me once more.

One night both Mother and my sister were out late. Mother was doing errands, and Hanne was at gymnastics. I was getting anxious for their return, when all of a sudden I heard an eerie, low voice outside the doorway mumbling, *"Hallo, hallo, ist jemand da?"* – "Hello, hello, is anyone here?" But the owner of the voice wouldn't make himself or herself apparent, and my imagination started to take over. The door opened slowly and I still heard only the ghostly *"Hallo."* While I slowly huddled against the nearest wall at the back of the room in anticipation of a monster about to pounce, a short, little old farm woman appeared and said, "You must be Emily. Is your mommy not home?" Just then Mother appeared, and greeted the woman with a friendly hello. The woman had been an old friend hoping to find a home for one of her German Shepherd pups she had had tied up outside. We didn't have the space or resources to adopt one of those adorable pups.

I tried to please Mother with masked smiles, unconditional obedience and even with white lies to help ease her frequent heart-wrenching anguish. "Children are meant to be seen, not heard! Speak only when spoken to! Ten boys are better than you two girls! There should be more beatings than feedings." Her vocabulary of swear words was quite impressive, considering she was convent educated. She liked to use sacred names in vain, sometimes in a succession of long, angry, one-word phrases like *"Jessas-Maria-und-Josef-aber-du-gehst-uber-eine-Leiche"* – *"*Jesus-Mary-and-Joseph! You'll-stomp-on-dead-corpses-yet."* That was directed at my sister's apparent cold indifference. When Hanne lost something, Mother screamed, *"Du wirfst Geld ins Fenster hinaus!"* – "You are throwing money out the window!" I felt so sorry for my mother. She had just had all of her teeth extracted and she complained a lot about dampness in the walls.

I can still feel the sharp sting on my cheek after receiving *eine Ohrfeige* – a smack on of the face, because I was not sitting or eating properly, but I took great pride in keeping a straight face. Crying or sulking would have been a sure invitation for a smack on the other side. I never got the strap, which held a high place of dignity hung high beside the pantry, but one parental glance in that general direction was all it took to keep me in line. Besides, I had already acquired the knack of punishing myself for imaginary bad behavior. By age eight, I had graduated from voluntarily running to the corner as a toddler, to kneeling on the sharpest corner of a piece of firewood to experience intense pain as long as possible.

One of my true sources of pleasure was Mother's sewing basket, which to me was a veritable toy chest to experiment with needle and thread. I even sewed a neat little lattice into the surface skin on the palm of my hand. One expression, *"Langes Fadchen, faules Madchen"* which means "Long thread, lazy maid" was meant to avoid terribly long strands of thread. For better results, shorter strands were considered best, though they called for more work with the extra cutting, threading and tying of knots.

On my way home from school I tried to find some logic in my eight-year old brain as to what "more beatings than food" meant, while a kindly older girl helped me find the bobby pin I was desperately trying to find in the middle of the gravel road. But as I wandered down the road toward the railway crossing and the creek, I cheered myself up by practicing a tongue twister Mother had taught me, which, in colloquial Austrian dialect came out as, *"Bschteck Tschpaedt Bschtoild"* which in formal German means *"Besteck zu spät bestelled",* and in English meaning "Cutlery has been ordered too late." Having mastered my most challenging tongue twister, I would ponder over whimsical sounding French words, such as parapluie (umbrella), portefeuille (wallet), and bibliotèque (library), which had been incorporated into our everyday language.

We were disciplined to exercise delayed gratification when everything was hard to come by and rationed out. Chocolate, or lack of it, especially comes to my mind. I was nine when I had received my first little chocolate Easter bunny. Mother put it up on a shelf for several weeks, and I yearned for it so much, that I don't remember actually getting any of it. There was plenty of farm-fresh milk, cream of wheat, potatoes, onions, sauerkraut, bread, butter, sugar and lard, and I enjoyed almost everything placed in front of me and it showed in my slightly chubby frame, but I was always hungry, most likely for lack of protein. I ate heartily, contrary to Hanne, who was a very picky eater. She favored pickles, sauerkraut, yogurt and soup, and she was usually gone before the main course. Somehow, Mother made everything look and taste good. She produced exquisite baking from the wood stove, one of which was a family favorite, "Linzer Gitter Kuchen." That's because *"Mit Liebe gekocht"* – "Cooked with Love", she said. And somehow she made sure our personal grooming and oral hygiene were impeccable. A teacher noted, *"Ihre Madel stechen aus mit Sauberkeit"* – "Your girls stand out in cleanliness." We also had to practice good posture. As we hiked along a country road she'd remind us, *"Brust hinaus, Bauch hinein!"* – "Chest out, tummy in!" Yes, Mother was very health and body-image conscious.

I don't know what happened late one night, but I found myself walking close to Mother's left hand side. She had a suitcase in each hand. Hanne was at her right side. We were walking down Mattigstrasse towards the Mattig (a small river which flowed north towards the mighty river Inn). *"Wir gehen zu Gott!"* – "We are going to join God!" she cried part way down the road. Obviously she had a change of heart, and we had turned around, walked back home, and went straight to sleep. We started the next day as if nothing had happened.

In one of my childhood dreams, Mattigstrasse conjures up a nightmarish memory: As I was walking to my house, I was being stalked by a tall, skinny man, lasciviously beckoning me, opening and closing his long black overcoat. In real life, that monster landlord had already smashed the exhaust pipe to our wood stove from the outside hallway. Even my sister was afraid of him. His little wife, dressed in black, was a constant, silent shadow in the background. Mother was upset about their goat kept in a stall at the back of the house past the outhouse and mostly locked up twenty-four hours a day. There was ample green space for it to roam in the back pasture, and Mother let the landlord know it.

~/~

Child abuse in many countries was rampant and hardly ever reported or documented in previous generations. Allegations wouldn't hold. The powers that be protected themselves. Mother was a victim of abuse herself. Deeply haunted, she lost her composure for what seemed the most insignificant triggers. I am sure her traumas manifested themselves in manic-depressive episodes. She could be exceedingly engaging, empathetic, encouraging, fun loving and giving when in a good mood, and almost smothered with affection. She certainly had a big heart, and went out of her way to help those less fortunate than we were, and she was definitely not afraid to express her indignation, or defend anyone publicly when justified.

On the other hand, when Mother was down, hellish hysterics broke out of nowhere. She'd swear, place guilt trips, use the strap or the *Pracker* – carpet beater, and she made suicidal threats. I took it all very seriously and Hannelore did not react at all, which really infuriated Mother, and labeled her "stone-cold and heartless, just like Father." Hannlore knew who she was and she had her own resources to resort to. She had developed a personal relationship with Raymond, our father, and with that came special memories and special privileges. I believe she visited him, which would explain some mysterious absences from home. She also took part in elite summer gymnastics camps at Wolfgangsee in the Saltzkammergut, while I roamed around the local neighborhood and countryside to pass the time until Mother came home from her shift work at the American-run aluminum factory in Ranshofen. Neighbors were jealous of her employment there, and spread rumors that she risked losing a finger or two at her *stanzering* work at which, co-incidentally, she excelled with the best of the mainly man-orientated workforce. *Stanzering*, as my Mother explained to me, means the shaping, cutting and molding of metal materials by manually maneuvering specialized machinery. She had been lucky to get the job, and I was relieved she hadn't lost any fingers in an industrial accident.

~/~

I delighted in playing with my beloved doll, doing needlework, newspaper folding (origami), and in constructing little medieval villages and farms with colored wooden blocks of all shapes and sizes, when Mother had brought them out as a special treat to keep me occupied. I sat at our traditional *Bauernstube*, a rustic kitchen nook crafted out of pine wood with a hand carved chandelier hung above it from the ceiling. It had carved Bohemian *Musikanten* – musicians, perched on its arms. I was also enchanted with my china tea set sent from Mother's cousin in communist East Germany, knitting dolls, creating string art, and doing gymnastics with my sister if she was inclined to, but always on Mother's coaxing.

And then there were the meadows and woods where I found total freedom to think and feel whatever came naturally. Full of bliss, I wandered back home, adorned with an array of flowers and leaves, drenched with sunshine and floral fragrance, and with a carefully arranged bouquet of flowers consisting of *Schlusselblumen, Dotterblumen* – cowslips, forget-me-nots, marigolds, and daisies, while anticipating Mother's joyous welcome by clapping her hands and then opening her arms wide to receive them, making me feel like a million dollars. I had a little secret, though. I had come across a clearing in the bush where I had seen the empty shell of an abandoned house. Its windows were shattered and walls damaged. It looked like the ruins of a modern house built not too long ago. It was obvious in my seven-year-old brain this had been the scene of horrible violence. It had to be gun fire. There was no charring by fire. I knew it would upset Mother if I told her.

Everything Mother said and did was emotionally charged, and whether she was happy or angry, mean or sad, I only felt pure love for her. This is the only truth I chose to believe. I have wrestled through a whole gamut of feelings I have harbored for and against her all of my life, and I have come to the conclusion that all that matters is love. If I could not bring myself to love Mother, who had the compassionate heart of a universal mother, I would have been incapable to accept and love myself or anyone else. A German boarder who lived with us for a while had taken note of our special relationship, and he commented, "You two are one heart and one soul."

When we found ourselves outdoors and removed from our everyday drudgery and when Mother broke into song, all was well with the world. Pure harmony existed between us, whether we picked berries and mushrooms, collected firewood, or gleaned for potatoes. I cannot ever remember not feeling exhilarated by the fresh air and freedom I experienced in those fertile, virgin forests of my native land. To keep me busy, while Mother and Hanne picked berries, I built fairy tale castles with all the unique objects one would find in a forest. With a stick I pried out as many similar patches of moss as needed to build up the walls of a castle. Mushrooms, cones, sticks, berries, leaves and imaginary characters completed my enchanted castle.

On some weekends, Mother braided my hair and taught me a song to prepare me for a day of begging. She gave me a bag with handles on it, and lovingly told me to be sure to be back by sunset. Mother had given up hopes of Hanne wanting to accompany me as her resistance was proving to be too strong, and Mother was resigned to shake her head and say, *"Du bist gans der Vater!"* – "You are just like Father!" and then let her go to be with her friends. As I roamed over the fields from farm to farm, I was lucky to get some buns and a few apples. Things were no more profitable in the more affluent part of the city, where mansions had gates with intercoms. I figured out if I pushed the button, my ringing allowed me to come into the servant's quarters. It was embarrassing to sing my song to the amused domestics, sometimes with nothing to walk away with.

I obeyed willingly and jumped when Mother said "jump," whereas Hannelore had a mind of her own and was willing to pay the consequences for rebelling. In her estimation, I was the favored one, but when it came to gymnastics, summer camps and new clothes, I was definitely not included in that league. I suspect Father may have subsidized Hanne's extracurricular activities until we left Austria, but that is only speculation.

I felt very adventuresome when I got to ride our bike (whenever it was not in use by Mother or Hanne) farther out into the countryside to see a farm couple Mother had encouraged me to visit from time to time. I could always expect a warm welcome there, and I remember the wife teaching me how to break an egg into a bowl. She and her husband made me feel like a darling little girl, and they always gave me an opportunity to tell them all about myself. I happened to repeat something I had overheard Mother telling Hanne, and blurted out, *"Wir haben schon achthundert Schilling gesparrt."* – "We already have 800 schillings saved up (around $80Cdn)." Several days later, Mother reprimanded me for having passed on our financial status. I felt betrayed by the couple's lack of confidentiality. My enthusiasm to visit them waned considerably. Who could I trust if not the people who had so doted on me?

On rare occasions, it was my job to do the errand after school when Hanne had missed fetching our daily milk early in the morning. I was still asleep when the poor girl had to get out of our warm bed even on the coldest days, before sunrise. I had forgotten one day, and I came straight home from school. Mother sent me right back out. It was getting dark, and when I thought I saw the farm house in the distance, it was pitch black already. I thought I heard a muffled sound from something approaching me about twenty meters away. It was a vague image of a man riding a bicycle, and threatening, *"Aber jetzt habe ich Dich, aber jetzt habe ich Dich"* – "I'm going to get you. This time I'm going to get you." I already had a habit of diving into a ditch or hiding behind bushes until all real and imagined impending danger, ambulatory, on bicycles, or in vehicles, had passed me by, but this time I did not feel guilty for being disrespectful, since Mother had trained me to greet all adults with a friendly *"Gruss Gott,"* – "Hello," preferably with a little curtsy. I had three choices: to dive into a ditch, in which case he would find me; quickly pass him and keep heading for the farm, but again he would get me; or last, turn around and race back on the road I had come from, along the field and toward the local tavern. The third option was the best one and I sprinted for dear life. Frightened but safe, having outrun him on his bike, I ran up the steps into the local tavern. I think the innkeeper recognized me through the smoke-filled pub as Margarete's eight-year-old daughter and found a gentleman to walk me home. Mother wasn't mad at me, but I was badly traumatized and bedridden for a few days. Rumors spread around the neighborhood that Emily Fahrmann was having strange attacks, and at school my teacher granted me time out to sit against the side wall by the radiator when she noticed signs of an anxiety attack.

Some Saturday mornings, Mother sent us to a Seventh Adventist meeting room in downtown Braunau where we were given biblical pictures to color. We wondered what we were doing there since we were Catholic, but they proved to be a safe contact when Mother had been suddenly hospitalized for a breakdown. She didn't show up at home one day, and Hanne knew just where to find her. Mother had made arrangements from the hospital to have us stay with a Seventh Adventist family who lived farther out in the country. An injured deer was convalescing in a closed-in pen by the edge of a forest, which reassured me I would be safe there too. The family had to stretch their limited vegetarian budget for us, and their parenting seemed even stricter than I was used to. The mother ripped one of the girls' dolls out of her arms for something I did not notice she had done, and she kept it away from her for several days. My Mother would never have denied me of my beloved doll. She even complained about the stained hand towel all six of us had used. And oh, when we were driving past our place on Mattigstasse on our way to school in Laab, my little eight-year-old heart just sank, and repressing my tears was impossible. We said prayers before every meal, at morning and at bedtime, and just before we left the house for the day as well. I longed for Mother's heartfelt tone of voice. I missed my mommy terribly and it was wonderful when we were together again, even in scary circumstances, such as the time we were stranded in a field next to a forest.

Under a late autumn sky, I had been patiently keeping watch over our broken-down, two wheeled cart, piled up with firewood that Mother and I had collected at the edge of a forest. Before the sun was beginning to set, a worker in the adjacent field next to an electrical station had spotted me and called out from the distance, *"Mochtest Du ein Bischen von meinen Brot?"* – "Would you like to share my sandwich?" I was tempted, but resisted, and shyly called back, *"Nein danke"* – "No, thank you." Mother had hiked into town a short while ago for a replacement cart, and she had told me, *"Sei braf und bewahrst das Holz, gel?"* meaning, "Be good and watch over the wood, okay?" Hours later, much to my relief, she reappeared again, looking fatigued, as if she had just burst out of a cosmic veil of a dark and scary universe, and she said, *"Du warst braf"* – "Good Girl". We then proceeded to transfer the firewood onto the new cart, and safely hauled it home.

On hot summer days, we hiked to a small pond to cool off. A horse's head floating at the other end didn't deter us, and I managed to teach myself to swim. There was also a city pool for a small fee, which served the purpose too, but it didn't have a shallow end, it was hard to hold onto the edges, and it was impossible to find a dry spot to sit on in a sea of mud saturating the surrounding grass.

During our stay in Branuau, we took some day-trips within Upper Austria. The first was to Mother's birthplace of Peuerbach, which is in the province of the Muhlviertel. After a short train ride, we ended up hiking over countryside to a farm house where distant relations used to live when Mother was little. The young generation were very friendly and they obviously thought I was really cute, when I showed off with *Purzelbaums* – somersaults on the wooden floor. Our welcome seemed short lived however, and we had to leave. While we were walking along the countryside for our return train, Mother broke into loud sobs. Her childhood memories had no doubt resurfaced, perhaps back to age thirteen, to her mother's funeral where large crowds had attended, perhaps to the tranquil days herding goats in lush pastures, and now we had all been rejected, and apparently I had been too rambunctious! As if it had been my fault, she cried, *"Warum warst Du so ubermutig?"* – "Why were you so rambunctious?"

The next trip was to the Wachau valley on the Danube, where Mother and I arrived at a farm house. She told me to wait outside and she walked up a long flight of stairs into the living quarters of strangers, and I meandered into an orchard in full bloom. I was nibbling on wild spinach when Mother called me for our trip back home.

Hanne's catechism class (above); she is in the third row, fourth from the left. Note the stark contrast of black robes among the white dresses. I'm in the front row, far right, in my grade 2 class photo (below); Mother marked an 'x' on my leg.

Hanne and Emily in matching outfits; Nanny Anneliese is on the right with puppy, and our sponsor and her daughters are in the middle.

With Anneliese, our nanny.

Chapter 3

1954: A SURPRISE VISIT TO OLTEN, SWITZERLAND

I woke up to Mother's voice telling Hanne, *"Emily wacht auf. Jetzt konnen wir gehen."* – "Emily is waking up. We can go now." I noticed water rising toward the top of my bed and flowing throughout our apartment. When we saw severe structural cracks developing in houses across the street, we rushed up the hill behind our house and watched, as one by one, the houses crashed into the river. We had no choice but to wait for assistance. It was in the summer of 1954, and the river Mattig across our street had flooded overnight and the dam upriver had been released.

The Red Cross relief society immediately arranged for all children, from ages six to twelve whose families had been affected by the flood, to be sent to Switzerland. My sister, being six years older than I, did not qualify at age fourteen.

Early the next morning, I found myself shoved away from a window inside the train by other children desperately trying to wave goodbye to their families. Mother noticed I had been crying and trying to force myself off the train, and just as I was about to step off, I saw my sister come aboard. Mother's frantic pleas had persuaded a Red Cross supervisor to allow Hanne to join me. My tears had saved the day of our departure, and they would save the day again on our final destination in Switzerland.

Halfway to Switzerland, we had an overnight layover at a school near Vorarlberg in the Austrian Alps. We waited in the school yard while one child at a time was called inside for identification purposes. My sister's turn had been unusually long, and I started to worry if they had sent her back home to Austria because she had exceeded the age requirements. Much to my relief, I saw her come out of the building into the school yard to tell me she was allowed to come along with me. I thought it was fun to be settling down with so many other children for the night, and it was comforting to have my sister at my side.

The next day, various children were dropped off at successive Swiss villages. It was our turn to get off in Olten. It was Red Cross policy to keep siblings together, but a volunteer asked us if it was okay if one of us went ahead to a neighboring village, in which case we would still be able to visit each other on occasion. I instantly started to cry, whereupon a lady took pity on us, stepped forward, and offered to take both of us. My tears had saved the day again.

The first impression of my new home was of impressive gardens, fountains, and a mini-forest at the periphery. As we entered a huge foyer, it reminded me of some of the mansions I had seen at home, except I didn't have to sing a song for a handout at this door. We were greeted by a cook and a nanny named Anneliese. We also met the lady's very handsome husband, and their two daughters, who were around our age. They stayed with their grandparents most of the time. I had a feeling they did not take too well to a sudden invasion of their own territory. In a photo, the darting eyes of the older girl tells it all. Our cozy bedroom on the main floor was furnished with huge four-poster beds and fluffy down bedding one could get lost in.

Every evening, the lady of the house worked on knitted pullovers for us, one in yellow for Hanne, the other in red for me. I was delighted to have strangers being so kind to us. Some mornings we woke up to identical outfits laid out for us, and eventually our old clothes and luggage had been entirely replaced. When the lady took us to a department store in downtown Olten to have our feet measured for new shoes, she chose more clothing for us. She had them packed and she didn't have to pay for them. We realized then that she and her husband were the owners of the store.

During our stay, we had a visit by two Red Cross representatives to check up on us. We were just fine. Of course there was no abuse to report, but if there had been, I would not have been able to express it. Children were told to speak only if spoken too, and even then, we were much too afraid to say anything.

Only one thing I remember not liking was how the cook prepared julienne carrots. She made a sugary glaze for the dish, which I just could not stomach. A more positive memory which stands out was the radiant smile the father had for me, and I for him. He said, *"Wie die lacht,"*—"What a smile," as he and his wife, both elegantly attired and looking ever so happy together, left the house for a social or business meeting. I hadn't experienced a happy family before, and for the first time in my life, I had a taste of what I had been missing.

After some time, we were pretty sure we would get away with a little teasing of our nanny, Anneliese. A song that came to our mind was titled after her namesake. It was a lamenting love song called *"Anneliese, ach Anneliese, Warum bist du Bose auf Mich?"* – "Anneliese, oh Anneliese, Why are you Angry with Me?" I thought it was quite bold of us to test her gentle disposition this way, but Anneliese took it all in stride and smiled, much to my delight and relief.

We had some picnic outings on alpine meadows and we chased wild horses. When the daughters came back from their grandparents, we created a puppet show with some of their friends, and we also went to the community pool where I rediscovered my ability to swim as I had taught myself in the local pond a year earlier. My fantasy dream life soon came to an end, however, and I hadn't even cried for Mother. It was getting well into September or October, and it was time to go home. We had already missed six weeks of school, as noted on my frayed grade three report card.

On our return trip, we watched the other children gathered at the various villages. Some did not look very happy or healthy, and I thought to myself how lucky we had been. I do not remember any solid food, but a lady walked up and down the train with a bucket full of hard candy. Hannelore let me lean on her shoulder, to snooze on the wooden benches while the train rolled through the mountains back into Austria.

The first thing Mother said when we had gotten off the train in Branuau was, *"Oh, Ihr habt zugnommen."* – "Oh, you've both gained weight!" Mother looked so different with a new perm. We had a Swiss greeting song and a poem ready for her. The poem was, *"Schwitzer Madle, Mogst'n Kaese?"* – "Swiss Girl, do You Love Cheese?" and the song was, *"Yuhee I Bin a Swizer!"* – "Yippee, I am Swiss."

No doubt Hannelore would rather have spent the summer with her peers and have started gymnastic classes at the very beginning of the season, but I was glad to have had her with me during our sojourn in Switzerland. I was also very proud to wear my beautiful new clothes to school.

Mother most likely exceeded her expectations of our Swiss sponsors through continued requests for support, and I really don't blame her. She had been struggling as a single breadwinner in a war-ravaged country for eight years, and she was prone to nervous breakdowns. We lost contact with our kind and generous sponsors and Mother would eventually find another who would help us. My time in Switzerland is my best childhood memory, beside my escapes to the meadows.

~/~

The following year, we were about to visit a gentleman in St. Gallen, Switzerland (not far from Olten, where Hanne and I had been staying with our Swiss sponsors. I wonder, in retrospect, if Mother had hoped to reconnect with them). I was all wound up in anticipation of our new adventure. I had the impression we were leaving shortly. I had been patiently waiting outside for quite some time and went back inside to ask Mother if we were leaving soon, since our luggage was packed ready to go, and a cherry cake, a *bisquit roulade*, our lunch for the trip, was cooling on a window-sill. She told me that she had yet to sew up a pair of travel pants for me to wear on the trip. I was really exasperated by then because I'd had the impression we were leaving that morning. My patience had already been tried, but I continued waiting outside, for what seemed an eternity. Hanne was much smarter in some respects. She amused herself with her friends, and seemed to show up just in time for our long walk to the train station the following morning.

The breathtaking vistas of the Alps, and beautiful Lake Constance (Bodensee), all lit up by the night lights of Breganz, kept us awestruck and we didn't get much sleep, so when we had finally arrived in St. Gallen, we went to sleep as soon as we were welcomed into a house. Something had gone wrong overnight, because in the morning Mother told us we had to leave quickly. We found an embassy barefoot, and someone there helped us retrieve our things, and put us up in a chalet on farmland. In the morning, Hanne and I took a walk along pastoral countryside. Cows, adorned with lovely bells around their necks grazed contentedly in pastures, and along the pathway, a nice man offered us candies. He thought we were very nice girls, *"Nette Madchen."* We visited a zoo, and took a long demanding hike up an alpine trail to a rustic old chalet where children took turns on a swing hanging perilously close to a steep mountainside. I felt quite privileged to have a turn at it, while wondering if someone was going to eventually serve bread and butter. I had spotted some adults drinking beer, but no one eating. We quenched our thirst from troughs filled with pure mountain water – the best! In a photo from that excursion, Hanne and I still wear the identical outfits we had received in Olten a year earlier. No doubt, Mother adjusted the buttons to the skirts, because we wore them for another two or three years.

~/~

When I was in grade three, Mother had found an affordable barrack in the suburb of Laab (where we ended up living for our last year and a half in Austria). Hannelore had dropped out of school and enrolled in a hairdressing course. The community of Laab was much closer to school, and we had finally gotten away from that scary landlord as well as from the pervasive dampness in the walls that Mother had always complained about. I was hardly aware of the presence of a municipal dump behind the barracks since I still had open fields and meadows to roam in, and Mother made sure no men ever came around again.

There was an open field between our barrack and our auxiliary church where we frequently attended mass due to its close proximity, rather than take the long walk to St. Stephen's church in downtown Braunau. Some youth offered me a hot potato cooked over a small fire in the middle of the field. I will never forget how much I savored that little potato; the best spud I have ever had. Not far away in the middle of the field, we had also discovered an entryway to a spooky maze of underground tunnels with partitions, in which frightened families had hidden away during WWII air raids.

Mother sent me to the auxiliary church to confess my sins. I told the priest I had seen a naughty picture, *"Ich habe ein hassliches Bild gesehen"*– "I saw a naughty picture". That's all I could make up. The priest came to my class once a week to teach us catechism. I felt stigmatized for being the child of a divorce. I could tell from how he looked at me differently, as if repulsed at the sight of me. Consequently, Mother sent me to the downtown school in the morning. I took a spare seat at the back of a classroom filled with unfamiliar students. The teacher asked me what I was doing there. "My mother told me to come to this school from now on." She put me on a telephone with my teacher in Laab (my very first experience on a telephone) and I returned to my school. Everything was okay after that.

Peeking out from the middle of the procession on our way to St. Stephen's Church for First Communion; Braunau, 1955.

When I told Mother that my grade three class was about to have its first trip ever by bus to an abandoned medieval castle, and that a hot lunch would be available for two schillings, she reluctantly gave me the two schillings, and told me to spend it only if necessary. I used one of them for a bowl of hot soup, and brought the other schilling back home, though I would have loved to use it for a buttered bun. At the end of the day, Mother made a glowing example of some girls of whom she had heard of, who did not spend any of their parents' money at all. I felt guilty for not choosing to go hungry that day, and I could have used my latest transgression in the priest's confession booth to *"beichten"* – "confess" my latest sin, if I'd remembered to do so.

I was used to going hungry at times. One morning before school, Mother told me to see the school's janitor at lunch time. He, his wife and two children were already having lunch in the school's basement suite when I showed up. I told them Mother had sent me there for lunch. I sat down on a nearby stool. Not a word was spoken, and not a morsel was offered while I watched them self-consciously eat their lunch.

Mother then sent me for lunch to the city's old folk's home in the Kapuziner Church, where I used to call on the friendly nuns on my way to kindergarten. I had never been in the old folk's quarters before. I was shocked at what I saw – impoverished sick old men and women dressed in dark rags, waiting for their lunch. I left as soon as I saw, whatever it was, simmering in a large kettle like an undecipherable, greasy concoction – most likely consisting of water, bread, and the previous week's leftovers. Walking there and back to school took up the whole lunch hour. After that, Mother sent me to school with the usual *"Butterbrot und ein Apfel"* – "Buttered bread and an apple" for a bag lunch.

Another day trip with Mother was to a road exhibition of oriental carpets in the town of Ried. When we got there, I had a glimpse of the interior of a large tent filled with oriental carpets. Then I was told to wait outside. No snack. No toys. Nobody. It seemed like hours until I saw Mother again, when she came out of the tent with a rolled up carpet under her arm, ready to catch the train back home to Braunau.

When Mother had heard it was bath day for the large family at the other end of the barrack, she sent me to their place. I found one *sitzbad* – a table tub full of hot water, ready for all the children. My turn came at the end and I couldn't wait to get out of that tub fast enough. One day, their father, a World War II veteran with a bad limp, included me with his children for a family boating outing across the river Inn. It was very nice of him to let me have a try at rowing, but when we landed on the sandy banks of an island, he sent all his children off to play, and he wouldn't allow me to join them. He made me sit on his lap all the while, and asked me to say nice things to him until they came back. Maybe he had the intention of giving me a little fatherly attention, but I felt extremely uncomfortable and told Mother about it.

The veteran's oldest son was about twelve years old. I was hardly aware of him, but one day, as I was returning back to our barrack from one of my explorations into the countryside, he came down the hill to meet me. He admired the flowers I had picked, and then he walked me back home. I thought that was the nicest experience I had ever had with a boy and, to this day, it may be my most romantic, distant memory, of a chivalrous, tall, blond, Austrian prince.

During our last winter in Austria, Mother had to use a sled to take me to the hospital for the second time in six years. She had noticed some yellowing in my skin and eyes. The nurses in the hospital gave me a ghastly daily drink which tasted like seawater, and I was put on a low-fat diet to treat jaundice. Apparently my case of jaundice was caused by ingesting bad lard. There were at least six or seven other sick children in the room. One little boy had candles lit on each side of his bed, and the nuns prayed for him all night until he passed away. In the morning the little boy's doctor was very angry at the nurses for not having notified him sooner, and the nurses were angry at Mother for bringing in a special treat I had always admired in the *Backerei Fenster* – bakery display window. It was little cake man covered with marzipan, something I was definitely not supposed to have at this time, and it had cost Mother one whole schilling or maybe two. *"Wo ist es?"* – "Where is it?" the nurse asked. Of course I had devoured it on the spot! I had also dropped an empty soup bowl and it had a chip and a crack. The hospital charged Mother for it, but I made sure they returned it to us. It was still serviceable, God uses cracked pots. I felt a little perturbed though, when, after my discharge, I found myself walking all the way home by myself.

One school day, I must have been sick with a cold, because Mother had me remain in bed under the down feather duvets, and I was delighted to see my sister show up on her lunch break from the hair salon and to boil an egg for me. I thought that was so 'cool' of her to do, and it made my day.

A cheerful memory of Braunau is of Mother singing on top of her beautiful lyrical range. She never smoked, but she did enjoy a beer or Schnapps, and it didn't take very much to get her dancing on a table top. Everyone wanted her at their parties. They said it was no fun without her. The others at those parties were *Auslander*, displaced people from the Sudetenland and surrounding countries. I noticed that their barracks were very shoddy compared to ours. Satisfied, and knowing Mother was safe and enjoying herself, I'd wander around the neighborhood, pick flowers, do some weeding in our communally run vegetable plot, and see whatever else I could find to amuse me. But soon we would be *"Auslander"* too, by crossing a vast ocean to a faraway land.

Six long and difficult years of my childhood in Braunau had given me the impression that the whole district seemed void of a safe place a girl could run to, except perhaps to the kind nuns in the Kapuziner church. To me, the atmosphere reeked of shame, defeat and misery, and in my estimation, Braunau should have been renamed to something which sounded nice, like Greenau. But Braunau it is, and in my mind it will always will be the birthplace of Hitler; a depressed, medieval settlement by the waters of two rivers.

~/~

By early Spring of 1956, Mother had made connections either through a local acquaintance who had already immigrated to Montreal from Braunau, or through an advertisement she or the sponsor had placed in the domestic section of a European newspaper, with a potential sponsor by the name of Mr. Otto Protzki. I was never quite sure which one of Mother's versions was correct. In any case, I always had two interesting options to the story.

Mother and Mr. Protzki, whom we soon called "Vati," exchanged correspondence regularly, and plans for our big move were set into motion. All we needed were official confirmations from two immigration diplomats. So, we took two consecutive day trips by train – one to Vienna and the other to Salzburg, where my sister and I stood quietly in a city park and watched, while Mother and official looking gentleman exchanged documents.

Mother included a picture (still in my possession) that I had drawn in one of the introductory letters to "Vati". It was a winter scene with tobogganers and skiers. Though she praised me lavishly for my artistry, it is not as grandiose she had made it out to be, rather a simple sketch on a precious piece of paper no larger than three inches by four inches.

It hadn't occurred to me to inform my teacher of our impending move. After all, a geographical move was hardly related to any of my school subjects at that point, and I had been taught to speak only when spoken to. Besides, I had called a red-haired girl *"Karotten Kopf"* – "carrot-top" during the previous school year, and my teacher had reprimanded me, saying she would never offer me a paper tissue for my runny nose again. So, when she approached me with an unusually friendly demeanor, and asked, *"Geht ihr wirklich nach Canada, Emily?"* – "Are you really leaving for Canada, Emily?" it felt like a dam had burst. She was obviously delighted with our good fortune, and my teacher, who had taught me both grades three and four, had actually smiled. Hope glimmered in her eyes and I could tell she was imagining a similar opportunity for herself someday.

~/~

Once our passports had been finalized, Father came to Braunau, from Linz to sign a waiver of paternal responsibility. Mother told me to wait in the courtyard while they entered a lawyer's office, and I'd had my very first, albeit fleeting glimpse of my birth father.

Mother's last affair in Austria was with a fellow she had met at the aluminum works in Ranshofen. I never met her sweetheart lover, but I had heard enough to know they were very much in love. One night I cycled into town in the dark to encourage Mother to come home. I knew where to find her. It was in a room on the top floor of the drawbridge tower which separated the left end of the *Stadtplatz* – city center, from the street leading to Ranshofen. When I knocked on his door, I heard lovely guitar playing and singing. Mother opened the door, and asked me to wait in the hallway. I have a feeling she would have liked to have this hand-some man join us in our new adventure to Canada, had he not lost his life in an industrial accident shortly thereafter.

Around that time, I had been observed as I improvised some dancing outside of our barracks, and I overheard Mother say to Hanne in a subdued voice, *"Dann sehen wir sie nimmer."* – "We'd never see her again." Apparently, there had been some talk about having me enrolled at the dance academy in Salzburg.

Mother approached the owners of the hair salon across the river in Simbach, where Hanne had been an apprentice, to ask if they would keep her until the completion of her hairdressing course, but they declined because they were afraid of the respon-sibility. They did say, *"Hannelore ist ein feines Madchen"* – "Hannelore is a fine girl."

Hanne had been very content working in that salon, and so had I been for a while, until I was reprimanded for having dipped into her 'tips' jar to buy chocolate at a confection shop just down the street from my school. But she had to quit her apprenticeship as well as having to give up her dreams of making it to the Austri-an national gymnastics team, for a new and better life in Canada. I wonder if Mother would have changed her mind, had she known

Hanne would be with child within three years, and that I would fail two grades and barely get through school in our new country, and that there would be chronic contention over her future inheritance.

Had we remained in Austria, the following year would have been my transition into grade five – *Gymnasium Hochschule*, a high school version for advanced students, and possibly music and dance lessons at an academy in Salzburg. I often wondered what our lives would have been like if had remained in our native country, but we were anticipating similar opportunities in a new land of golden opportunities.

While Mother was busy packing and selling the furniture, including the oriental carpet and the *Bauernstube* – the breakfast nook with the rustic chandelier and peasant musicians perched on top, and while she was having two crates constructed just outside of our front door, I decided to join a father passing by with his child in a stroller. They were going to look for berries, and I nonchalantly tagged along. We found berries. Lots of them. I had no container so I ate them to my heart's content. When I came back several hours later, I was surprised to find Mother, for the first time that I can remember, showing quite a bit of concern over my absence.

The day before our departure, I spotted Hannelore embraced in the arms of her boyfriend, saying her last goodbyes. I'd had no clue she had been romantically involved with a boy, and it was very touching to see her so emotional with anyone. He lived with his widowed mother and young twin siblings just across our common entry way. Mother had occasionally donated food to the pitifully poor family. In the two years we had been neighbors, I had never seen the twin girls playing outside, nor had I heard them playing inside, as if they had still been cowering inside a bomb shelter. I enjoyed my own company in my own imaginary world, with Mother and my sister, and I really didn't have to say goodbye to anyone. I hadn't even been able to relate to the two classmates from normal middle class families Mother had tried to connect me with. Their

contented and easy going manners bored me. But, I decided to walk
to the other end of the barrack to say goodbye to the veteran father
with the bad limp. He wouldn't acknowledge me. He simply grumbled something inaudible. He was still mad at me.

We were leaving Braunau to get away from it all, to learn a new language, to acquire a new culture, and have a better life in Canada. Mr. Otto Protzki, our new "Vati," would be waiting for us on a pier, in Montreal, in July of 1956.

Our last three photos taken before the journey to Canada. Family portrait, 1955; me on the bike with Hanne's boyfriend, 1956; and all the little kids on the block.

Chapter 4

1956: LEHAVRE, FRANCE
By mid-July of 1956, we were off via rail for a stopover in Paris for identification, disinfection and inoculation purposes. The aseptic smell was an affront to my sensitive nasal passages, and I did not understand why the Parisians did not seem impressed with us 'Germans.' We then took the train for the port city of Le Havre. There, we stepped straight into a huge Cunard ocean liner named *RMS Askania*, and we set sail across the vast Atlantic Ocean.

Our personal cabin had three separate bunks and a port-hole with a view into the deep blue yonder, which made me feel slightly claustrophobic. Good thing we didn't spend much time in the cabin, except to sleep at night. We had been used to sleeping together in one bed so far, but we didn't suffer any separation anxiety. We were introduced to American style food such as cornflakes, peanut butter, hamburgers and hot-dogs, and it was the first time ever we had been waited on as a family. As usual, Hannelore took every opportunity to disappear with her new friends, Mother socialized with other passengers in the lounge most of the day, and I ran up and down the ship, exploring every nook and cranny at the different levels until I got tired and returned to check up on Mother, who had made a special friendship with a single lady, Paula, with whom we would develop a lasting friendship. Paula also hailed from Austria, and had left her young son with relatives until she could afford to send for him.

In the lounge, Mother always liked to introduce me in a lyrical singing voice, *"Das ist mein Baby"* – "This is my baby." Satisfied with her acknowledgment, I'd continue with my explorations. I happened to come across my sister and some young sailors playing tag on a deck, but I knew better than to try to join in on the fun. I kept my distance. I could have been slapped on the face, just like I had been on Mattigstasse, trying to get in on a similar game with her peers. With the mealtime announcements, we always managed to reunite. As I look back, there was a conspicuous lack of literature, games, toys and activities in the picture, let alone a movie. The ship, *RMS Askania,* which had been launched on December 20, 1923, in Newcastel-upon-Tyre, England, and had been used as an armed merchant cruiser in WWII, started to feel like the personification of "Boredom City." All I could do was to run up to the stem, stop–then run back to the stern–stop, and repeat my routine with the port on the left side and starboard on the right. At my different pauses along the way, I'd prop myself against the ocean liner's surrounding rails and gaze until I was mesmerized at the different patterns of waves produced in the wake of the ship propelling itself so confidently across the ocean, and I wondered what my future in our new country held in store.

We were already in the Gulf of St. Lawrence, past the Strait of Belle Isle, yet we were still so far away from our final destination. I had never been briefed on geography, or on any language other than German, and I really did not know where on Earth we were in this vast ocean. I had never seen a map of any ocean dividing two continents, let alone one of Europe or Canada.

Finally we landed at Quebec City, and were able to wander around the lower part of the city for a few hours. It was so good to feel the earth beneath our feet, touch the brick of old structures and look up the huge walls leading to the upper part of the city. I would soon learn in school that were called fortresses. I was very much looking forward to see our "Vati" in person. If the priest in Braunau had asked me to draw another picture of God, I would probably have used Vati's image. I had made him my earthly hero.

We still had about 150 miles to go up the Saint Lawrence River for our final destination. Mother had prepared me well on how to greet our new Vati. *"Lass alles von Deinen Armen, laufe zu Ihn, und gib Ihn ein grosses Busserl"* – "Drop everything, including your doll, run to him and give him a big hug and kiss as soon as you see him." So that's what I did. And we didn't know that it had been our ship *RMS* Askania's last journey, and that she would be retired in December of 1956, and scrapped by January of 1957.

~/~

MEETING 'VATI' IN MONTREAL, PQ

Vati's friend chauffeured us up Rue Saint Laurent, which is the street that divides Montreal east from west. The street went on with unusually long distances between intersections, and there were no trees. I perceived it as an endless tunnel. I didn't know, at the time, I was claustrophobic. For the rest of my life, Rue Saint Laurent would always have this forbidding *je ne sais quoi* – a mystery about it, as referred to by a CBC commentary on Montreal.

Newly landed immigrants, windblown, on the banks of the Saint Lawrence River

The chauffeur finally turned right onto rue St. Zotique, then right again onto rue Casgrain. And there we were – at our new home. Hannelore and I looked at each other with big eyes. We were not impressed. This seemed worse than Heidi (in the movie) having to leave Switzerland for Frankfurt. There was no yard, no trees, just blocks of attached tenement apartments and row houses with long stairways to the outside.

In one of his letters, Vati had mentioned that he had purchased a new bed and matching dresser for Hanne and myself, and when Mother had read the wonderful news to us, she practically yodeled with excitement. True to his word, Hannelore and I

In Canada on rue Casgrain, Montreal, with my Vati; Hanne at 17 (right).

now had a bedroom all to ourselves. There was a bathroom with a real bath tub, a toilet, and hot flowing water. Vati's bedroom was sectioned off with drapes, dividing a good size living room in half, and Mother shared Vati's bed from the day we arrived.

The next day, Mother and Vati consulted a notary public to transfer the title of the apartment building over to her for the total sum of one dollar. On the second day, Mother and I walked to the local farmer's market to fill Vati's refrigerator with produce. Soon, she had the spare room in our flat and some apartments on the upper floors sectioned off with partitions to accommodate additional new immigrants. Mother was in her glory, cooking up a storm in the kitchen, getting a new enterprise started, learning how to manage the apartments, and attend to Vati's needs as a diabetic. The needle Mother used to administer his daily insulin shots was huge by today's standards.

Soon, several fine young men took Hanne out on her days off from her *au pair* nanny job, while I, as her inquisitive little sister, basked in the limelight of her suitors, one of whom allowed me to drive his motorbike up and down the back alley until I got stuck and he came to my rescue. That was truly an exciting time for us.

And for the first time in my life I savored ice cream more than once or twice a year. The corner store sold an ice cream cone for five cents, and I frequented the shop with the iconic soda fountain as often as I could manage to procure a nickel out of Mother.

The main entry to the bachelor suite on the main floor came from the back alley, but it was connected to our flat in the interior with a locked door, unless Mother unlocked it to let the renters in and socialize. I had a lot of fun aiming marbles under their door, and then wait to see what would happen. To my delight, they were sent back via the same route. Being the landlady's daughter, I had the special privilege of visiting anyone I wanted to in the building, and I was always very warmly welcomed. Being naturally curious, I had a lot of questions for them, mainly about where they came from and what they were planning to do. If I really liked them I offered to babysit and do their dishes.

Vati with "his girls," and around the dinner table (below).

The summer of 1956 had come to an end, and plans for returning to school had to be made. I had attended four years of elementary school in an all-girls' Catholic school in Austria, and I expected to attend the all-girls' Catholic French school located just around our corner from rue Casgrain. But on the first day of school, the nuns turned me and Mother away, and directed us to an English Catholic school a good, brisk, half hour's walk away. At that school, early morning pre-classes church service attendance was highly encouraged. On the second day, it took me a while until I found the right church. Mother taught me not to hesitate to question strangers for directions, but it didn't occur to me to put my thumb out for a ride, as we often did together.

The nuns at that school were very kind, and I really appreciated a hot bowl of soup for lunch for a pre-paid token, so much better than sometimes going without lunch all day in Braunau. That year, I found myself winning bags of marbles after school. I almost felt sorry for the poor kids who had lost all their marbles by the end of the day. When I arrived at home, I usually found Vati Otto sitting in his favorite chair reading an Agatha Christie novel or other classics. As per Mother's prodding, I dropped everything, ran to him, gave him a compulsory hug and a kiss, and then played with my prized marbles (sometimes under his feet) on the paisley patterned carpet with perfect circles woven into it for something to aim for.

As my first year was progressing, Vati liked to ask, *"Sprichst Du schon etwas English?"* – "Can you speak some English already?" I'd bashfully answer with a *"Ja."*

One of my chores was to polish furniture with lemon oil. I made sure I got into all the nooks and crannies, waited five minutes and buffed it all over again just as Mother had instructed. I loved to dust and tidy up, especially around Vati's delicate china figurines. I enthusiastically set the dinner table. I checked it twice to make sure the plates and utensils were perfectly aligned. I also felt privileged to dry and then put away his fine Alfred Meighen dinnerware after every meal, and not in a million years did I imagine that I would someday be willing to pay one thousand dollars in legal fees to keep it.

On Saturday nights, we huddled together on the couch and watched the shows that were all the rage in the mid-fifties. When it came to especially exciting parts in a movie, Mother had me interpret what she hadn't caught on to. She'd nudge me with her elbow, and asked, *"Was hat geschehen, was ist passiert, was hat er/sie gesagt?"* – "What happened, what has transpired, what did he/she say?", and while I was trying to translate it into German, I would miss out on the next line(s). Oh so frustrating! But it was great to stay up late and watch the Ed Sullivan Show, the Juliette show with her tag-line introduction "Now, let's meet, and greet, your pet, Juliette!" and all of the other specials, including wrestling (after which I was usually tired enough to go to bed quite willingly).

I delivered Mother's surplus cooking to new immigrants who lived upstairs. There was never an idle moment; if not sweeping the kitchen floor, then the back courtyard littered from the upstairs balconies.

It was getting very late one night, close to midnight, when I had been helping Mother in the kitchen after a big dinner party. I felt exhausted and I just had to go and lie down. I had gone into a deep sleep, but Mother abruptly woke me and made me finish the cleanup. She also slapped me for helping myself to a single slice of plain bread. I am happy to say that was the last time I remember being slapped.

A minister of German ancestry once said in his sermon, "If I had to do it over again, I'd rather be an Italian. The Italians are emotionally free to express and wave their hands and hug each other." He also touched on violence in German child-rearing practices, and he admitted some anger towards his mother for her harsh tendencies, but as the landlady's daughter, I felt somewhat protected with my special status. One of the nice Italian mamas even volunteered to relieve me of a load of ironing. The aroma of fresh baked, stuffed apples wafting out of their kitchens is still a tantalizing memory.

I also had some lessons on marriageability. Mother mentored, "A future mother-in-law did not approve of her son's potential wife because she had not sliced the cheese the right width. A French kiss is asking if the main door is open. Once you have sex, it becomes addictive and you'll never be able to concentrate on anything else." Well, I was going avoid sex if it was going to sabotage my life, hinder me from doing the things I wanted to do, have my independence and pursue the things that made me happy.

Once we were settled in Montreal, Paula, the lady we had met on our voyage overseas, liked to visit us on her days off from her nursing job at St. Mary's hospital. She was like a breath of fresh air, and she never failed to cheer me with her genuine, enthusiastic, and welcoming manner, and she always had a little something special for me. She even took me to a professional photographer because she thought I was so *neat*. She said to me, *"Du bist wirklich ein reines Madchen"* – "You really are a great little girl." Most of all Paula showed me exceptional warmth and kindness. She was like a favorite auntie. She was also a very popular nurse at St. Mary's Hospital. She married a German immigrant and had lovely children of her own. They left the province of Quebec for Ontario, and we lost contact when my own family moved to Alberta. My heart still swells at the thought of Paula. Apple Hill, Ontario, you will always have a treasure in heaven.

~/~

By the age of twelve, I had graduated from believing, *"Ein Storch hat dich gebracht"* – "A stork brought you, to a more romantic yet realistic version, *"Du bist unter meinen Herz gekommen"* – "You arrived from under Mother's heart." A few months later, Mother tried to prepare me with a story about the birds and bees. *"Setz dich hin, Emily, jetzt muss ich dir etwas sagen von die Voglein und Bienen"* – "Sit down Emily, I need to tell you something about the birds and bees." I cut her off promptly, knowing she was going somewhere I didn't want to go. I said, "I know, I know!" and took off. Catholicism kind of supported ignorance in that department, with subliminal messages that lack of knowledge about sex and reproduction meant being protected from all the negative connotations associated with the whole topic. Pretending to be ignorant and avoiding attraction was the way to go to maintain an idyllic, sinless self-image. I was in a fantasy world.

One day, Mother surprised me with a vinyl record of *Peter Pan*. She had really splurged this time, but it was well worth it. Every time I played it, I not only learned English, but I got totally lost in that fantastic world of piracy and make believe, and I couldn't play it often enough. Mother could see it was money well spent and tried not to get exasperated at having to hear it played over and over. Unlike the big ocean voyage we had been on not so long ago, the animated setting of *Peter Pan* was an exciting, if delayed substitute for all the fun, music and entertainment I would have liked to experience on my real life voyage across the sea.

~/~

Someone had told Mother that Protestant elementary schooling in Montreal was superior to the Catholic system, and consequently she had me transferred from the all-girls' Catholic English school to a mixed English Protestant school. It was Peace Centennial School on rue Jean Talon. I had to repeat grade five at Peace Centennial School, and Mother had us converted into Protestant Lutherans, mostly to avoid the extra tuition fees levied on non-Protestants. My compulsory navy blue school uniform from grade five didn't fit anymore, so Mother decided to sew one up overnight, with a home dyed cotton bed sheet. I was never more mortified than to walk into the classroom in an A-shaped tunic that had been quickly assembled and unevenly dyed, but today, it might have passed as a really cool tie-dyed creation. Mother eventually did buy me a tunic with three pleats going down in the front (a new style), and I enjoyed keeping the pleats perfectly straight by ironing them with a damp cloth placed on top. I loved how the sizzling steam from the cloth emitted the scent of fresh linen.

My new grade five teacher at Peace Centennial on rue Jean Talon was a buxom Jewish woman who didn't seem to particularly care for me. I had gone from angelic nun teachers to a fearsome matron. She didn't give me a role in the Christmas play either, so I volunteered to sweep the stage in the background. I had already done a lot sweeping in my lifetime, and I'd had my first taste of subtle discrimination. It never ceased to amaze me how she could possibly manage to read or even see her shoes over her humongous bosom. Sinful thinking was my sweet revenge. However, I was tickled pink with myself for having come up with a poem with two lines rhyming "a butterfly" with "a crust of pie." I felt nothing short of a literary genius, and a bright light in my brain had suddenly fueled a lifelong passion for words.

I got through my second year in Canada relatively unscathed because all I lived for were the extracurricular activities which were all the rage at that time with hula hoops, ballgames, bolo bats, roller blades, skip-ropes, comic books, and a new bicycle from "Vati", Otto Protzki. I thought I was in a dream world when he took me downtown to Eaton's to pick out the bicycle of my choice. And then, one day, what a delight to find an upright piano waiting for me after school. Another day, he walked me straight to a local jeweler for my very first watch. Before winter had set in, Mother donned a beautiful black sheep's wool coat, which she wore it very selectively as she did not want to appear too affluent. That was the most fun year of my childhood, but little does one know, at an age of innocence, what lies ahead.

Mother made sure I took my homework and piano practice very seriously. She bought me a leather school bag the size of modern carry-on luggage from which I developed calluses from carrying its weight to and from school every day. By then I had a lot of personal items to maintain. I had a leather schoolbag and shoes to be polished, a piano to be dusted, and a bicycle to keep spotless (including the spokes) and free from scratches, and walk over curbs to preserve its integral structure. I also tried to keep Mother's expenses down by peeling my bus tickets in half, until one day the bus driver noticed.

There were huge city parks with wading pools and play-grounds just a bus ride away. My future looked rosy. I was relieved to have a really nice elderly teacher in grade six, in contrast to the buxom matron. I won a seedling umbrella tree as a prize for a composition about the benefits of trees. I loved school. I delighted in the new pencils, a ruler, and an eraser in the new pencil case. The following year, grade seven, might have been a good year too, if I hadn't been made to skip it.

I was in no particular rush to get home from Peace Centennial School on rue Jean Talon, and often chose to detour and stroll through the commercial street of rue St. Henry to admire the goods and fashions in windows displays of shops I imagined someday frequenting. I was absorbing a lot of bilingual infor-mation. I also noticed some boys and girls entering a building from which I could hear kids splashing. It didn't take me long to realize they were in swim programs. I think it was the YMCA. I entered, and had somehow made myself understood. I wanted to swim too! The lady instructors gave me the address where the required swim suits were available. It was dark already when I found the outlet in an industrial area, and sure enough, someone was the door of the back alley to sell me a swimsuit for two dollars. I trained at that facility twice a week for the winter, and I won a little trophy for the breast stroke I had excelled in. I did it all by myself. I walked the distance there and back by myself, and I never expected anyone to cheer me on, or remind me to bring my towel.

By springtime Vati was no longer sitting in his favorite chair when I came home from school. Mother had decided to occupy him outside of the home. She had contacted his old company colleagues at Canadair, and had arranged a steady pick-up time for him, three p.m., for the evening shift. Mother liked cool, well ventilated rooms to help her with her pre-menopausal symptoms, and as soon as Vati had left, she opened all the windows. When I came home, frozen from the blizzardy, snowbound hikes from school, all the windows were still open, and I kept my coat on to practice piano. She showed me how to prepare Vati's bed for his return and tidy his counter tops, and she told me how important it was to respect the change he liked to keep on his dresser (not that I ever touched it), and then my bedtime routine always included eighty brush strokes to maintain my hair's lustrous glow.

Meantime, Mother was waiting for a response to a letter she had written to her former doctor in Braunau. In her letter she had placed evidence of what she had suspected was symptomatic of a mysterious illness. She had found these tiny dark nodules in her bed. In the doctor's response, via airmail or *Luftpost*, he told her that these nodules were not organic, but they were the plastic tips that had come off her bobby pins.

Soon, an overnight babysitting opportunity came along for a young German couple who had heard about me as a reliable babysitter at age twelve. I took the bus to downtown Montreal and discovered that their humble abode was actually the furnace room of the apartment building. It may have been a little noisy, but it was warm, the baby slept through the night, and the next day I had a dollar in my pocket as I rode the bus back home through claustrophobic rue Saint Laurent.

Vati was hospitalized for complications of diabetes on several occasions, and I visited him as often as possible. It helped if he had a cookie or a cracker waiting for me at his bedside. At one point, both Mother and he were hospitalized simultaneously. She had been admitted for gallbladder surgery, and she joked over having improvised a word for stomach – *Magen*. She referred to it as her "eating box" when her doctor asked her what was bothering her. We chuckled over that one many times. I'd make consecutive trips by bus to their respective hospitals, return home, do my grade six homework, and get ready for the next day amongst boarders and tenants coming and going.

Before Mother's discharge, I had washed, starched and ironed all the doilies, dusted, and vacuumed to my best ability. She showed me her red and swollen scar – *eine Narbe,* which appeared to me like a miniature railroad track, starting from under her bosom, and running down below her bellybutton, all connected with ties for stitches like a railroad track, spaced at one inch intervals along my poor mother's convalescing body, but it didn't seem to take very long until she was her normal self again.

Then one day, Mother asked a German immigrant to take me to Montreal's Belmont Amusement Park, which was situated near the banks of the St. Laurent River. He was an upstairs tenant, waiting to be reunited with his wife and two girls from Germany. The day went all right. I won a doll, except it felt like he had been on a tour of duty with me. My future brother-in-law, Hermann, told me later when I was an adult, that Mother couldn't wait until I left the house for school in anticipation of a rendezvous with the father. I was offended to hear that because she had always handled these situations very discreetly, but I noticed that Mother was taken a little aback when the father's wife and two girls arrived from Germany after all.

I helped orient the two fair haired daughters to our school, and we found our first experience with Halloween absolutely exhilarating, running around the neighborhood in fresh crisp autumn air, collecting lots of candy just for saying "trick or treat" at every door. I felt sorry for my friends' family because we obviously had a much better start with Vati's help, while they had a hard struggle like most immigrants. They were a little jealous. Whenever I went upstairs to see the girls, I saw their father lying in bed looking absolutely defeated. I was thankful I didn't have a father who was that dejected. One afternoon Mother abruptly took me to the movies. I cannot remember the movie, but I remember having bad cramps (a charley horse) in my thigh.

The German family had moved out of their apartment while we were at the movies. There must have been an altercation behind the scenes earlier that day, because Mother told me to pay no heed. We never saw them again, but I think I may have recognized the older girl on a Montreal transit bus four or five years later, around 1962. I kind of recognized myself in her lost demeanor, and I wished I could have run up to her, embraced her, befriended her again, and help each other out in the mutual challenges we were about to face as relatively new immigrants, but I was too embarrassed, having been the privileged ex-landlady's daughter, who had possibly flaunted her special status.

By the end of the second summer in our new country, Hannelore had completed a year as a live-in *au pair* nanny in order to learn the English language, and she was planning to go into hairdressing, which is what she had started to do in Austria. She also took a night course in English for new immigrants. Mother gave her a terrible verbal thrashing for not having received better than just average marks. Since Hanne was in-between jobs that summer, Mother decided to get us out of the sweltering city, and had someone drive us to various sites in search of a retreat in the country. We checked out a country lodge by a lake, where we observed kids swimming and diving into a lake from a raft. Hannelore and I would have liked it there. However, since Mother was always looking for a better bargain, we ended up on a child-less couple's farm in the midst of nowhere, with not even a cow's trough to cool off in. I needed water. We were water people, the *Fahrmann's*, who had traded on a *Floss* – a barge, up and down the Danube River and tributaries centuries ago. I was so bored that I begged the husband to make us a pair of wooden stilts to walk on. That's all we had for amusement, and Hannelore had been stuck with me once more.

In the fall of that year, Mother and I accompanied a Russian botanist on a field trip in search of butterflies and bugs, which he processed and added to his impressive collection. One Friday after school, Mother decided I would enjoy spending a weekend with him, and she sent me to his address at the other end of Montreal. He wasn't there, so I roamed around the adjacent snow covered industrial field, hoping to spot him coming back from his work site at Canadair. I then waited inside the staircase of his apartment building to keep warm. I am still not sure, from the expression on his face, when he showed up, if he was actually expecting me, but I was glad to come in from the cold, have a hot meal, and see his butterfly collection again. In the middle of the night, I woke up in the arms of someone dripping wet in sweat. The voice said, "You have a cold. Let me help you cure it." When I objected and resisted his advances after he had carried me to his bed, he relented and left me alone. The scientist soon disappeared out of our lives, but I was quite touched when he mailed me a beautiful white rat in a cardboard cylinder.

I came to love the white rat as a cute pet. It was so tame I could let it roam freely in the back alley. I had to bring him in for the winter, thinking it would be safe in the spacious undeveloped basement used to store Vati's old pharmaceutical inventory, including a case lot of his generic toothpaste we tried to use up. Old furniture left behind by departed tenants was propped against the walls at the back. The floor was packed with soil, and I assumed my pet rat would feel right at home, having its cage to escape to if necessary, but one Saturday night, when everyone was out, I listened to the agonizing screeches of my beloved pet being attacked by wild rats. And then there was total silence. I was too frightened to go all the way down the stairs to rescue him. I searched for him the next day, but I couldn't find him.

~/~

Early in the spring of 1958, another family had arrived in our complex. I watched them from our courtyard below, pretending to be sweeping the area while they were walking along the narrow third floor balcony towards the back entry of their new apartment. A father, mother and four teen-aged girls, all dressed in the long flowing skirts and bobby socks of the fifties style, had just come off a ship from France.

Whenever I noticed someone walking along the back balconies, I said a little prayer, because one day after school, Mother told me someone had fallen over the railings that afternoon. He had been leaning onto the second-floor railing when he fell onto the back alley, and he was taken away by ambulance. It sounded serious.

Meantime, I took the bus to Eaton's downtown and spent my babysitting money on a fancy silver-plated serving tray for Mother's 43th birthday. She expected no less.

Soon I befriended Suzanne, the youngest of the four French girls whose families had just moved into our building. She was thirteen. I was twelve. She liked coming down to our main floor apartment to join in on our activities. One sweltering day in July, as we were searching for a public pool to escape the heat, she noted that my walking strides were too long and not lady-like. Hers were short and feminine. A girl was to walk like a "Parisienne," she noted. I tried, but it felt awkward. She was as delicate as "Collette" from the opera. I was a sturdy "Heidi" from the Alps. We flirted with the young student who temporarily boarded with us in order to complete his last year of high school before he was to join his parents in California. We were quite dazzled with him, and we teased him while he was working on his impressive geometry designs.

Suzanne and I were sent to a farm in the Laurentians for a week. We were allowed into the house for our meals only, and at night, we were sent to a separate building for sleeping quarters. There was little supervision during the day or night, and our teasing of a sixteen-year-old boy could have led to more serious consequences than just being shocked seeing him at our door with a full-blown erection. We screeched, pulled our blankets over our heads and waited until he retreated into his room. We heard him say, "I hope that will teach you two a lesson." It did.

In the fall, Suzanne's parents had made plans to move to California. One Canadian winter had been enough for many of our tenants. I had forgotten all about Suzanne because Mother had sold the apartment building and we had already moved to NDG (Notre-Dame-de-Grace) across town, when Suzanne unexpectedly showed up at our new place on Beaconsfield Avenue and asked me for the German student's new address in California. My first reaction was, "I don't have his address" (which I didn't). My second reaction was, "I could probably ask Mother." I had turned into a selfish, jealous thirteen-year-old, and watched Suzanne leave in a huff and puff. I never really forgave myself for letting her down. When I traveled to Los Angeles six years later and looked up her name, Suzanne Auberge, in the Los Angeles telephone directory, she would not take my call. Ouch! I had never imagined that she had been serious about our young boarder, but I never forgot the adventures Suzanne and I had in the summer of 1958, and neither would my Christian conscience ever allow me to forget that I was born flawed with Adamic sin. I had been somewhat wicked, and there would be only one Redeemer to save me from that sin, among other trespasses.

~/~

Vati died almost three years after our arrival in Canada. During his final hours, Hannelore and I stood at each side of his hospital bed while Mother urged him to accept Jesus Christ as his personal savior. He nodded "yes", and then looked far into the distance as he reached up with his arms as if he could see where he was going, and we saw him take his last breath and then relax into the arms of his savior.

I will never know whether Vati had approved of the extra commotion he experienced during his last years on earth. Personally, I do not believe he had bargained for the intrusion around his personal space, but then maybe he enjoyed the distractions that came with it. He will always hold a very special place in my heart. I pray that God has abundantly blessed his soul, and I hope he has found his generous reward in heaven for being an exceptionally Good Samaritan.

Sadly, Mother was still abusing Hannelore. I can still visualize an ash tray flying across the dining room table in her direction because she had objected to handing over most of her hairdressing wages. That seemed to be the final straw which drove her into the arms of a father figure.

~/~

Mother first met Hermann as a door to door salesman, when he had knocked on the front door of the apartment building and introduced himself as an immigrant roofer from Dusseldorf, Germany. He had been surveying the neighborhood for work from the roof top of the Catholic Church just around the corner on rue St. Laurent and rue St. Zotique. Mother most likely proved to be too old fashioned and set in her ways for a serious relationship with a divorced father twelve years her junior.

He, in turn, twelve years older than Hanne, charming, generous, and experienced, had come to her rescue. This may sound like a soap opera, but it is true. Hannelore and Hermann took an apartment right after her last altercation with Mother, and soon they had to get married because she was with child. That was the scenario two years after we had left Austria, and twelve years later, her lovely wedding gown would come out of storage for my own wedding, under different, yet precarious circumstances as well.

I had quickly learned it was up to me to get a proper education and "go places" in life. Hannelore had quit school at the age of fourteen due to lack of academic interest, and I was not to follow that path. At one point even Hanne said, "You are the only one in this family with a chance at success." But she was neither stupid nor mentally challenged. She had developed into a skilled, lovely, and dignified looking young woman, and to me, she looked like a true Grace Kelly.

~/~

Within three years of our arrival, Vati had passed away into the arms of his Savior in June of 1959, my white pet rat had died, and my beautiful long pony tail had been cut off into an awful, short, permed hairdo in tight curls which I thought had made me look like "Little Miss Piggy", and my adored sister had to get married. I had just completed grade six at Peace Centennial School. My German and French friends from rue Casgrain had moved far away. Mother had quickly sold the six-flat apartment building at the urging of my newly married sister and her husband while I was away. Mother subsidized them generously from the proceeds, and then purchased a property where Vati would have liked to live in his retirement years. We were about to move to NDG (Notre-Dame-de-Grace), at 4142 Beaconsfield Avenue, Montreal West.

This was not the happiest transition in my life. I had not been involved in the physical move from rue Casgrain during that time, since Suzanne and I had been sent to the country, and I found myself disoriented and in a blur to have found my things moved into a strange house in the interim. Mother didn't seem very happy either, preoccupied and concerned over Hanne's "situation".

All I had ever wanted and hoped for was serenity and unity within my family, and in my prayers, I asked my heavenly Father and his angels to look out for me, now that Vati was gone, and not knowing the inheritance he left would lead to ongoing family squabbles.

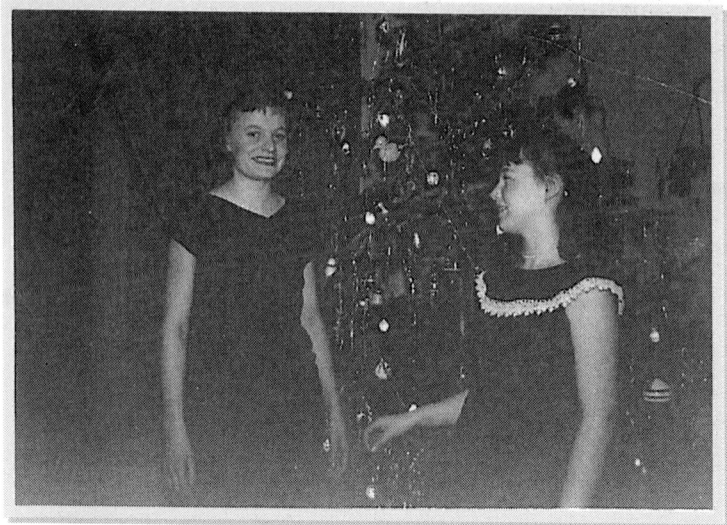

An adoring glance for my sister on our second
Christmas in Canada, and at my piano (below)
photograph which mother had published in the
German newspaper.

Vati, our beloved
sponsor; his
funeral in the
spring of 1958
(below).

Hanne's
wedding party
in the summer
of 1958.

Chapter 5

1959: ROOM #1

Upstairs, the first room to the left was divided by a partial wall dividing it into two small areas: the inner section had a single bed with no other furnishings except a closet, and the outer part facing west had a large desk the previous owner had left behind. It was made of solid oak and took up most of the space. The previous owner had left the desk behind. On it was a marble pen holder with a tall official looking black pen perched on top, and I anticipated many hours of serious study at that desk, and I called my suite Room #1.

Room #2 next door to me was occupied by a German tradesman whom I rarely saw or heard. Rooms #3 and the attic #5 were still vacant, and Mother took occupancy of room #4. Every room came with the bare essentials—a bed, closet and possibly a desk and chair—no décor, no pictures.

A two-car garage took up the space that once had been a back yard and provided another source of rental income for Mother. A portable, five-rung ladder, propped up on the back landing against the wall of the garage's tarred rooftop next to the kitchen door, lent access to the clotheslines. The undeveloped basement had a cot for an extra guest, a hot water gas tank, rough plumbing, a tub, fixtures for a future toilet, a wringer washer, several indoor clothes lines, and two laundry sinks by a window facing north, from where one could see the house next door.

As we were inspecting our new home, I noticed fancy figurines and beautiful china horses gracing the shelves of the previous owner's hutch, and I worried what it would look like empty, since the hutch and some of the furniture came with the house. I asked Mother, *"Lassen Sie auch die porzellan Pferde."* – "Do the china horses come with the hutch?" The China was not for sale, but I was astounded when Mother tried to cheer me up by giving me one hundred dollars in cash to spend at one of the fine import outlets near the docks in Old Montreal, for figurines similar to the ones I had admired so much. I knew just where to go, because when we were still living on rue Casgrain, I had passed by there via city bus to visit Vati in the hospital, and I had noticed the beautiful china in the store's display windows. The sales staff certainly thought it unusual to have a customer barely thirteen years old with that amount of money, but they were exceptionally sweet in their treatment of me, and I certainly didn't think anything unusual about the whole scenario. I was used to thinking and working like an adult. I had just finished grade six and I was about to skip grade seven, I had a room of my own, and I was the landlady's daughter.

While we were settling in, Mother had befriended a couple who mentioned that they spent their summers at a cottage near Val David, in the Laurentians. So, one very hot day, she took me to their summer retreat on an impromptu visit. We got off the bus, started walking down a country road, and with the help of inquiries along the way, we found their cottage. There were startled looks on their faces when we showed up at their door, but they let us in. We hadn't brought swimsuits, but Mother suggested a swim, for my sake, and I had my very first skinny dip ever. The feeling under the moonlight was almost supernatural, and I wished we could stay near that calm and warm lake all week. But we were not welcome to stay the night, and walked to the local motel, took a rundown room next to a noisy bar, said our prayers, and took the bus back to Montreal in the morning.

Mother then set me up as a mother's helper with a Jewish family vacationing at a cottage in the Laurentians. I was assigned a cot next to their two children's beds. Their father came up on weekends, and their grandparents visited as well. While the grandmother observed me cleaning up after supper, respecting the dairy and non-dairy sets of cutlery in the Hebrew tradition, I heard her say, "You are going to have a very lucky husband." Hearing that was music to my ears, not so much at the idea of making a good housewife someday, but the fact that this sweet lady gave me a sincere compliment in a genuinely warm tone of voice, in contrast, her daughter, who was rather bossy, had made me wash my handkerchiefs and my underwear separately. My wage was $1 per day and Mother had designated it for my upcoming school supplies. Within the third week of July, Mother had someone sent for me, either Hermann or a boarder. I forget exactly who. I felt guilty for abandoning this family, but Mother was having a crisis and she needed me. A pattern had been established permanently and would take root in my psyche.

By mid-August, I experienced severe abdominal pains and the doctors at St. Mary's Hospital were not able to determine the cause of my symptoms, so with Mother's approval, they took my appendix out. Our new neighbor, Mrs. Mueller, had given me a lovely pastel chiffon housecoat (peignoir) to wear in the hospital, and I brought my reading material which consisted of tabloid romance magazines, which caused quite a stir with the staff. As I was walking down the hallway in my lovely peignoir, a nurse stopped to ask, "Where did you get this fancy negligee! Aren't you a little young to be wearing this?" Then a supervisor showed up at my bedside and said, "You shouldn't be reading these magazines." She took them away and handed me a respectable age-appropriate book, probably a Nancy Drew, which I thought extremely boring.

The lady who brought the juice and snack wagon around every afternoon was exceptionally kind, and I soon realized that we were able to communicate in our Austrian dialect. I also discovered that she, her husband, and young son had recently arrived from Vienna, and I immediately relayed my exciting news to Mother. We soon developed a lasting friendship with the Yurmans, alternating with Sunday get-togethers and exquisite meals prepared by either Mother or Mrs. Yurman. We usually concluded the day with a drive into the countryside, or a climb up the stairs to Saint Joseph's Cathedral to light a few candles in one of its numerous chapels. It meant a lot to me to be associated with a family that lived in harmony. They worked hard to get ahead from entry level hospital work to responsible positions in surgery wards, and I didn't know that they had hopes for their son, two years younger than I, of eventually making a good match.

~/~

Mother didn't have parents of her own to serve as healthy and traditional role models, having been trained in religion and the domestic sciences in a convent run by nuns, and she didn't think it was important to come to school events, other than to convince the principal of West Hill High School to have me skip grade seven and have me accepted straight into grade eight, in order to make up for the year I had lost due to my immigration. "You look as bright as a button." he said, and I found myself moved straight into high school with students the same chronological age again. I didn't need to ask for any money for my school supplies. I had worked for them. And as I entered grade eight, I still sported that unwanted, tight, curly, short perm I had received in a beauty salon on rue Casgrain, making me look like "Little Miss Piggy."

My grade eight teacher had a strong English accent. She was very nice and caring, but I could tell she had been traumatized, most likely from the war, because she once ran out of the classroom in an emotional outburst, seemingly unprovoked. When she introduced English literature, Shakespeare, Chaucer, Latin and French, I could have run out of the classroom too. I was definitely overwhelmed and challenged from having missed the rudimentary basics taught in grade seven. However, I knew that there was a swimming pool somewhere in the expansive school, and hoped to get a chance to use it before too long. Little did I know it would be almost five years before I got to realize that wish.

One day, a girl in my class befriended me. Her name was Anita. She said she liked me because I was very quiet, and I thought she was exceptionally nice. She also happened to live on Beaconsfield Avenue, just down the street. Soon her family opened their home to me, and I even got rides to school, but I actually preferred the exercise and fresh air by walking. I'd noticed the difference a brisk walk could make in my ability to concentrate in class and in my general sense of well-being. No doubt the Tomasons had already met Mother, who had never been shy to introduce herself as a struggling single mom. When I showed up at their door, Anita's father always welcomed me with a very exuberant "Emileeleeleelee!" Sometimes I lived with the Tomasons while Mother was away on live-in jobs, and I was Anglicized with basement romper room dinners by the television set, peanut butter sandwiches for afternoon snacks, the presence of a formal yet rarely used living room full of antiques, and by learning how to shave my legs, American style. Anita and I climbed trees, frequented trampoline parks, skated in an outdoor rink, and attended teeny-bopper dances at the church right next door to her house, where I won a box of chocolates in a spot dance. I was planning to take it home to show off to Mother, but the boys got to it and ate it all.

~/~

Our new neighbors, the Muellers, had just arrived from Germany, and had rented the house adjoining ours. They had two preschool age boys, as well as a teenager who was so quiet I was hardly aware that he was part of the family. Through our mutual walls, I could hear the music of Mr. Otto Werner Mueller, a future maestro, practicing his conducting skills. I started babysitting their darling little boys, Michael and Peter (Pippo), and I automatically helped Mrs. Mueller around the house. She was an opera singer, not a domesticated housewife. I liked visiting Mrs. Mueller. She had a freshly baked *Gugelhupf* – Bundt cake, cooling on her kitchen table, while I put her hair in rollers. She also liked to sip on a glass of wine. She commented, *"Du bist wirklich ein suesser Backfisch"* – "You are really sweet, considering you are a teenager." Mr. Mueller usually sat at the other end of the kitchen table study-

ing another language to add to his impressive linguistic reper-
toire. I was little embarrassed when he said that he could hear me
playing my piano through the wall. I thought I was under his scrutiny, because he never did mention if I had any talent.

My routine was firmly set after school; change out of navy blue
school tunic and white blouse, practice playing the piano, babysit,
observe Mother's cooking instructions (we wore aprons in the
kitchen), do homework, observe the boarder's routines, iron tunic
and blouse, polish shoes and try to get to sleep by eleven p.m. I
tended to be a night owl, even then. Mother raised her eyebrows
when I came down for my favorite bedtime snack, which was a
hand-full of raisins mixed with nuts. She had finally given me some
slack on her staunch 'no snacks' rule to prevent cavities.

~/~

For the first ten years of my life in Austria, we had observed the
Christmas season on the first day of December, with an Advent
calendar, a wreath with four candles on it hung from the ceiling,
and a visit by old Saint Nikolaus, who arrived with a fully decorated Christmas tree, lit with real candles, lots of singing, and some
presents.

Things had changed in just three years. When Vati was still
alive, and when my brother-in-law had first joined our family, we
had continued to observe our Christmas tradition. We had all
been really happy together, and there were presents for everyone,
even skis. But that Christmas, in our new house on Beaconsfield
Avenue, I felt totally overshadowed, utterly rejected, and depressed. We were groomed and dressed as if we were going to a
royal affair (with no festivity or special dinner planned) and there
were no presents for me at all, nor for anyone else that I could see.
There was a box of chocolates from our guest. My heart was briefly moved with joy however, having had permission to hold my
one-month-old baby nephew, Miles, for one fleeting moment. In a
photo, I lovingly smiled at him as his proud thirteen-year-old
auntie, and my perm had relaxed and grown out enough to make
me look pretty again.

Mother had started complaining a lot about Hermann, which really upset me, because he had been like a favorite uncle to me since he had come into our lives, and I simply adored him. I thought he was a genuine, fun loving, and generous man. He had cared enough to tell Mother, *"Das sind Klamotten an Ihr. Bekleide Sie doch besser."* – "For heaven's sake, dress that girl a little bit better. She looks like a rag-a-muffin." It would have been painful for me to think he was anything but angelic. I couldn't take the awful undercurrent of disharmony among them and doled out lots of idealistic, well-meaning advice (of a teenaged girl).

Hermann took us to a ski resort one weekend. Mother remained in the ski lodge to look after little Miles, and Hanne and Hermann took the T-bar up the hill, while I was left to my own devices, while getting a lot of exercise paralleling up the hill, and hoping to make it down to the bottom without having to track down a runaway ski. Mother still refused to spend money in restaurants or cafeterias, which meant going very hungry until we got home, and a snack was out of the question. Old habits die hard.

I cannot remember seeing much of my sister during either of her pregnancies with Miles or with Brittney. But I clearly remember her saying, "You'll never get to touch my baby." What she said just didn't make sense to me, because I loved children. I had been highly recommended as a babysitter and I ended up babysitting my niece and nephew quite a bit after all. I am not so sure about the old expression, "Sticks and stones may break my bones, but words will never hurt me."

The least I could do was to be eternally grateful for the promises of a bright future built around my faith. I loved being an auntie, having a nice brother-in-law, lovely quality hand me downs from my sister, and school friends I would see again in the New Year. I gave thanks for the multitude of blessings I did have and I always said my prayers at bedtime.

Emily at 14, on
Beaconsfield Avenue,
NDG.

Hanne and
Hermann, with baby
Miles, 1959.

I had NO presents that year—so sad... but...

...when I got to hold my little nephew, I smiled.

With my
Grade Nine
classmate
Anita on
Beaconsfield
Avenue.

Chapter 6

1960: ROOM #3
I must admit that we were an attractive trio, and the establish-ment was certainly impressed with us girls, relatively new from Europe. Mother, when dolled up, was a stunning looking matron with a regal posture, Hanne looked like a composed model, and I was okay too, except my nose was considered pudgy and my body a little chubby. When we conversed in High German, or in the fun-ny sounding Austrian dialect I loved so much, eyebrows were raised. I was proud of having maintained a good command of my native language and I thank Mother for having passed that on to me.

When Hannelore came walking up the street, serenely pushing Miles, her firstborn, in a stroller, it was quite the sight. She was barely twenty, yet she looked like the sixteen-year-old gymnast from Austria. My teen friends wondered what on earth she was do-ing married to an older-by-twelve-years, excuse me, "smoking fuddy duddy," as they liked to refer to her husband.

People also must have wondered how Mother had so quickly acquired her status as a single home owner, having so recently immigrated to Canada, and whatever had happened to Father? Well, Mother had briefed me on two versions, whichever to suit the occasion: the dead or the alive one.

~/~

In the spring of 1960, I unexpectedly found my personal things moved out of my room #1 to room #3 while I was at school, and one quick glance into my vacant room, my world suddenly collapsed. Mother had rented my room out to someone else! Ronald, who was in grade ten and sometimes helped carry my school books, had co-incidentally dropped by. When he happened to see me crying, crouched on top of the staircase, he took off! I wondered why God allows so much suffering for a fourteen year girl, but there is virtue/purpose in suffering as Paul writes to the Romans 5:3-5: "We rejoice in our sufferings, because we know that suffering produces perseverance; perseverance, character; and character, hope." When He comforts us in our affliction, we can comfort others with the same comfort (2Corinthians 1:3-11). Then we become more resilient as "wounded healers."

Room #1 had been my very first room completely to myself, with an official looking desk and marble pen holder. This was the room in which I had learned to shave my legs, where I had secretly honed my sewing skills with Mother's remnants, and where I had hidden my creation-in-progress under my bed, a secret that had to remain well guarded, because I was clandestinely using Mother's remnants on her state of the art Phoenix 1956 model sewing machine, gifted from Vati, with all the bells and whistles of the day. It had to be shut down quickly, since the cabinet was located in the upstairs foyer, and there would be traffic coming up the stairs from boarders. Mother would soon be returning from work as well, and no trace of threads or pins were to be left visible at my "scene of crime."

Our new boarders, seniors of Jewish descent, usually greeted me with a warm hello from their slightly opened door, which used to be the door to my former room #1, until one day as I was going up to my new room #3, I saw the husband standing behind his partially opened door. He had parted his housecoat and fully exposed himself to me. I was shocked and pretended I never saw anything. Mother had mentioned to me that he had been abusing his wife and that he would need surgical treatment to curtail his sexual appetite. I was relieved to know that the wife finally got a break after his "treatment," and they had found an apartment of their own.

After the initial shock of having been uprooted, I settled into room #3 quite nicely. It was the largest bedroom of the house. The professional size desk with the marble pen set did not come with it, and I don't know what Mother did with it. It seemed odd that my new desk was so small that I had trouble arranging my homework on it. The room did have decor however, with heavy, wall-to-wall, hunter-green, velour drapes, making it extra cozy. The rest of the house paled in comparison to the drapes alone. Then, Mother surprised me with a used white alarm clock radio. I had come a long way at the age of fourteen. I felt that there was a very special person in heaven who cared for us deeply. I gave thanks with repeated *Vater Unsers* – Our Father who art in Heaven.

When I came home from school one day, Hanne and little toddler Miles were visiting from their apartment on the corner of Sherbrooke Street and Vendome Avenue, and sat around the kitchen table watching Mother prepare an Austrian treat such as *Zwetchken Pofesen, Apfel im Schlafrock, Palatchinken* or *Kaiserschmarren* – all deep-fried, high on sugar, fats and carbohydrates, but very delicious. Hannelore's greeting to me was, *"Gott, Du best genau die Mutter"* – "God, you are just like Mother!" I wasn't sure exactly how to take that comment. I certainly didn't take it as a compliment from the way she said it, but it added to my conviction that she always had and always would resent me. In photos of that particular visit, little Miles didn't look too happy either that day, but he certainly laughed out loud for me whenever I took him to the park.

~/~

There was another girl living in our block whom I rarely saw, except when she walked by my house on her way to school. I had heard that Priscilla was a book worm. One day she invited me to her house and showed me one of her sweaters to try on, and said, "You are definitely a sweater girl. It's yours if you want it." In a photo, I stand next to Anita, wearing the beautiful red sweater and a lovely fleece lined beige coat which Hanne had passed down to me. I had definitely acquired a taste for fine fashion.

My fourteenth birthday was coming up on June 2nd, and I had remembered Mother's threats about not getting anything because I had interrupted a conversation between her and a hospital employee several months earlier. I had been impatient, because I had been waiting on her all day. Sure enough, she did not acknowledge my birthday, not that she ever made a big deal over it anyway. I would feel terrible about my birthdays for most of my life, but forty-three years later, I was going to be compensated with a lavish surprise birthday party with musicians, hosted in the mansion of someone special from the Okanagan Valley.

Ironically, Mother always expected a generous present and a big fuss made for her birthday. So, on her 46th birthday, I tried to set up a fancy tea service on the tarred rooftop of our garage, which I liked to visualize landscaped with grass, bushes and flowers. I carried the tea pot out separately from the china cups I had arranged on a tray, and apparently I didn't make it look good enough for our neighbors, just in case they were watching. Mother exploded, and that was the end of our tea party, and life went on.

Bathroom and kitchen schedules had to be observed. Mother would take me aside and explain the boarders' circumstances: a lady who had just had a mastectomy, a single mother with a school age daughter who tried to annoy me while I was studying, a carpenter, a Victoria Order nurse from the Kootenays, a young mom with a toddler whose father worked on a cruise line, the oversexed senior with his exhausted wife, and the occasional over-nighter in the basement. I was briefed on who was staying in which room, and sometimes our original tenants from rue Casgrain came by to see how we were doing.

Mother had great business acumen. She was an excellent task master and I felt like I had special grownup status as a landlady's daughter. I was very proud of my mother. Her enterprising spirit left me feeling in awe of her as an unusual woman of the day, so I was indeed happy to be her little side-kick, and I hoped that someday with a good education, I would become financially secure, and turn into a successful entrepreneur too, just like Mother.

Anita's brother, Stuart, had taken a liking to me ever since he saw me walking down the street as the new thirteen-year-old kid on the block. He was heavily involved in Rovers and soccer. He was a big history buff, and he was away for a year for French immersion with a Quebecois family in Richelieu. His family invited me to their annual Bible camp vacation in northern Ontario, but I wasn't too keen on the idea. I had the impression it would be all about rigid Bible study and prayer, not realizing how much outdoor recreation and fun they really did enjoy every day. Besides, Mother was in the process of arranging another domestic job for me.

Things with Stuart seemed to go *flat* consistently. A year later, Stuart had invited me to a Bistro for our first date. We had French onion soup with croutons. All went well, but as we had gotten off the bus and walked up Beaconsfield Avenue towards our houses, a severe burning sensation gripped my stomach, which to this day seems to be the worst case of indigestion I ever had in my whole life. *Flat!* I couldn't wait to get home. I dubbed the theme of my relationship with Stuart *"Flat,"* because it resurfaced throughout our teens and right into our senior years.

I had already walked into the path of a sizable wet snowball that caught me *flat* in the nape of my neck as I was entering my house. *Flat!* I remember a stinky bomb thrown *flat* through my mailbox slot, disrupting my teen party. *Flat!* A bicycle tire gone *flat* on a date; a marriage proposal gone *flat*; and when we were seniors, a plan to reunite went *flat* too, due to an accident. He was a jealous high school History buff with a big crush. Ah, such is the nature of romance. I might add that surprisingly, Stuart suffered significantly from real culture shock as well, when his transition from Ottawa to Montreal during his elementary and high school years had not gone smoothly. To this day, it is still a thorn in his heart.

That winter, I conveniently forgot to study for my grade nine mid-term exams because I had become addicted to playing board games with Mother and a journalist, visiting from the USA. I believed that he was a serious writer since he kept a typewriter beside his cot in the basement. I had already won a lot of change, and I thought my winnings would never end, until he returned to the USA, and learned that the love of money nearly caused me to fail most of my subjects.

It was generally known that our house was an open house on Friday and Saturday nights, and that we danced to Rock-n-Roll music until well past midnight. Some neighbors must have had the impression that we were a pretty wild bunch since some of the teenagers smoked, and somebody always brought a case of beer. I wondered how Mother had managed to spend all those hours upstairs in her bedroom, without a telephone or television, but towards the end of the evening, she always came downstairs from her room to say hello and socialize, and after our last guest had gone, we made sure the main floor of the house was spotless. I still wonder if the neighbors thought we were crazy with the vacuum cleaner going in the middle of the night. I found it very comforting to see Mother's opened Bible on her bed stand when I stopped by to say goodnight, and then to say my prayers, giving special thanks for feeling safe and content, knowing Mother was nearby.

During one of our parties, someone had thrown a stinky bomb into the mailbox slot which took a while to air out. I found out, fifty-three years later, that it was Stuart, my latent high school sweetheart, the jealous *outsider* at that time, but very much in my life now. I also found out why he did it. He claimed he did it because he and his 'Rover Club' buddies had never been invited to my parties. However, it had been no secret that my parties were "open house" and no one required an invitation as long as they kept a certain standard of decorum. It was a simple case of silly juvenile rivalry.

Loa's parents, botanists at McGill University, gave us a lovely slide presentation party of their latest adventures in Iceland and Europe, and provided a sampling of traditional Swedish goodies. Loa had to observe a strict curfew and had to leave my parties early, by 10 p.m. sharp! I think Loa was envious of my apparent "freedom" from dual parenting. Though her parents had always been very kind to me, they did not fancy having their daughter staying at my place for too long. Loa didn't particularly fancy Mother either, but I do know she was eternally grateful for having had arranged double dates for her, and for having included her in my social life. We were true soul mates.

Well, it seems I had become a bad example when Anita started to host parties on her own (myself excluded) when both her parents and Stuart had been away. Something had gotten out of control, and Anita's parents didn't take it lightly.

It was usually Mother who greeted my young suitor who'd come knocking at the door on Saturday afternoons. I would hear a melodious "How are you, Mrs. Fahrmann?" There was a certain familiar tone in his voice he wouldn't have dared use if she had been married. It was exciting to have a young male visitor show up at my house, if not a little embarrassing, because he would find me ironing on the padded kitchen table, hanging up laundry on the tarred roof of the garage (often with curlers in my hair), practicing piano, knitting, writing letters in German under Mother's tutelage, or doing homework in my room.

For the first time, and only time, things got a little steamy with my good friend Nelson, in my room #3. Good thing Mother called us down for a snack – just in time! Nels helped me with my homework a lot. He was in grade eleven! Awesome! He became a tenured professor of Psychology at Western University in Ontario, and we reconnected via e-mail, sadly, just a year before his passing at age 70. His last words to me were, "You were lovely."

One day, my home room and math teacher, Mr. Manson, told me, "Emily, you have a good head on your shoulders. You can do anything you set your mind to." By the same token, he had given me failing mark, and I had to repeat grade nine. My English teacher singled me out in class as well and complimented me on my looks and behavior. He said girls like me were brought up right, to speak only when spoken to. And right in front of the whole class he said he liked full lips on a woman, and that I would be a beauty someday. He made me feel special and I had a real crush on him. He was handsome. He also offered me a ride home after school. I didn't accept. He happened to be a coach for the year-end field day. When I came back from my run he said, "Emily, you will never be alone and you will never disappoint anyone." Boy, did he ever get that wrong, but the affirmations from my teachers were all the assurances I needed to keep me going for a while.

On the other hand, I most likely had a mild case of ADHD (Attention Deficit Hyperactivity Disorder), affecting attention span and cognitive reasoning, exacerbated by limited language skills as a relatively new immigrant. I had never in my life to that time, and for an additional three decades, without exception, been able to read any fiction books throughout to the end without losing track of the story, and even then, I did not fully understand it. No wonder I consistently failed English Literature and composition, but I excelled in music, sports, the sciences and math.

At one point, I felt real pangs of homesickness and told Mother about it. For a moment she didn't know what to say, she took a big breath, and then said "Emily, it'll pass. What would we go back there for." So, our past life in Austria was rarely brought up again. It pained Mother to have to reflect on her own childhood, particularly on the circumstances around my birth, and when my pride in my Austrian heritage inadvertently came through among my friends, I often found myself quickly shot down with, "Then why don't you go back there!" as if I had spoken about an arch enemy. More often than not, some of my Canadian acquaintances came up with this old favorite, "Isn't that where all the Nazis are?" when I had a need to share a little bit of my identity and recollections of my home-country. What choice did I have as a fifteen-year-old? Run away and destroy everything we had built up in Canada in five years? We had just received our permanent Canadian Citizenship papers. It seemed like I was responsible to hold up the fort. All I could do was to dampen my personal enthusiasm, adjust, adapt, try to live up to everyone's expectations, and maintain my image of a well-adjusted, accomplished, trilingual, supportive daughter of a single immigrant parent. How could I destroy this fantastic scenario?

I saw my mother's business as an unconventional, yet practical livelihood which, no doubt, raised eyebrows from the establishment. I never witnessed Mother's affairs (and I thank her for her discretion), nor when and how she received her rent monies, and I treated my babysitting earnings just as discreetly as she did her own income. I hid it, lest she claim it for one reason or another. It was my business to fit in, accommodate, present myself impeccably, run errands, interpret, and make polite conversation. I was *not* to get pregnant and have to marry like my sister had to. I was to get an education, and then Mother's inclusion in any future marital arrangement was a "given."

After a few visits from two young Mormon elders, Mother suggested we move to Salt Lake City and become Mormons too. If I had said "yes", we would have moved to the United States and our future would have changed drastically based on my decision. It was my concern for my sister that would keep us in Montreal.

I had four piano teachers over a five-year period. My first lessons started in grade five at Peace Centennial School with black keys painted on cardboard until the school obtained a real piano. When "Vati" surprised me with a piano of my own, Mother arranged further lessons with a student teacher who taught out of her home. I noticed that she was an immigrant daughter too, and not content with what she was doing, and I imagined her parents pushing her too hard to succeed. Aside from the relief I found from entering a warm house, having been chilled to the bone by blistery cold winds at lengthy waits at bus stops, I do not remember having made much progress, or having been inspired by the young lady. After our move to Notre-Dame-de-Grace (NDG), Mother connected me with a very friendly German piano teacher and I made respectable progress. I thought it very nice of her to invite me for lunch anytime, to boost my morale. It was Mother's idea. To my amazement, Mother appeared at my first and *only* recital at year end. I was so nervous I could barely play, and felt like I had disappointed her. I made a fool of myself and vouched never, ever to play in public again.

My piano teacher's husband (a professional musician with the Montreal Symphony Orchestra) happened to visit the Muellers next door quite often, and he started to show up at my door after his visits there, and tried to force himself on me. Thank goodness I was swift and strong enough to fend off the burly barrel-chested bass player. For unrelated reasons, my piano teacher decided I would make better progress with someone new, and she referred me to an elderly male teacher (anyone over fifty seemed ancient to me). He challenged me well, and I advanced to Grade Eleven Conservatory. When my weekly tuition had increased to five dollars, Mother expected me to further my studies on my own, and I lost interest. She said, *"Du kannst es jetzt selbst lernen. Du bist sehr begabt"* – "You can do it on your own now. You are very gifted." I can't help but note the first syllable in *gifted* means *poison* in German.

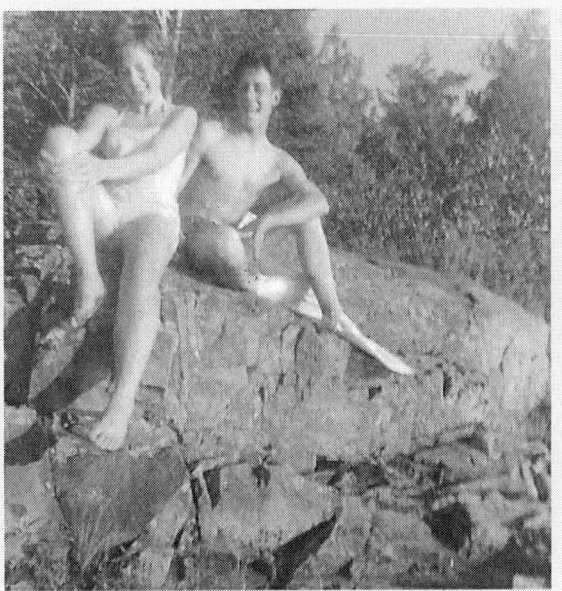

Summer fun at 15 with Karl, in St. Andrews by the Sea, 1961.

Sweet 16 in May of 1962; taken by a photographer downtown on St. Catherine Street, Montreal.

Chapter 7

1961: THE ATTIC, #5

Mother asked me to move out of my current room #3 with the hunter-green drapes, into the attic Room #5, and I jumped to it because living in an attic had a certain allure to it, promising distance from my world as I knew it. Besides, I was getting used to being moved around. She had the Jewish senior couple move into my current room #3, so she could have my original room renovated into a semi-self-sufficient suite, and soon had a stove and a refrigerator installed where my big desk used to be, and rented it to a young mother with a little boy, and later to a nurse from the Kootenays.

A narrow, dark, curved stairwell led to the attic #5, and it was indeed a really cool hideaway from the comings and goings of the boarders downstairs. I could stand upright only in the center of the attic, with the pitched ceilings all around me. Soon my friends, Anita, Ron, Loa and Nels agreed that it was a great place for any teenager. We played hide and go seek from the basement up and out through the attic window onto the roof–when Mother was out, of course, not that she didn't tolerate our shenanigans quite well. She enjoyed our youthful company vicariously. After all, she had spent her teen years in a convent.

Having a telephone in the attic gave me a sense of security. Mother allowed a strange man to come up to say hello. I had just returned from my bath downstairs, and was all wrapped up in my terry towels. He said, "Now you are squeaky clean, just like a brand-new baby," and then returned downstairs. He impressed me as a true gentleman. I didn't have to fight him off.

Another day, Mother came up to the attic to see how I had settled into my new abode, and she made a remark that resonates to this day, *"Du wirst nie eine Schonheit."* – "You'll never be a real beauty." I'd recalled when I was eight years old, she had told me, *"Du hast Zahne wie Schaufeln, und dicke Lippen."* – "Your teeth are like shovels and you have fat lips." I knew I was not going to meet her standard of beauty my sister had achieved with a smaller frame and long blond hair. I had a picture of a beautiful young lady on my wall, whom I had admired very much and aspired to look like. That hope certainly went on hold quickly, but the back of the frame kept serving as a good spot to hide my babysitting earnings, and Mother soon talked me out of keeping my telephone, to save the cost.

I did receive an allowance, and I worked hard for it. I ran errands. I was Mother's interpreter in French and English. I curled her hair and scrubbed her back regularly. She noted, *"Du hast begabte Hande."* – "You have gifted hands." I did the lion's share of the housecleaning, including the windows. I stripped the floors with steel wool, waxed the floors, polished the furniture and ironed. I also did mending and some of the laundry. Mother had always made work sound like it was a privilege. *"Du darfst das tun."* – "You may do that." I loved it, silly me. But I did not like giving her a mandatory kiss on the mouth when I came in or left the house, and I didn't appreciate her incessant talk. Annoying yes, but I thought she cared and meant well.

After the senior couple had moved out of room #3, an elderly Parisian lady took it, when her son, a medical intern, had found the accommodation for her, and we soon had students coming and going up to that room for French lessons. Never missing an opportunity, Mother immediately arranged French lessons for me as well. I didn't understand why I was full of trepidation at first. I had to be coaxed out of the attic for the tedious and boring lessons. I sat beside her at the tiny desk I used to study on, and I read out of an old, little French classic, possibly *Les Miserables*. However, my French marks improved dramatically throughout the rest of High School.

The French lady's son and his colleague dropped in one evening, when my teenage friends had gone home after a party, and asked Mother for permission to take me somewhere overnight. She left it up to me. I said "NO!" I was going on sixteen and still a virgin. Molestation and sexual assault didn't count. I was grateful for my teenage friends, and I happily said my prayers in the safety of my bed.

Mother and I shouted at each other over something I cannot remember, but I ran outside and started sobbing against the wall beside the basement window, where one could see the laundry sinks inside. And then I felt a bucket of cold water pouring over my head. "The teacher thought this would cool you off! You could have used a father!" and she retreated into the house. Yes, I certainly could have used a father (for emotional support and as a mediator). Another argument flared up. This time I barred myself away by jamming the door to the attic with furniture. I picked up a stone paper weight, banged it on my head repeatedly, and then I hid myself in one of the crawl spaces for what seemed like twenty-four hours. Mother tried to enter, but she left me alone until I came to my senses.

The French neighbors to the right side of our house were a well-to-do young Quebecois couple who drove a brand-new vehicle every year. The wife, on Mother's prodding, invited me over for a cup of tea and a biscuit. I sat rigidly on an antique chair in her formal parlor while I waited for her to appear with a silver tea tray in her arms. I was afraid she might have noticed me from her house, even with all the lights turned off, using the sink by the basement window to purge myself clean.

My neighbors may have felt sorry for me, as some of the boarders did, when they had noticed me crouching for equilibrium, dizzy from working too fast. If I happened to appear relaxed while cleaning, Mother said, *"Dummel Dich nicht zu schnell"* – "Don't get carried away now." I didn't like the sarcasm in her voice. We went through a period when we found leaving notes for each other at random places worked well, leaving them at the most unexpected places, and I rather enjoyed our new form of communication since there was no vocal intonation involved and it gave us plenty time to think things through.

In one of Mother's pensive moods, she asked me to come and sit beside her. There was something she needed to disclose which had to do with something before my birth, and then she stopped. I wish I had urged her to continue, but I decided not to push the issue if it was too painful for her. For the rest of my life my imagination wandered from one possibility to another, wondering if I had a twin that she had given up for adoption, if I had a secret brother, or if she had had an abortion, and if my sister knew about it and had had to keep yet another sinister secret about me.

One Saturday afternoon, I had turned on the gas water heater for a hot bath. Meantime, my good friend Loa and I strolled down the street to see Anita for a while. When we came back, the house was filled with a foggy mist. The heater had overheated. Hot water was bubbling out of the toilets and sinks. It took a little courage to tiptoe and fumble my way through the foggy steam, down the stairs, along to the back of the basement, and find the switch to the heater. I feared that at any moment, the house would go up in an explosion, just like a home which had been decimated a year earlier only a block away. I managed to find the switch! But, while I was in the basement, Loa had gone up to the attic, where she said she had fainted, but she reassured me that she had come around quickly. I needed to say my *Vater Unser* – The Lord's Prayer, that night, and to my knowledge, no one else ever found out. She took it to the grave with her and I would too, except it's all out now!

The Parisian teacher had moved out, and at Mother's prodding, I took a few more French lessons at her new residence. I can still vividly remember her chic chignon, her sophisticated appearance, and her slow meditative stroll down the street with her hands clasped at her back. I remember her son taking an interest in me, and on another occasion, giving me an injection for pneumonia (possibly due to an over-strenuous and fashionably underdressed day of skiing with Ron), and I will never forget the time she instigated Mother to pour a bucket of cold water over my head.

With fifteen dollars I had accrued in babysitting earnings, I bought myself a pastel suit with a pleated skirt and a pair of matching shoes from a boutique on Sherbrooke Street (far too classy for a teenager), and I proudly wore it like a princess on Sunday afternoon outings to St. Joseph's cathedral with our friends, the Yurmans. I loved beautiful clothes and how they made me feel. I wanted to appear stylish just like my sister, but I did not understand why I always wanted to appear in different outfits, as if I needed to constantly change my identity.

~/~

At the end of Grade Nine, Mother took a job as a domestic cook for diplomats from New York City who took their annual golf vacation at their Canadian summer residence in St. Andrews-by-the-Sea, New Brunswick. We were full of anticipation and took the bus to Eaton's to buy brand new suitcases. My luggage set was white – such luxury! The sendoff from our house on Beaconsfield Avenue made me feel like a virtual celebrity. Even a boy I had never seen before showed up at my front door, absolutely smitten by the sight of me in my brand-new pastel suit, which I vividly remember being a shade of tangerine, apricot, or soft salmon. I felt like I had metamorphosed from the gawky rag-a-muffin munchkin at age thirteen, into a glamorous Scarlett O'Hara from the movie, Gone with the Wind, as poignantly depicted on my 'Scarlett and Her Suitors' collector plate commemorating the fiftieth anniversary of the movie. But I wouldn't know my final grades since my school was to forward my report card to St. Andrews-by-the-Sea.

Since Mother liked to keep me busy at all times, she took me straight the wool shop in the village of in St Andrews-by-the-Sea, and helped me choose the necessary supplies for knitting a sweater. I chose dandelion yellow wool. In the evenings, the American housekeeper and I liked working on our projects together. We even compared our knitting speeds. When the lady of the house had noticed my excellent knitting skills, she presented me with a special knitting tote from the wool shop to carry my supplies in. I wished she had not felt the need to say, "There won't be anything else," because I, the cook's daughter, did not expect any gifts from her in the first place.

Mother had quickly befriended Karl, a recent emigrant from Vienna and apprentice tailor from the local navy base. On our mutual days off, he took us on various outings and dances in Calais in Maine, USA, just south of the border. When he came to fetch us, he found me climbing a tree in the middle of the retreat's expansive garden. I was still climbing trees at age sixteen! I had a lovely time while it lasted. I took my knitting project to the beach every day and produced a beautiful sweater with perfect cables knit down the front, and I also found out what physical contact with jellyfish felt like while swimming in the ocean. When my final school report had arrived in the mail stating I was to repeat Grade Nine, I wasn't too concerned. I was having a wonderful time, and thought it would never end.

Every morning, I woke up to a jubilant Mother serving me a beautiful breakfast in bed. She had free reign to shop, cook and serve fine cooking, and she was being paid for it. She was in her element, and we also had a handsome and enthusiastic young Austrian fellow to chauffeur us around. I had also earned a little pocket money by doing some of the housekeeper's jobs (Mother's idea). Unfortunately, our employment was cut short due to some rivalry between Mother and the permanently employed housekeeper.

~/~

As soon as we had returned to Montreal, Mother said, "Pack your bags, we are taking the train to Long Island, New York." She had just found out from Hermann that he had an uncle in the USA, and she decided to visit Mr. Steiner, Senior. We were warmly welcomed by his French wife and her sister, who put on quite a spread for us at every meal. But I wouldn't eat much anymore. I just picked at it. They ran a fishing outfit with rental cabins and a tackle shop, and their son took us out on a fishing trip. The sea was rough and it was very early in the morning. Fishing, especially at that time in the morning, was not, and never would be my cup of tea.

The next day, I walked through an unfamiliar, impoverished territory to check out the beach on the other side of Long Island. It was too cool to swim, so I put my things down on the sand and waded by the edge of the ocean for a while. That is where the beloved dandelion-yellow, cable-knitted sweater I had created in St. Andrews by the Sea disappeared into the hands of a crafty thief. I probably wished we hadn't had to leave St. Andrews-by-the-Sea for New York, so abruptly.

The following Sunday, Mr. Steiner's son invited me to come to church. I thought he tithed generously with a five-dollar bill. After church, he wanted to hold my hand as we were walking along the pier beside the ocean. It felt very awkward. As friendly and sincere as he was, he impressed me as an older man looking for a wife, and to me that was a very scary concept.

While we were with our hosts on Long Island, I remained fit with a daily minimum of two hundred sit-ups. I'm not sure why I started to pick on my food like a bird at this time and obsessively counting calories, when the ladies of the house had put so much effort into preparing sumptuous feasts every day. Mr. Steiner Sr. took us to Manhattan to see a Follies show on Broadway before we returned back home. He was such a grumpy old man though, and I was glad to return to Montreal and see my friends again.

In my new pastel suit, with our good friends, the Yurmans and
my 'designated' young suitor, at St. Joseph's Oratory. (His right
hand is only an optical illusion.)

Christmas 1962, with the whole family, next
door at the Muellers'.

Chapter 8

1962: ROOM # 4
I was in my second year in Grade Nine, and just before the onset of Winter, Mother had announced that Karl was on his way from St. Andrew's, New Brunswick, and that I would be automatically relegated down to Room #4 from the attic #5. She hadn't given me any advance notice to the effect he was moving to Montreal, let alone of moving in with us. Mother did not consider having a room to herself a priority, so she vacated room #4 for me, and moved her sparse wardrobe and personal items into the entry closet downstairs and slept on a makeshift bed in the living room. Karl quickly found a job and a social life of his own, and soon declined our invitations to join us for dinner, and never joined my parties, probably because he was already twenty-two years old and I was having a lovely time with my peers. That year, school was a breeze the second time around.

For my sixteenth birthday, Ron invited me on a date for the first time. I was a little stunned that he knew about my birthday, and wondered how he had found out, because I was trained never to mention my birthdays, let alone expect gifts. Mother may have spread the information through the grapevine, but it turned into the loveliest birthday ever. He took me to the local Swiss Chalet restaurant for my first ever taste of barbecue chicken with their special sauce and all, and then he stopped at a pâtisserie for some take-out pastries to savor after a vigorous hike to a shady spot near the summit of Mount Royal. He had been such a gentleman, and my sixteenth birthday remains as a wonderful memory to this day.

~/~

By mid-June, Mr. Otto Werner Mueller, the budding young musician and conductor next door had been invited by the Vancouver Symphony Orchestra to conduct The Magic Flute, an opera by Mozart, and since I had been minding their two little boys and generally helping out all year round, I was automatically designated as their ideal mother's helper, with Mother's blessings. The Mueller's oldest son was going to catch up with us after taking summer school at West Hill High.

The Muellers had to leave before the end of my school year, and since my marks were quite acceptable from my second time around in grade nine, the principal waived my final exams. Mother thought it was a wonderful plan, and I was thrilled with the opportunity to travel across Canada and spend time with the musical family. However, something was askew already. While we were loading up the car, and while Hannelore and some of my friends were wishing us bon-voyage, and after Mother had handed me a five-dollar bill for the summer, she suddenly broke down crying and pleaded with me not to leave. It was a nightmarish scene right in our front yard, but since we were practically on our way, I lovingly suggested she turn to my sister for support, and I hesitatingly left the scene to join the Muellers, who were waiting for me in their brand-new car.

~/~

It was truly a spectacular trip across the landscapes of Canada via parts of the USA. The two little boys, Peter aged two, and Michael aged five, flanked on each side of me in the rear seat of the car were a pleasure to look after. Pippo, the younger, helped us find our motels at the end of the day by trying to repeat "No vacancy," but it came out as "No bacon seat." The Muellers were very kind to me. They did not make any untoward demands, and they were completely satisfied with the way I managed the children and anything else I offered to help with. We were greeted by the owner of the house we were to stay in, on King George Street. It had already been vacated by his family, but the doctor remained behind for a few days to help our orientation. His family had already gone ahead to vacation in England. The doctor and I had a few long conversations, and we even danced the cha-cha in the music room.

The boys and I enjoyed many hours at English Bay beach, though Pippo sometimes cried for his mommy. We practiced our own little version of the Magic Flute, with easy songs like "Pappa Pappageno, Pappa Pappagena" as the song goes between the two love birds. Their mother, Margo, was able to enjoy most days with her husband at the rehearsal hall without any worries. While the boys napped, I got my exercise by running around the spacious home in circles, and by doing my sit-ups.

We took the bus to the Queen Elizabeth theater downtown to watch the boys' mommy and daddy rehearsing. All dressed up, we also attended the opening and the finale of the opera. I met another conductor, Zubin Meta, now maestro with the Vienna Philharmonic who looked so serious that he gave me the impression he didn't like me. One day, Mrs. Mueller called from the theater to say we were having company, so I started an impromptu buffet supper for the cast. One of the lead singers tried to approach me after I had gone to bed, but he respected my reluctance.

I had kept Mother updated on all of my new and exciting experiences in weekly letters, but about three weeks into the summer, I received a desperate letter asking me to come home. I had no money and she did not send any. Once more, I suggested she turn to Hermann and Hannelore for support, and I told her we would be returning in a few weeks.

I had also received an incredibly beautiful love letter from Ronald, who lived several houses down the street from Stuart, my other suitor. Ronald was a life guard at a public pool in Lachine that summer, and he wrote, "I am surrounded by the cream of womanhood, but none surpasses your beauty." In his letter, he also added a new word to my English vocabulary. The word was "hypochondriac." He called my mother a hypochondriac because he had heard that she had been hospitalized in a psychiatric ward. He also felt that Mother had not been treating me right, but his letter boosted my morale somewhat during this time of uncertainty.

I tried to suppress my tears on our way back to Montreal. The Muellers and their older son, who had joined us, just looked at each other in disbelief. They couldn't understand why I wept so much. They never asked me what was going on because they could not possibly fathom why I had fallen into a deep depression. I was in grief and I couldn't explain what was happening to me, and it hadn't registered in my mind that Mother had already sent for me from other summer jobs and that it could happen again. Mother's co-dependency with me would leave some serious psychological scars.

Visit with Mother at the Allen Memorial Institute after electroshock treatments in August, 1962.

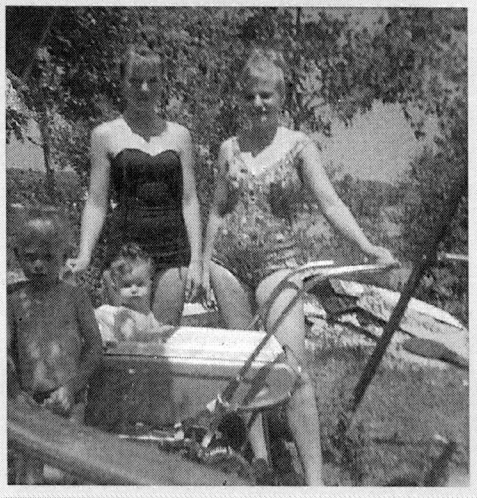

Emily (17), Hanne (23), Miles (3) and Brittney (1) enjoying a weekend at their summer cottage in St. Donat, 1963.

Chapter 9

WEST HILL HIGH SCHOOL, MONTREAL, PQ

Upon our return from Vancouver, I was greeted by a strange couple who informed me where Mother was staying, and then left for their home in Sudbury, Ontario. I immediately jumped on a city bus for the Allan Memorial Institute, and found that she'd had the infamous experimental electroshock treatments that resulted in a major scandal against the director of the hospital and the CIA in the United States, as has been documented in books and film. I could not recognize her in her heavily sedated state. I had a few consultations with a Dr. Engel, whom I impressed as a stable and confident young lady. He encouraged me to start writing. I thought he meant "riding" horses. Here I am, 53 years later, *writing.* Mother was eventually sent home into my capable hands as it were. I must have subconsciously rationalized that if I had been there for her, this latest calamity could have been prevented, and I suspect my family had a part in this scenario, since it was easier for them to harass Mother for her money without me being around.

I wasn't aware that I had suddenly ceased to menstruate and that it was not going to occur for another seven years. I had been restricting my calories the previous two years, but my full-fledged eating disorder had taken root that summer. No one knew about it, and everyone seemed to approve of my slenderness, so I felt quite acceptable on that basis, but it seemed I had lost control of everything but my body image. My friends and their families were leaving the province of Quebec, and I was unable to make new connections. And since Karl had been boarding with us for several years, people had mistakenly assumed he and I were an item or seriously involved.

Our visits with the Muellers next door had dwindled. I wasn't aware that they were preoccupied with a permanent move to Vancouver, and I had been working as a part-time script girl for their friend and film maker who had hired me to coach two little boys in French and English for a film documentary based on Montreal's clothing industry. On our last visit with the Muellers, I asked Mother to go ahead first because I wanted to do my sit-ups, so I'd appear fresh and happy when I arrived.

~/~

That fall, I received a telephone call from Ron, inviting me to dinner at his place, just a few houses away. His family was out, and he had the whole place to himself–a rare occasion, since he had two other teenage brothers. I arrived dressed in my favorite pleated wool skirt and matching sweater. He had dinner ready in the oven, and he filled the two layers of cake he had baked with custard, and topped it with a chocolate glaze for what should have been my first taste of genuine Boston cream pie. He gave me a tour of his house, took me to his room upstairs, and showed me his sports equipment which tumbled out as soon as he opened the door to his closet.

The romantic picnic he'd taken me on for my sixteenth birthday in June, and the love letter he had sent me in Vancouver later that summer, had fueled my romantic mood, but we had gone straight downstairs to sit down and eat when the phone rang. He answered it, said something into the receiver in a muffled voice, looked at me and said, "I'll be right back." He took off like lightning. I sat at the table for at least forty minutes, watching dinner getting cold and not touching a morsel. When he came back, I excused myself and went home. Though my disappointment with Ronald was profound, I felt enveloped by a gentle aura, and I thought I had seen guardian angels out of the corner of my eyes, and I felt His presence, as if trying to reassure me, that whenever the going gets tough, God gets even tougher.

~/~

As soon as Mother had recovered from her electroshock treatments, she took an evening shift as cook for a fraternity house at McGill University. Before she left for work, she had prepared a plate of *Apfelradl* – pancakes, with a tall glass of chocolate milk by its side, which I enjoyed with gusto. I could almost hear her say, *"Ess dass was wird von Dir!"* – "Eat, so something will become of you!" None of the boarders at that time needed to use the kitchen, so I settled right into my studies at the kitchen table. It was nice to have it all to myself. When temperatures tumbled to below freezing, I enjoyed being able to turn on the oven for some lovely heat coming out of its opened door. I felt a twinge of guilt because the thermostat in the hallway was encased with a lock, and Mother's electrical bill might show a difference.

I felt somewhat protective of Mother after her ordeal with experimental electroshock treatments at the Allan Memorial, and I was really concerned when she and two salesmen sent me out of the kitchen one day. There were some muffled sounds and I thought they were going to harm her. I asked if everything was all right, through the swinging doors to dining room. When I was invited to re-enter the kitchen, I discovered that she hadn't been harmed at all, and everything was all right indeed. Whew!

Meantime, Hanne and Hermann usually had me babysit Miles and Brittney on their nights out. Weather permitting, I had conditioned myself to sprint from my place on Beaconsfield Avenue to their four bedroom apartment on the corner of Sherbrooke and Vendome, like a deer. They, like Mother, also had rented their spare bedrooms to recent immigrants, and sometimes a boarder would try to get too chummy with me, but I instinctively knew how to handle these situations. Their resident budgie bird kept me amused however, when it nonchalantly perched itself at the end of my knitting needle for a bouncy up-and-down fun ride while working on my latest project.

When my grade ten morning class at West Hill High had been dismissed for lunch break on November 22, 1963, I walked into the school's hallway to find most students looking at each other as if in shock. I heard stunned words reverberating in disbelief, "John F. Kennedy has been assassinated!" I had never followed politics, but I felt so sorry for his lovely wife Jackie and their beautiful children. My other thought, "How could this happen in America?" not aware that I would eventually feel disappointed about my own life in a land of the free and golden opportunities.

I still heard Karl coming and going, up and down the narrow staircase to the attic. "Does he have a girlfriend?" I naively wondered, while I was diligently studying for my grade ten exams. Our summer romance two years earlier in St. Andrew's-by-the-Sea, the trip to New York, and my summer with the Muellers to Vancouver seemed as if but fleeting moments in a make believe, far away world.

Once in a while, Karl, Mother, Hannelore, Hermann and I did frequent the German Hofbrauhaus night club in downtown Montreal, and I felt a little out of place (under-age). Otherwise, Karl hardly ever came back to the attic much before midnight, but he was keeping his foot in the door so to speak. He was willing to wait until I graduated. So was the German carpenter who had quietly occupied Room #2 since I was thirteen. I didn't realize he was doing the same thing, until I found him waiting for me in the early morning hours, after a graduation dance. I fought him off just like I had so many others, and as I drifted into deep sleep, I felt pleased with my ability to say my prayers in German, English, as well as French and give thanks for His protection.

~/~

There was another boy, by the name of Dale, who, like Stuart, had been adopted into fine families and raised in NDG. Dale had familiarized himself with most of the students in the community, including my own friends from West Hill High, so he knew a little about myself and my circumstances. He knew that I was the daughter of a divorced or widowed homeowner. He had noticed me in the hallway of the school before he had dropped out of high school after an attempt at one or two private schools. This is when he had originally told himself, "This is the girl I am going to marry someday."

When he asked me out for the first time, I included Mother on the date. I really didn't want to leave her alone all evening anyway. Besides, I wasn't entirely sure if I could trust him, because there was absolutely nothing boyish about him. He didn't object to taking us to the movies in his father's car. After he had dropped us off, Mother said, *"Der hat dunkle Augen, aber Er hat schoene Lippen."* – "His eyes are really dark, but he has nice lips." Though Dale appeared as an exceptionally stable, mature and intelligent nineteen-year-old man, she implied his eyes expressed a dark side.

I accepted his second invitation on condition we double date, and I invited Stuart to join us with his own date for an evening of bowling. I beat each one of my three competitors with a score of 185. The closest score was 160.

I took advantage of ski trips my high school had made available on Saturdays, and I am sure it had been noticed in the neighborhood that I had been lugging all of my equipment before sunrise to and back home again in the dark from the drop-off location at the school, which, during the week, had already been daily work-outs in and of itself with a load of books cradled in my arms. Mother must have known that I would take to skiing like fish to water and didn't hesitate to give me the money for the bus fare and ski lift tickets. My brother-in-law had given me the skis and poles for Christmas at age twelve, and I had only used them once for a family outing several years earlier. All I had to to is get myself and my equipment (skis, poles, ski boots and backpack) to the bus early in the morning, and be mentally prepared to use T-bars and chairlifts for the first time.

Soon, Ron from down the street joined me for the next school ski trip. As we were heading up the snow-laden slopes in our chairlifts, he royally entertained me with all the French folk songs he had recently learned at Scouts, and I taught him the folk songs I knew in German, including one of my favorites, *"Mein Vater war ein Wandersmann"* – "The Happy Wanderer." However, he was an unusually aggressive skier, and I actually had a hard time keeping up with him by the end of a day of non-stop skiing. I was chilled to the bone and came down with pneumonia the following day. However, I had basked, unpiqued, in the limelight of a charming boy's undivided attention all day, much to the intrusions and slight provocations of some envious young girls.

Soon, Dale offered to drive me to the ski slopes with his father's car, though he hadn't taken very well to skiing himself. He must have heard how much I loved the sport, and he was perfectly willing to wait for me all day. I think the best part for him was innocently allowing him to warm up my chilled toes under his derrière while he drove me back home.

I am sure it was Dale who took me to the theater to see the Rogers and Hammerstein production of the musical, "The Sound of Music." I was totally unprepared for what I was about to see, but soon realized the movie had been filmed in Salzburg, Austria, and I felt like a cruel joke had been played on me – a reminder that I once lived in that beautiful country, and that I had been ripped away from a world I once knew. I think I was deeply traumatized by the reawakening of memories that had subconsciously tugged at my heart since we had left that country six years earlier.

Dale soon invited me for Sunday dinners with his family. His mother doted on me with an extraordinary kindness and nurturing I hadn't experienced at home. Sometimes his sister's family joined us from Ottawa. He eventually took me to football games, hockey games, and some movies without Mother, but he never took me to a dance. He had dropped out of school and was employed by Western Electric Telecommunications through his father, a financial controller in the firm. His job took him out of town and we lost touch.

~/~

During my last two years in high school, I had entirely forgotten about menstruating. I was obsessed with studies and fitness, but I didn't miss out on any dances. Staying fit and slim, and graduating was my focus. It was all about not gaining weight or it'd be the end of me, so I thought. I have had night dreams in which I am literally terrified of not making it through high school. In one dream,

I find myself sitting at the back of a class as a shamed little old lady, still struggling to make the grades. I also had bad dreams of being terribly hurt and abandoned by my adoptive families, the Muellers and the Thomasons. It seemed to me that they chose to forget me because of my problems.

Mostly everyone I had known had moved away, and I was the straggler, entrapped by an insidious disease, making me think, "You have lost a lot, but you still have control over your body, and if you gain weight, you will lose that too." I found myself devouring anything fast-and-easy to eat in a starved frenzy – a box of Ritz crackers, cookies, bread or ice cream. Before Mother had a chance to notice anything missing, I rushed to the store to restock the pantry with my babysitting money. Ironically I had also been studying recipes in-depth and probably had the knowledge of an experienced chef, just like Mother, who served healthy, balanced meals to fraternity students at McGill University, while I threw out bread at home to make it seem like I ate much more than I did. I hoped she would bring home a tasty left over meal, but I wonder if I would have actually eaten it.

Mrs. Yurman, the Austrian lady I had befriended four years earlier, while I had been hospitalization for appendicitis, came by to check on me at that time. She wondered about the bread that hadn't flushed down the toilet completely. "I had too much to eat and got sick," I explained, before she left to be with her own family. I had turned into a full-fledged bulimic/anorexic and I had become socially withdrawn. Suddenly oblivious to the comings and goings of any boarders, I went on long runs in what seemed like a deserted neighborhood and made feeble attempts on the piano. My lessons had been cut off for some time and I had lost interest. I studied well past midnight and got up again by five a.m. to review the homework I had just done a few hours earlier because I was terrified of sleep 'deleting' all the facts I had just memorized. The pursuit of knowledge and facts kept me sane, protecting me from going crazy. I went without food all day, and spent my lunch hours strolling through the school halls and around the expansive school grounds, and I developed tremendous headaches and eye twitches. Then I stopped at the public library before heading for home in the dark, because I believed this was what serious students did. Besides, the room #3 next to me was occupied by an impoverished single mother and her nine-year-old daughter. The mother seemed to be permanently chilled, with her arms tightly wrapped around herself, and the girl was repeatedly trying to get my attention while I was studying. There was nothing I would have rather done than to play and have fun with this needy little person, but my survival depended on my studies. I had to graduate from high school. Playful fun was no longer an option. I still said my prayers, believing God had isolated me for a reason.

~/~

Mother's seasonal job at the fraternity house had ended and she started to bring my suppers up to my room so I could carry on with my studies uninterrupted. I looked at the tray she had placed on my desk and thought to myself, "I know you mean well, Mother. You are concerned about me, and you want me to eat." I would take a bite and tell myself, "Oh, this is nothing but fattening grub." I waited until I could inconspicuously sneak the plate out of my room to the bathroom. When she came back to retrieve the tray, she asked, *"War es gut?"* – "Did you like it?" I answered, *"Ja, Mutti, sehr gut"* – "Yes mom. Very good."

Mother had expressed her concern to Hannelore and Hermann, when they showed up one evening, as I was hovering over my books. They asked me to stand up so they could see how nice and slim I looked. "Look!" Mother said, pointing at my bones poking out of my hips, when Hanne responded, "That's nothing to worry about. It's just a phase. She'll gain it back." I was somewhat pleased with the attention I had received from my family, but Mother insisted I see her doctor. I told him I preferred lean meats, vegetables and fruit, and that I had eliminated all fatty foods. After the examination he concluded, "You are made like a fine Swiss-made watch." and we all thought I was just fine.

During the latter part of my final year, I had an opportunity to move to Germany with a fellow who was going into the military and join an army base in Germany. However, I didn't know who this tall, dark, and good looking fellow was, who had shown up at my door, face beaming, to practically propose marriage. I was put on the spot and slightly stunned to put it lightly. Mother liked the idea, but then she may have been the one to have set it up with good intentions. Just a few dates and family meetings, with time to consider it could have swayed me in that direction. Nothing would have made me happier than to see my home country again, and maybe even to start a family without feeling guilty about dropping out of school and leaving Mother on her own. I was afraid of being thrown yet into another situation beyond my control, and I never imagined that he would be willing to wait a few months until I graduated, as if all arrangements had already been booked for the very next day, with having nothing to say in the matter. I had yet to learn much about myself and my family, and about my creator's purpose for me.

~/~

Then one day, I had a totally unexpected invitation to lunch at one of my grade eleven classmate's home. I accepted, not in my wildest dreams thinking that it would turn into an extensive lecture with five other Jewish girls to support her, as they sat around her dining room table, and lectured me on the atrocities the Germans had committed against the Jews in World War II. There was no lunch; not even water. I was not prepared to defend myself against my accusers and I just let it pass over (pardon the pun), making sure I did not do or say anything to draw attention to myself. I remained silent. I was an innocent, naïve, immigrant girl from Austria, starving herself. Maybe they had decided it was a good time to start dieting themselves since one or two of the girls were seriously overweight. The thought of reporting the incident never occurred to me. Nowadays I am sure that would be considered 'bullying'.

I found myself reading up on World War II, and I just about keeled over when I learned that Hitler was born in *Braunau am Inn*, my home town, the town I lived in from the age of four to ten before we emigrated in 1956. That was the first time I felt truly cursed by the world. I had suddenly become the underdog, and championing the less fortunate in this world became a personal mission, though twenty eight years later, my husband's opinion on my passion was, "You only associate with losers."

I was actually envious of Jews. I could have posed as being Jewish with a surname like Fahrmann. All I would have had to do is to perhaps take off one "*n.*" I fantasized about having Jewish blood in me. Their pain was recognized. Mine was a silent torture. Had I been of English, French or Jewish descent, I would have been able to identify with a major ethnic group living in Montreal at that time. As it was, I felt shunned, and having worked for Jewish families as a German girl from *Braunau* only added to my anxiety. Mother had referred to Jews as "*Die Juden*" in a certain subdued voice, so she may have been aware of what had happened. In defense of Mother, I must add that she herself had been threatened by the powers that be, because she had spoken out against Hitler's religious policy by asserting her faith. I have a document stating that she had been reported to the regime's headquarters in Wasserburg-am-Inn, Germany, stating "*Bei der Polizei angezeigt*" – "Reported to the police." She had risked being blacklisted. It was a mild warning. She had done what her conscience had dictated, and she had her best intentions as a witness for justice, peace and love.

I have read literature in which German offspring of the war have the same collective survivor guilt that Jewish offspring have. They ask themselves, "Why me? Why did my grandfather have to starve? Why did my mother have to suffer? Why am I comfortable? And what do I have to do to earn the right to that comfort?" And so many of us tended to give priority to others, as if doing so would make up for the injustices inflicted during the war.

~/~

Towards the end of my last year in high school, my English teacher took me aside and accused me of plagiarism, and I admitted to it. I had copied some material out of an encyclopedia, and she made me write a new essay, while her scolding brought me to tears. She also unsuccessfully discouraged a very nice new student I had befriended from associating with me. I don't think my English teacher regarded me as a 'nice girl,' though my open-house parties had ended long before the end of my second year in Grade nine, and I only went out to dances on weekends. I am sure my lack of sleep and stress and malnutrition may have given me the appearance of leading a disreputable or erratic life style.

The marks in my grade eleven were respectable, except the 47 out of 100 in English Composition. I did not know why I hadn't been able to read a book through from cover to cover or concentrate on a story line, let alone in the written form. No one has ever seen that failing mark still discernible on my faded grade eleven matriculation report card, and don't ask me how I graduated that year or how I was admitted into first year college (with that mark). And no one knew that I was lonely, and suffered from anxiety, depression, and anorexia.

"See ya!" was one of my favorite expressions according to my 1964 Grade 11 Yearbook It is no coincidence because I went out of my way to avoid pronouncing "r"s like the plague since it caused me so much trouble and teasing by rolling it the European way. Years later, I was flattered when my teenage daughter took an interest in my yearbook and actually "claimed" it. I could obtain a copy of it through West Hill High's classroom website, but my memory of grade eleven still makes me sick to my stomach.

~/~

Right after the graduation ceremonies (June of 1964), I joined a group of students at the corner coffeehouse. Dale Tinsley, who had dropped out of school a year earlier showed up too, and sat beside me. I tasted my first cigarette in that cafe, and all I remember is feeling so sick I abruptly left for home. I forgot to take my graduation certificate with me. I had left it in that smoky coffee shop with the juke boxes blaring, and I never went back to collect it. I hadn't expected any form of recognition or celebration anyway, so there was no disappointment, though I imagined my fellow classmates enjoying special family celebrations for them. But I did manage to hold on to a Royal Life Saving Society of Canada certificate, and bronze medallion I had earned by taking advantage of the high school's swimming pool program several months earlier.

~/~

As soon as I had graduated, Mother promptly set me up to work for two families in the Laurentians. This time, I alternated back and forth between two co-joined cottages, to wash dishes, sweep, make beds and babysit, all in kosher style, for two families. It was a good deal for them; two for the price of one. I was delegated to share a room with a pre-teen boy who, in his own bed, masturbated endlessly. I am sure any girl would have run away at that point, but not me. Who was I to complain?

I am not sure if Karl had moved out of the attic by then, but within two weeks, he showed up at the cottage to bring me home, which was a tremendous relief from my daily drudgery, although I had to quit yet another summer job due to Mother's mental health. Karl had been in search for new employment, and soon left for Los Angeles, California shortly thereafter, and I realized that Mother had sold our home on Beaconsfield Avenue while I was away. She was in the process of packing our household goods. Where was I to go, what was I to do? To please Mother, and show her that I was willing to eat more, I asked her for a second boiled egg.

Room #1 had been my very first room at age of thirteen; room #3 felt like a princess's room; room #5 was a private hideaway in the attic. In room #4, I had heard the rumble of my ex-boyfriend Ronald's motorcycle rumbling past my house, while waiting for a chance to inconspicuously dispose of my cold dinner down the toilet, and it felt like my life was drifting away into uncharted waters toward another unknown territory, and I was fearful of what lay ahead. But I still said my prayers, because that's what Mother reminded me to do every night: *"Tu beten. Alles wird einmal gut."* – "Say your prayers. Everything will be alright someday."

High school photos of Stuart
in 1962 and me in 1964.
Party time (below).

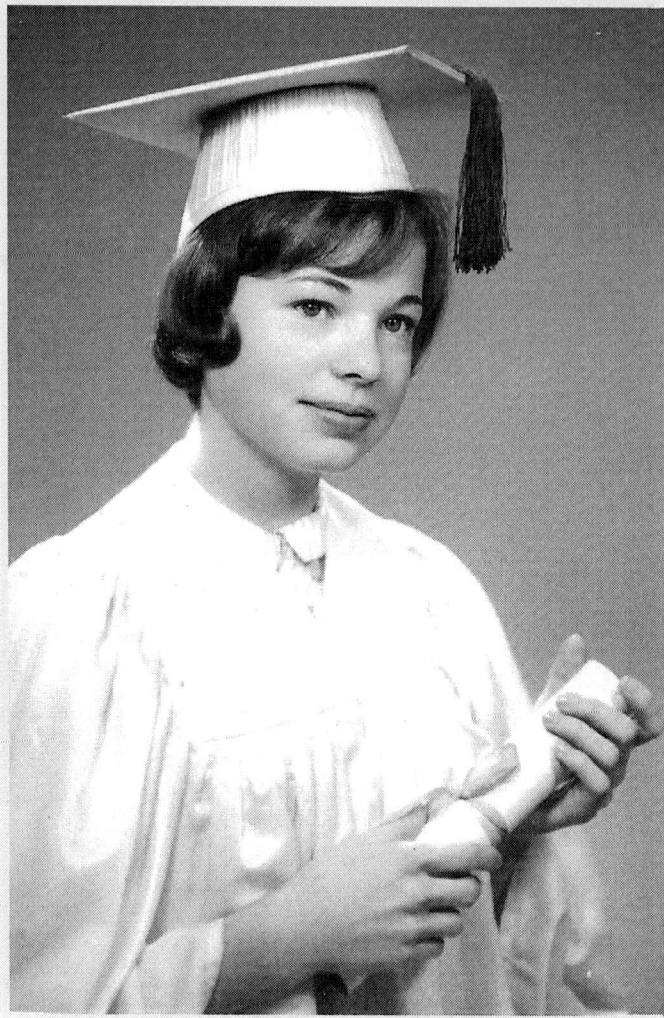

High school graduation photo, 1964.

Chapter 10

1964: MACDONALD COLLEGE; ST. ANNE-DE-BELLEVUE, PQ
My grade eleven home room teacher at West Hill High had passed out pamphlets offering bursaries to MacDonald College in St. Anne-de-Bellevue. The college specialized in three fields: Agriculture, Home Economics, and Teacher Physical Education. Agriculture was male oriented; Home Economics was female oriented; Physical Education was gender neutral. I opted to major in the latter because I loved physical exercise and needed to stay in perfect physical shape, while assuming I would eventually feel comfortable with the 'teaching in English' part of it. I wasn't worried about excelling in academics.

Commercial art had originally appealed to me, but Mother quickly talked me out of a career in an "economically uncertain and male oriented field," as she alluded to it. I dismissed the possibility of going into Nursing at McGill University because I believed McGill was an institute designated solely for the privileged upper crust class with financially well-heeled backgrounds, and I hated to go to Mother for extravagant expenses. Besides, I was still carrying that big eating disorder secret.

~/~

After the sale of the house, Mother took a live-in job as homemaker in the suburb of Pointe Claire. Her new employer, Mr. Wilson, had been recently widowed with two adopted school age children. Since Pointe Claire was a relatively short commute to MacDonald College, I accepted the invitation to share her room with her. What else was I to do under those circumstances?

I had one last chance to see my old home on Beaconsfield Avenue, in NDG (Notre-Dame-de-Grace), when Mother had asked me to go back and check if we had forgotten any Christmas ornaments during our move. I rang and knocked on the door for quite a while, until a black teenage girl answered. She seemed extremely shy. I explained who I was and what I had come for. I had to convince her for some time that I would have only a very quick look In the basement storage area, until she finally allowed me inside and down the stairs into the basement.

I could not find any Christmas ornaments. What I did see were a couple of raised cots with an array of equipment used for sex and bondage, including chains and whips. I climbed up the stairs and dashed out of my old home as fast as I could, and I was hurrying down the street to catch my bus when I noticed a man of color approaching the house. When he saw me, he sped up to catch up and started to yell, "What were you doing in my house?"

I told him exactly what Mother had sent me for. Then he warned me if I told anyone about what I had seen in the basement, I'd be in big trouble. I reassured him I wouldn't tell anyone. I felt so sorry for that young girl. Her family may have been the first people of color to take up residency in NDG. This is my last memory of 4142 Beaconsfield Ave, NDG, Montreal.

~/~

Most of the students at MacDonald College lived on the campus. I had long forgotten how to make friends, but I accepted a compassionate student's invitation to lunch in the cafeteria one day. I was very self-conscious and I thought all eyes were on me as I picked at my food. I had been retreating into one of the stately living rooms in a remote area of the college during lunchtime and between classes, with my books and a handful of candy by my side. I must have been considered an odd ball student with peculiar habits that no one understood.

If I'd had the courage to approach the authorities and asked if I qualified for room and board on campus, I would no doubt have had a chance at improving my attitude towards food, with three square meals available every day, without feeling that I was imposing on Mr. Wilson's or Mother's budget, as well as widening my social circle and eliminating a fairly long commute by foot and bus. However, Mother's mantra always was, "Cheapest is best," and Mr. Wilson's mantra at the dining table was, "We all need to lose a few pounds."

Several months later, Mother had received a telephone call from a Lebanese businessman, father and divorcee, who had interviewed her for a job while we were still living on Beaconsfield Avenue. He took us to lunch at the Mont Tremblant Ski Resort, and he proposed to me right there and then. Mother didn't object to the idea when he asked, "May I have your daughter's hand?" I decided it was not a particularly good idea to marry a stranger while I was in my first year of college. I had a thirst for knowledge, zest for life, a beautiful body, a keen awareness of my physicality, and I was blessed with a deep faith in the promises of God. And deep down inside I knew that the love and peace of my heavenly Father was the answer.

I remember many invigorating hikes through pristine, white, glistening, sun-kissed, or moonlit snow, on my way to and from my classes, my strolls through St. Anne-de-Bellevue, the college's town, with its quaint little village shops, orchards that produced the sweetest and juiciest apples I would ever taste, and Mr. Wilson's children anxiously waiting for their bedtime stories: small pleasures such as the little things depicted in the song, "My Favorite Things" in the musical, *The Sound of Music*; things one should never be denied because of society's pressure to succeed in the corporate or academic worlds. To quote Emily Dickinson, *"The mere sense of living is joy enough."*

~/~

Speak of things going *flat* again. I had only seen Stuart on rare occasions that year, until he called me and asked me to a college dance, which meant driving twenty miles out to Pointe Claire to fetch me at the Wilson's. Late that night, instead of taking me all the way back to Pointe Claire, he dropped me off at an address

Mother had provided me to people she apparently knew. The extra gas expense had also been a consideration for the cash strapped university student. It was after two a.m., and the occupants had kindly left their door open for me, or so I thought. I entered the home, and settled into the first vacant bedroom by the entrance. I slept well, and I was greeted next morning by a kindly lady who had no idea who I was. I had slept in the bedroom of her parents who had been away for the weekend. Over tea and toast, I showed her the address which Mother had provided, but they had no idea about any such arrangements made by a Mrs. Margarete Fahrmann. I was in the wrong house. Before I left to catch a bus, she introduced me to her brother, who was a quadriplegic. I felt so badly for him. He was delighted to see me, and asked to see me again. God and my guardian angels had looked after me once more, though I never did find out where I was supposed to be staying or with whom, and I would tell a shocked Stuart about that night fifty years later.

Meantime, I enjoyed the lectures, the physical education classes in the gym, in the pool, and on the sports fields of MacDonald College. However, having isolated myself, the thought of having to finally speak up in a compulsory small group discussion towards the end of the last semester made my knees knock so hard against each other that I had to grab them to stop them from trembling. I just couldn't speak up. I failed again! I failed myself, and I didn't dare tell Mother, let alone confide my nervousness and my problems to a guidance counselor.

I arrived late for student practice teaching at a suburban elementary school because I had trouble finding the remote location of the school by foot. The principal welcomed me by saying, "You immigrants sure get all the breaks with your grants." My chance at student teaching in the grade four class was rigid and uninspired, but I really did appreciate the little student's polite attentiveness, as if they had sensed my insecurity. I also arrived late to catch the gathering of approximately 30 male and 40 female classmates for a fabulous year-end class photo.

My report card from MacDonald College stated that I did not pass. I had failed, and I automatically precluded any possibility of continuing my studies there. I might have done well by switching majors to the Home Economics (Domestic Sciences) department, but I tossed my report card out so no one could see evidence of my disgrace. The most logical option was to enroll in Montreal's Sir George Williams University Business program, but I felt like a real cop-out by then, and I was no longer the proud landlady's daughter, but an immigrant daughter who could not succeed in the proverbial land of golden opportunities. To share those feelings with anyone seemed unimaginable, *verboten*, forbidden for fear of ending up in the fires of hell, an allegorical concentration camp or worse, heading in a direction I did not want to go, limited to a "box," chained to it, and I couldn't get off. Maybe it was God's way of protecting me until I was ready and strong enough to face the real 'tzunamis' that lay ahead in those choppy waters of mine. If it hadn't been for my God-given physical strength, spirit and determination, I probably would have self-destructed before I turned the age of twenty-one.

~/~

DOLLARD-DES-ORMEAUX, PQ
I hadn't been included on a family trip back to my homeland since we had emigrated nine years earlier, and I took it as punishment for having failed my first year at college. Mother (age 52), Hanne (age 25), Miles (age 5), and Brittney (age 3), were going to Austria and Germany for the month of July, 1965, and I was asked to take care of the Wilson family (with pay) during that time.

All went well and I enjoyed the cooking, and taking care of the children and the household, but I also welcomed the chance to get away from my job when Hermann invited me to spend a weekend at Lake Placid, near the Adirondack Mountains in Maine, USA. We had always gotten along very well, and he had always respected me as his wife's little sister. Nothing had ever gone on between us romantically or sexually, and our time at Lake Placid was totally platonic. He was twice my age, almost forty–an old man in my eyes. However, I should have known rumors were going to fly.

On another weekend, Hermann asked me to assist him with a buffet supper for a party he had hosted for his business associates. I did not stay too long into the party. There were mostly men, if not all men, and it felt like it was a stag party about to turn into something else. I was uncomfortable and I found a ride back to the Wilson's by 10 p.m.

I was disappointed when Mr. Wilson declined to include me on their camping vacation with his girlfriend and his children, so I decided to use my earnings of $240 toward a train ticket to see Karl, who had occupied the attic and had relocated to Los Angeles. I had a seater all the way there, and I was offered a free meal in the diner when the concierge noticed that I had not been eating very much.

Father and his second wife, Christine, in Linz, Austria; 1964.

With my lovely niece, Brittney, in 1965.

Chapter 11

1965: LOS ANGELES, CA
As soon as he had spotted me, Karl jumped over the guard rails for a big greeting. Then he took me to his boarding complex, where he had arranged a shared room for me, and while he still had to work on the first day of my arrival, I used the time to recuperate from my arduous journey by relaxing by the poolside. Karl had given his roommate permission to escort me to an amusement park. While we were having lunch, his friend said, "You sure are in the right city. I think you should be a model or an actress."

Karl brought out his convertible sports car, and took a week off work to show me the attractions in Los Angeles, in Tijuana and Ensenada, Mexico, across the border. He had assured me that I could continue my studies at the University of Southern California, UCLA, if I were to stay and marry him (though he mentioned that he had a very jealous girlfriend in the sidelines), and he was also willing to wait for sex. I was relieved at that because I thought I was frigid, but I was definitely ready for a little adventure.

Something pulled me back to Montreal, however, or perhaps even back to Austria. Like a powerful tide wanting pull me under, I thought my family needed me. I was somewhat geographically disoriented as well. I needed someone like Stuart to ground me in South Western history and geography, so he may have drawn me back subconsciously. I had already turned into somewhat of an intellectual snob, and I couldn't see myself with anyone intellectually inferior, though Karl was a very clever guy. I should have been in my glory, hand-in-hand with an adoring young man, strolling in the sand of a moonlit ocean-side, yet found myself bursting out with tears. Since then, I have come to appreciate the incredibly powerful need to remain connected with one's roots, as depicted in the 2016 movie 'LION', in which a severely traumatized and displaced little boy develops a serious identity crisis as a grown man, and is torn between his loving and well to do adoptive parents in Australia and his long-lost impoverished family in India.

~/~

I had an icy reception when I called my family from the train station's pay phone in Montreal. I heard a flurry of chatter in the background and I got the impression that picking me up at the station was a huge inconvenience, and I had to insist on a ride home since I had nothing left of my $240. Reluctantly, Hermann did give me a ride, but even he gave me the cold shoulder. In the back of my mind I had to ask myself, "What happened? What have I done now? Has Karl already telephoned them from L.A. to have expressed doubts about my weak commitment to him?"

Apparently, Mother and Hannelore did not have a particularly pleasant trip overseas, one reason being they did not get along very well with their in-laws in Dusseldorf. Mother expressed outrage over their need for daily afternoon siestas, and they were in a terrible kerfuffle over something else. I surmised that it could have been over my outing with Hermann in Lake Placid, or the party I had helped him host when they were away. I couldn't understand why they were making such a big fuss. Hermann was no angel, but their suspicions might have been related to something entirely different. I hate to say this about my beloved brother-in-law: he was predisposed to gossip, which sometimes turned out to be a mockery of others, especially of Mother's excessive frugality. The absence of spiritual leadership of his family was evident to me, and that was sad, considering he liked to socialize with the pastor, who's church he had been contracted to built.

Mother must have sensed I was still too vulnerable to be living on my own, being a student, and compensated Hannelore and Hermann for taking me into their home that fall. Mother had her money securely invested and her household effects in storage, including my piano. Her mold as a paid, live-in domestic had been firmly established right out of convent, so without rent, food or overhead expenses, she was, no doubt, happy to see her savings grow. She did suffer from pressure to relinquish her assets to her son-in-law at times, but she stood her ground with the advice of her lawyer.

I was back in college again. Mother had a new live-in position. Hermann was a prosperous building contractor, and Miles and Brittney were in preschool. Even before extensive future renovations, I thought their home was beautiful. It was decorated with teak furniture throughout and it had a beautifully landscaped garden. Hanne seemed to have it all: beautiful children, lovely home and private membership to a country club. I suppose I was envious of her home and family, and she was most likely jealous of my freedom.

~/~

Stuart and I were both students at Sir George University that year. He majored in History and I enrolled in Business Administration. He occupied a room near McGill University because his parents had moved ahead to Ontario. We saw each other between classes and we liked to frequent a quaint European coffee shop after school. He came out to my sister's in Dollard-des-Ormeaux for a costume party that Hermann hosted in his Bavarian-themed basement party room. Hanne was dressed as a hula dancer, Hermann was a pirate, Stuart donned a Samurai warrior outfit, and I looked like Tinkerbell. Since all of the other guests were already married with children, we were the kids of the party and we probably acted our part, because we danced the night away in a world of our own.

That autumn, we had a cycling date. Stuart had already biked a good ten miles from downtown Montreal to my sister's house in Dollard-des-Ormeaux, from where we had planned a day trip of cycling. About five miles out of Dollard, Stuart's bike had a flat tire and we had to get rides home. *Flat* again.

Embracing
Stuart at
a costume
party, 1966.

Stuart was a sociable and consummate gentleman, always willing to offer lively, stimulating conversation on history and music, but I never truly realized how deeply he felt about me. Later that year, when he dropped me off at my sister's house after a dance, he trembled as he was about to propose to me, and I gently declined. Another *flat!* I couldn't see marriage in our cards at that time. Hanne's words had flashed through my mind to the effect that I didn't know if I was a man or a woman, and deep down inside I was aware that I had serious psychological issues which needed to be addressed before taking on any life-time commitment, and I doubted if our parents would have approved of marriage, since we were both in school with no money and no place of our own.

Besides, we didn't have to get married. We'd never had intercourse for religious reasons, to honor God. I had forgotten I should have been menstruating, and I was far from feeling safe and serious with any man at that point. Stuart married a girl named Leona, on the rebound, and that soon went *flat* as well.

Toward the end of my year at Sir George Williams, Mother called me from her live-in job to say she could not see anything. She was afraid she was going blind. I was so distressed, I dropped out of business school. Mother was fine again after her surgery for glaucoma, and I looked for my first official job.

~/~

My sister pressured Hermann to move me out of their home shortly after I had been employed with Fischbach and Moore Engineering Co. Suddenly, and unwarranted, he asked me to pack my things. I thought, "What have I done this time to deserve such a sudden harsh kick?" and I figured, since my sister and my mother had been out of their nests at my age, there was no reason why I shouldn't be out there too. Hanne had married at age eighteen, and Mother had been admitted into a convent at age twelve. I had blocked out any trace of a possible resentment on the part of my sister, and I understood that she was tired of being expected to look out for me. She had her own family, and she had enough of having to take on Mother's role. I asked him to take me to the downtown YWCA, the only safe place I could think of.

Being an outcast in downtown Montreal was one of the most painful times in my life. It was in the peak of the sweltering summer heat in July, almost unbearable in a stuffy, non-ventilated, non-air conditioned room, trying to keep grapes and apples cool in the washroom sink filled with water. I aimlessly wandered around the old city and around Mount Royal. I tried to mask my loneliness, but it was obvious to two concerned fellows who asked if I needed help. Of course I denied it. At work I pretended I had a normal home life, and acted as if nothing had happened, but I kept botching up on the simplest tasks. I had just endured the bitter taste of homelessness, and felt robbed of the pride and security I had once enjoyed as an Austrian landlady's doting daughter.

When Mother returned from a trans-Canada bus tour, she was appalled to hear what had happened. Had she been around, they wouldn't have dared to evict me that way. She immediately had me move into her one-bedroom apartment on Barklay Avenue, where I found myself among many recent immigrants again. For a while I felt like I was going back in time rather than forging ahead. Mother claimed half of my monthly salary right off the bat, but it was a safe roof over my head.

Meantime, Hermann invited me to join his family for a seaside vacation in Atlantic City, NY. He was still sorry for having taken me to the YWCA earlier that summer, and he had contrived a plan in order to include me as a paying family member. My sister was very pleased when I handed her two hundred dollars for my expenses, and I was a very happy aunt, wedged between my niece and nephew in the backseat of the car, on our way to sand, surf, sun, and fun! We enjoyed the boardwalk attractions in Atlantic City, we had our individual portraits sketched, and we had a lovely time on the beach. When they went out on the town in the evenings, I babysat the children.

~/~

I was pleasantly surprised to find how much I loved having the apartment to myself when Mother had taken a job in Ottawa to care for a gravely ill senior. I tried to make a cozy nest out of it. I cleaned it thoroughly, and on its shady balcony, while under the curious scrutiny of occupants of some surrounding apartment buildings, I altered the wall-to-wall living room drapes to fit properly around Mother's stacked up storage boxes. My biological clock must have been ticking for a nest of my own.

I anticipated some quality time with Mother when she extended a heartfelt and enthusiastic invitation to visit her in Ottawa for the weekend, but she took off as soon as I had arrived, leaving me alone for the day with a strange old man on his deathbed. I took the train back to Montreal the next day, and I didn't take her up on a second invitation.

Back at work, one of the vice-executives, Vincent, had taken a particular liking to me, despite all of my typing errors. One day he drove up to my bus stop in his convertible, and he offered me a ride home. He said, "I think you are very pretty." I fabricated where I was living because I was embarrassed to be living in a rather shabby one bedroom apartment with Mother, and I had him drop me off a block away. I knew he had a penthouse suite from personal letters he'd had me type up, and therefore I surmised I was too lowly in status for a nice, upwardly mobile Jewish bachelor.

~/~

I hadn't seen Dale since my graduation day at the local corner coffee shop in NDG, until he looked me up on Barklay Avenue two years later, in the fall of 1966, and asked me out again. I remember asking for take-out chopped liver (I was starving), and enjoying a drive to Magog in the Eastern Townships, and as we were walking along a country pathway, he asked me to marry him and settle down in the townships. I suppose I found it odd that he never wanted to kiss or cuddle. I told him I wasn't ready for a full time commitment with anyone at that time. Besides, the term "marriage" did not mean anything to me. From what I had seen so far in my life, happy marriages were non-existent, at least few and far between.

At Fischbach and Moore's company Christmas banquet at Ruby Foo's on rue Decarie, an obviously influential government official was seated next to me. He entertained me royally with animated stories of his experiences on the ski slopes of St. Agathe and Mount Tremblant, and he asked to take me home. I figured he probably had a wife and kids and I opted for the city bus. I was ashamed of having just come out of the YWCA, of my relatively shabby living conditions with Mother, and of course of my eating disorder. I later read that the gentleman had been involved in a government sex scandal. God sometimes did come to my rescue, and he made sure I was busy with exercise classes, evening courses at Sir George Williams, a weekly German refresher course at the Goethe Haus, and with a spirit that kept whispering, "Keep the faith, and believe in my promises (for the ultimate reward)."

One day, a tenant in the Barklay apartment complex stopped me in the hallway and asked me if I would be willing to pose as a model for a class at a Technological Institute where she taught industrial designing classes. She was looking for a substitute for her regular model. Five dollars seemed like reasonably good money for just one hour of posing in the nude. I simply disassociated myself in order to get through an hour of painstakingly sitting on a chair that had been placed on top of a table, for an all-male class. I was nervous as heck and perspired profusely. The five dollars didn't include the time or the bus fare across town and back, but I was prepared to do anything, except sell myself or rob a bank, for a bit of extra money, because – I loved beautiful clothes!

And then, one day in March of 1967, my boss came out of his office and said, "This is not your cup of tea. You are not strong enough for this job and we are letting you go with one week's severance pay. You really belong in a typing pool full of girls." I then told everyone I had quit of my own volition, which made it look just as bad, because one way or the other, I had shamed myself because a job in those days was supposed to last a life-time. Mother took me aside and asked, "What is it you truly want?" The only answer I could conjure up, "To learn, of course. Without knowledge, I may as well be dead." She had an astounded expression, and I hadn't known that I had something in common with Henry Ford, the industrialist who had created the Ford Model-T car in 1908, when he echoed:

Anyone who stops learning is old, whether at twenty or eighty. Anyone who keeps learning stays young. The greatest thing in life is to keep our minds young.

~/~

During my period of unemployment, Mother suggested I consult her doctor again, who, at my initial consultation, had advised, "Get yourself away from your mother, as far as possible because she is evil." He admitted me to St. Mary's Hospital for amenorrhea. On the second day, the doctor sent the attending nurse out of the examination room. He then told me that he had a cure for me, while he pulled down his trousers, exposed his private parts and reached for my hand to touch him. I wouldn't co-operate, and with the privacy curtains drawn around my bed, I wept a lot for a couple of days until I was discharged. I never heard from him again and it never occurred to me to see another doctor. If sex with a doctor in a hospital examination room was the cure to my illness, I decided I'd rather go untreated, even if he thought I was made like a fine Swiss-made watch.

After my discharge from St. Mary's Hospital, I applied for a position as a stewardess at Air Canada. I was told I was too young, and it was suggested I come back in a year or two. I was 20 years old, looked like a million, and I spoke three languages. Personally, I most likely looked too young and too innocent for my age to qualify for a job that was considered very glamorous in the sixties.

I had channeled all of my energy into functioning normally, acquiring various skills, avoiding an unorthodox lifestyle, including an unwed pregnancy, a loveless marriage and last but not least, in not letting my family down, and I was beginning to feel like a rejected alien in a country called Canada, adrift in uncharted waters, as if trapped on a desert island to which I had lost my passport.

A huge block deep in the recesses of my mind had started to make me behave like a robot. The wall I had built around me had had become impenetrable. My brain dictated, "Don't be vulnerable! Don't get involved! Stay strong! Get a grip! Don't fall off! Save yourself for the big stage. Meantime, no one can hurt me up here. I am intelligent, attractive and fit as a fiddle and no one will ever catch me. I am the strongest and fastest, and I am willing to wait."

On testing the waters, I invariably slipped into a delirious high, made a fool of myself, and ultimately retreated back into the safety of my box. One day I realized just how silly I was, acting out in total abandon with a strange young man in a Montreal subway. I wasn't the kind of a girl one would have called loose and wild. I aspired to portray myself as a classy, well dressed, well-adjusted, studious, hardworking immigrant, and reaching out for help from authority figures would certainly result in judgment or condemnation. All the while my body was trying to betray me because it had developed and matured against my will, and the monthly cycles had been willed away through restrictive dieting and rigorous physical exercise.

According to Shakespeare's quote, "All the World's a Stage," everyone has a unique part on his or her stage. I had hoped hard work, dedicated study, physical exercise, bible study and eventually being a good mother and wife would someday release me of my chains, but I had no idea I had been psychologically arrested and that my future was going to be circling around my primary relationship with Mother for the rest of my life, and that sustaining that pitch of survival would be permanently exhausting.

~/~

Hermann occasionally met me for coffee during the work week, and he also treated me to an outfit at one of his business associate's clothing outlets. I tried to help him understand why Hanne seemed so aloof with people, and I encouraged him to go home and be a good husband and father. He had been like a favorite uncle to me since I was twelve years old. Yet, Mother accused us of being seen together in public, and I was made to feel guilty for being happy in his presence.

In my spare time I practiced yoga, I was an avid swimmer and runner, I skied, and I was always enrolled in a night course or two in a Continuing Education program. I had a few dates with some German fellows Mother had connected me with. One Austrian fellow, Bruno, told me it wouldn't work because I was preoccupied with an upcoming basic law exam. He thought, *"Du denkst zu viel."* – "You think too much." He was right. I was always deep in thought. Another German fellow from our apartment building that Mother had introduced me to, took me to New York City to visit his sister, and while they had gone out to do some grocery shopping, anorexic and starving, I helped myself to a good proportion of her lovingly baked Christmas goodies. I am still mortified at having left this lovely lady such an awful impression. On our way back to Montreal, he parked his car on the roadside and expressed romantic feelings, and sadly my heart was in a tight knot, and I could not reciprocate his tender emotions.

In the winter of 1966, I joined a newly formed ski club that had been advertised in the German Club's newspaper. One of its members gave me and others rides to the club's chalet in the Laurentians. After a day's skiing, we enjoyed tasty buffets by the fireside of the communal ski chalet. There was usually a full house of skiers and it was run responsibly. I liked the fact that there was no sign of rowdiness, drunkenness or inappropriate behavior, but for the first time, I truly believed that Hanne and Hermann had actually tried to slander me by insinuating to Mother that I must have been engaging in sexually promiscuous behavior while in that ski chalet.

I missed the stress-free weekends in St. Morin's winter wonderland, but I needed to earn a living, and I was on the job hunt for the second time. I had to dismiss the appealing idea of going to a trade school for hairdressing, commercial art, or of even joining the armed forces. My old girlfriends, Anita and Loa had dropped out of high school to attend the Montreal School of Fine Arts, and I believed they saved themselves a lot of frustration by following their passions, and they excelled at it, whereas I had mistakenly considered the vocational trades as beneath my calling, and the arts as luxuries only the rich enjoyed in their spare time.

There was a lot of political unrest with the FLQ (Front de Liberation de Quebec) separatists at the time. Pierre Laporte, among others had been assassinated. Bombs were exploded in mail boxes. The terrorism in Montreal was a bit unsettling, but I felt the storm would soon blow over and felt reassured it would never amount to anything close to the scale of WW II, though I was quite confused over my national identity. Nowadays, fortunately, it is cool to have multiple cultural identities.

~/~

I tried to run the office for a small leather import company in the far north east of Montreal, where the superintendent of the building took a keen interest in me. He took me for coffee and drove me around town, and told me he was married with children. I asked him to stop at a wool shop for a new knitting project I was about to preoccupy myself with (instead of giving in to the pursuits of a married man). My position had actually called for an experienced office manager and bookkeeper, and I ended working in the warehouse part-time, unloading, sorting and hanging leather coats and jackets. A mature lady with extensive experience in bookkeeping eventually took over.

In the spring of 1967, the upper duplex of Mother's investment property in Roxboro became vacant, and we decided to move out of our apartment on Barklay Avenue, overnight. Close proximity to family in the neighboring community of Dollard-des-Ormeaux where my sister's family lived, sounded good. What was I thinking? I was still longing for harmonious family life, and didn't want to believe that there were trustworthy and good people all around me who would have embraced me if only I let them, nor that I had the whole world in the palm of His hands, but I was on a run-away train.

Various dances and parties in Montreal, about 1966–67.

Chapter 12

1964: MEETING FATHER AT AGE 20
It was Expo '67 year in Montreal, and my sister had invited Father over from Austria (his very first overseas destination). I waited several days until I was invited to her house to greet him. We said *"Gruess Gott,"* – "Hello," non-ceremoniously shook hands, while he placed an Austrian souvenir wallet into my hand. The next day we all attended Expo '67 for an enjoyable afternoon. Unfortunately, Father cut his visit short because he was not comfortable at my sister's house, or perhaps of Mother's proximity in the neighboring community of Roxboro triggered a traumatic memory of their war years apart, or more likely of their divorce just before my birth, and I myself was just about to experience my own first intimate relationship, and leave my nest permanently.

Later that summer, Mother had received a visitor from Salt Lake City. The gentleman happened to own a summer cottage in the Laurentians, which, to my surprise and delight, we enjoyed for several consecutive weekends. I climbed the hills, jogged on the country roads, and swam in the lake to my heart's content, and Mother even asked a neighbor to take me out on water skis. I had craved for this kind of summer recreation all of my life. I simply loved life at that lakeside cottage.

During the week, it was a long bus ride from Roxboro across Montreal to my job location at the leather import company, and our gracious visitor had offered me a ride in the morning. Mother absolutely forbade him to do that for me. I don't know what she was thinking, because they knew I had fallen head over heels in love with Fred, the guy I had met across the way from the cottage in the Laurentians. He happened to be a twenty-eight-year-old divorced father of a little boy, who lived with his mother.

On a stifling hot and humid day in a non-air conditioned upper duplex, Mother and I simultaneously lost our tempers in the heat of the moment over something (or maybe over nothing at all). I hadn't done anything to annoy Mother, such as using her hand soap or her shampoo. I called Fred, who had been temporarily living with his parents, and he suggested we search for an apartment. Mother's visitor returned to Utah, and shortly thereafter she was briefly hospitalized at the Jewish General Hospital for a break down. I wondered if it had taken special connections to be admitted into a Jewish hospital, as a German/Austrian.

During our search for accommodations, I lost my virginity at Fred's parent's place while they were away. It was disappointing. I had saved myself for *that* for so long? I'd remembered Mother telling me that on her first time, at the same age of 23, on her wedding night, she had also been extremely disappointed. Moreover, we had sheets tumbling in their washing machine when his parents showed up unexpectedly. Very embarrassing. Nevertheless, it seemed like I had a fairly stable man in my life. We found a seventh floor apartment on rue Pie IX, Montreal East (as far away from Mother as possible, as the doctor had suggested). I eventually found a better job with another company, I enrolled in a couple of night courses (Law and French) and I enjoyed taking my jogs around the expansive Botanical Gardens across the street, working out after work in a gym with a sauna and professional masseuse who gave terrific massages for two dollars an hour.

We took Fred's little boy for ice cream one Saturday, but Fred would not allow me to have any because, according to him, I had to learn to discipline myself. Neither was I allowed to consume bread at any time. Mother had given me a gentle warning. She had spoken to his ex-wife who told her she went through a nightmare with that man.

I was in awe of Fred, however. He was already junior executive at the Montreal Gazette. He was furthering his education at McGill

University, he was tall, dark, and good looking, ambitious, fit and health conscious, and he frequented the YMCA gym regularly. He also recklessly drove a sporty black convertible in which we came perilously close to a few head-on collisions. We split our rent and utilities down the middle, including his car repairs, but he also insisted I pay for our furnishings with a line of credit through a furniture store. The idea of being in debt totally went against the strict financial principles I had been raised with. I was twenty years old and I felt financially ruined! The sex was not satisfying, as he withdrew every time. Neither was I a virgin, nor married, and I was in debt!

When Hermann employed me in the office of his construction firm in the interim of my unemployment, he asked me to work overtime one day, and since Fred usually worked late, I was in no hurry to go back to our apartment. I wondered what my brother-in-law was doing when he set up several rows of chairs and an over-head screen when his business associates showed up and took seats. I sat on top of a work bench against the back wall, and to my horror I was watching the first of a series of pornographic videos. I was the only woman in a dark room full of men silently staring at the screen. I looked down for most of the show. When it ended, I took my high heels off and jogged through the dark, vacated indus-trial area, all the way home to rue Pie IX. I must have had an angel looking over me that night, because even the men in Hermann's office seemed to have been embarrassed for me. I hadn't connected it to the stag party Hermann had hosted at his house when I was still in college. I had forgotten that I had walked out on that all-male party as well.

Fred rarely returned from work before ten o'clock at night, and when he found me in the recreation room on the top floor of the building, socializing with other tenants who'd invited me to take a turn at the drums during a jam session, well, as soon I saw him, I dropped my drum sticks. I knew there would be trouble brewing and I felt guilty for thinking that I had done something wrong. He dragged me down several flights of stairs while pushing me against the walls of the staircase all the way down to our apartment. But when I had indisputably caught him being unfaithful, he simply retreated into a pouting denial mode and refused to speak about it.

The next day I didn't want to return to the apartment after my daily jog and took the elevator to the top of the building and huddled in a corner, soaked by rain, until Fred showed up and took me inside. He was decent enough to run a hot bath for me and give me a shot of cognac.

Mother must have sensed that something was wrong between Fred and myself, because she offered me a loan of $450 for the airfare to see my father in Linz, Austria. It was an extraordinary gesture on her behalf. I was pleasantly surprised, because we were not on the friendliest of terms anymore. We had hardly seen each other since I moved out of her duplex in that terrible kerfuffle a year earlier. It didn't occur to me then that she may have been attempting to spirit me away from Fred, or that she had even conceived of the idea I could still use a father in my life. I was in denial about Fred having abused me, as well as having had abused his ex-wife (according to Mother), and that he had even propositioned my married sister.

~/~

I was twenty-one years old, and I was about to spend time with my birth father, meet my uncle, aunt and cousin Gildis in Vienna, and possibly her distant cousin, Kaethe, in Frankfurt, on the river Oder, East Germany, whose family history I had been well acquainted through the letters and photos we had already exchanged since I was a child. It had totally passed me by that I had already met Father at my sister's house one year earlier.

All I cared about was this delightful opportunity to see him again and I was already flying high weeks before my actual departure.

Mother had always reassured me that during the war, Father had been involved in work related to rationing food and supplies. Therefore I was spared any undue association with regards to the "SS" or Nazis, unlike some of author Ursula Hegi's immigrants who were ashamed of their fathers who had controversial connections to the infamous Nazi regime.

My head was in cloud number nine in anticipation of forming a permanent relationship with my father. I took three weeks off from Laurentide Finance, and I flew out of Montreal for Vienna at Easter time, two months short of my 22nd birthday.

Fred took me to the airport, and when I had boarded, a flight attendant told me that the pilot would like to see me. It took me a while to muster up the courage to take him up on his invitation because to be in the cockpit with a pilot seemed like a very daring thing to do for a young lady. We made light conversation, but I was much too shy to take him up on his interest in me. Besides, I was focused solely on my father.

Mother had arranged to have one of the adult children of a deceased couple she had been closely acquainted with in the 30's and 40's, to meet me at the airport. I was greeted by one of the siblings, and I called my cousin Gildis' home to let her know I had arrived in Vienna and where I was going to be staying for the time being. Her mother told me that I would still be able to catch Gildis performing on stage at the Vienna State Opera House, and we managed to catch Gildis singing an aria. The young man then took me to his family home. The atmosphere was strained because his brother's girlfriend was terribly jealous at my appearance. I spent a night there, and in the morning I called Gildis to set up a time for us to meet later that day. I then set out to explore Vienna via tramway.

The first thing was to look for a *Caffeehaus* for coffee and a strudel pastry, and later indulge in my favorite childhood sandwich, *heisse Leberkaese* – hot Bavarian meatloaf on a bun. All the while I felt like announcing to everyone going about their everyday business, "Hello, I'm home – Austria's child is finally back at home. The lost child has returned! Aren't you all absolutely overjoyed to have me back again?"

Before I knew it, I was being pursued by a very well dressed gentleman, who refused to leave me alone and tried to talk me into accompanying him to the Middle East where he apparently had a car dealership. I welcomed some company to explore Vienna though, and we started to walk about, but he kept wanting to stop at every bar for a drink and to get chummy. He was coming on as too strong and overbearing. I didn't know how to get rid of him, so I took him with me to my cousin Gildis' home and introduced him as one of the brothers who had put me up the previous night. I think Gildis' family suspected something was awry and somehow we lost contact with him.

Gildis' family gave me a very warm reception. Their flat was located above a delicatessen they had operated until their retirement years. My cousin Gildis never experienced hunger, the lucky girl. She gave me an impressive musical performance, accompanying herself on her piano and her accordion and I felt both awed and intimidated by her confidence and accomplishments. Gildis was mostly preoccupied with her boyfriend who remained behind the scene. We were obviously two worlds apart. Apparently, her association with her uncle Raymund (my father) had been quite limited. Gildis called him stoic or something to that effect. I remember Gildis' father taking me for several jolly strolls around the neighborhood, arm in arm, and I was thinking, "I hope this is what it will be like when I see my own father."

I was invited to stay with Aunt Mitzi, my father's sister, who lived in a spacious condo across the street from Gildis' home. Aunt Mitzi told me all about her deceased husband's career as an opera singer. She was preoccupied as a care giver for an ailing senior, and she was still grieving her husband's death. But every morning, before she left for the day, she set out fresh hot coffee in a thermos and some lovely fresh pastry; a *Moongipferl* or *Nussgipferl* – a poppy seed or a nut crescent. Delicious! I didn't see much of her otherwise.

Gildis took time out of her busy schedule to give me a tour of the Vienna Zoo, where I had a chance to hone my skills with a fancy camera Fred had taught me to use. We had been waiting to hear from Father for almost a week. It seemed as if he was trying to dodge me, or have me checked out to see if I was okay. If Mother had reported him to the Russians in 1945 while pregnant with me, his estranged daughter might possibly spell trouble too.

Father's family in Vienna. Left to right: Aunt Lia, Uncle Hermann, Uncle Franz, Cousin Gildis, Aunt Mitzi.

Finally Gildis tracked Father down to the resort town of Bad Schallerbach, less than one hour out of Vienna. As I stepped off the train, I saw Father wearing a long all-weather coat, standing there, tall and straight against the hills of the resort. It was a calm reception, but my heart fluttered just the same. He walked me to a bed-and-breakfast chalet where he had reserved a room for me, and then he took me out for *Backhendel*, an Austrian version of barbecue chicken. The next morning while Father took his spa treatment, I explored the countryside, up and down the surrounding hills and pathways. I must have appeared like the young Maria in the Sound of Music, or at least like a mountain goat prancing up and down the hillside in total abandon.

Two very handsome suitors showed up out of nowhere that day. One, dressed in a business suit, invited me to sit beside him on a bench. He looked out of place in his finely tailored attire in the middle of farmland, and his enthusiasm proved to be too overwhelming for me to handle. I couldn't figure out what he wanted or what he had in mind. Besides, I had come to see my father.

The other gentleman was there for a vacation. He looked like the consummate athlete. He was extremely keen to get to know me, but I was in a hurry to see my father. We quickly exchanged pictures and addresses. Father took me to the local dance hall that night. I accepted a few dances but I just wanted to be with him and get to know him; a difficult task to accomplish with a "Fahrmann," according to Mother.

Father's spa week was up, and we returned to his home town of Linz, where he resided with his second wife, a war widow and who had given him refuge from the Russians in 1946 (the year I was born). He had a modest one-bedroom apartment in a post-war suburb called Neue Heimat. His wife was very sympathetic towards me, and seemed almost apologetic in her demeanor. They gave me their bedroom, and every night Father had slipped a chocolate bar under my pillow. We spent the next couple days roaming around Linz. I was introduced to his pals and enjoyed *ein Bier* at his *Stammtisch* – his regular table at the local pub. I was so surprised when he brought out his motorcycle from storage to take me for an overnight trip along the banks of the Danube River, up and down the Wachau Valley. We stopped in a small village for H*eisse Leberkaese Semmel* – hot Bavarian meatloaf in a bun. I held on tightly with my arms wrapped securely around my daddy.

There had not been enough time to make arrangements for a temporary passport to see my distant relatives, Kaethe and Kurt Gladis, and their son Eberhard, in East Germany. Father saw me off on a train to Vienna to catch my flight connection back to Montreal. The last thing Father said to me was, "*Du bist sehr bescheiden*" – "You are a very sensible girl," and he slipped 80 Schillings into my hand.

I had been too proud to let on that I had been a lost and confused soul and I assumed everybody already knew about my problems, particularly since Mother had prompted them. I wouldn't dare have asked for anything. I had hoped they would have insisted I stay, move back, and let me recapture some of my childhood and my identity. But the past was veiled in a mask of secrecy. Father was a kind and sensible man, but he showed no emotion as hard as I pried, and he staunchly refused to talk about the past, especially of the war years or even of his own childhood. He was very much a "Fahrmann," according to Mother, meaning they were non-demonstrative people. Mother often accused Hanne, *"Hannelore, aber Du bist ganz der Vater!"* – "Hannelore, you certainly take after Father."

So when nothing magical happened with Father, I told myself I still had a family, a job and a boyfriend in Canada. I flew back to the only life I knew, and I had just missed my first golden opportunity to take the plunge off my "box," out of my trap, and change the direction of my future. I wish I had known that it was not necessary to feel guilty or embarrassed for clinging to one's country of origin.

Fifteen years later, Hanne informed me of Father's passing. She had always claimed to be his sole heir, and she never did tell me if she had inherited anything.

Father's greatest gift to me was to have had opportunity to meet him in person, and to no longer have to carry around the fantastic blown up fantasy I had created of him. Maybe he never realized how the absence of a parent impacts the life of a child, but I eventually allowed my heavenly Father to fill his place perfectly. After many worldly disappointments in my search for love and unconditional acceptance, I eventually came to trust God completely and allow him to fill that void for comfort and joy!

~/~

When Fred met me in Montreal, he said, "I wondered if you were coming back." He obviously knew more about my emotional and psychological makeup than I had given him credit for.

I returned to work at Laurentide Finance the day after I arrived in Montreal, and I had hoped that my life with Fred would improve, but nothing had changed and I decided to leave him and the furniture I had paid off in installments.

I moved into a furnished suite in October of 1968, and continued with my course and my job at Laurentide. One day I returned to Fred's apartment to retrieve the skis I had forgotten, and I was shocked to see another woman answer the door so soon after I had left him.

I don't know what had suddenly gotten me into the smoking habit because I found myself chain-smoking at my desk next to several other heavy smokers, that is, until I came down with severe bronchitis that scared me enough to quit.

I was twenty-two years old, and completely out of touch with the events that had transpired so far in my life (possibly in survival mode), and also (out of touch) with my old buddies who had been well on their way to successful careers. However, by sheer coincidence, both Stuart and Dale, my two old high school rivals, happened to come across each other at a bus station in downtown Montreal in mid-December of 1968, and Stuart had informed Dale that I was living with a man named Fred. Dale somehow found out that I had left Fred and immediately traced me to my new apartment. He never told me exactly how he found me. I didn't have a telephone. Stuart had a hard time forgiving himself for having inadvertently tipped Dale off as to my whereabouts, because if he had known that I was on my own again, he would have divorced his wife and proposed to me once more.

Dale immediately showed up at my apartment to find a nice Yugoslavian gentleman visitor whom I had met at my friend Marianne's wedding, at which we had been best man and bridesmaid. Actually, the gentleman had just brought me back from a day of skiing, and yes, just like Dale, he had also been willing to wait in the chalet all day. But as soon as Dale saw my friend, he told me to give him the boot, and I am embarrassed to say that I asked him to leave, just because Dale said so. What I pushover I was! Dale then asked me to join him for a holiday that had been long in the making. He also vouched that I'd never starve with him. He said he needed a much-deserved break from several years of uninterrupted work with Western Electric Telecommunications in the

Maritimes, and it didn't take much convincing to join him and visit his parents in Sarasota, Florida, where they had been snowbirds every winter for six months since Dale was fifteen years old (leaving him with his least favorite aunt, who had moved into his home). My future father-in-law had retired early due to a genetic heart condition and I knew they would be pleased to see me again. They had always been fond of me, especially his mom, judging by the fuss she liked to make over me. I was in Grade ten the last time I had seen them, when she had lovingly administered a nasal decongestant for my runny nose.

I immediately quit my job at Laurentide Finance, dropped my courses, gave up my suite, and I was surprised to see Mother absolutely thrilled to accommodate my furniture among her furnishings in her upper duplex in Roxboro, because 'brand new furniture' (no matter how much it crammed her apartment) used to be a symbol of great wealth to old-world immigrants. Dale had just purchased his dream car, a metallic blue '69 Mustang, ready for its maiden journey to Florida, and I suspected that his father, a conservative Christian and a pillar of the church, was no doubt leery about this sudden development.

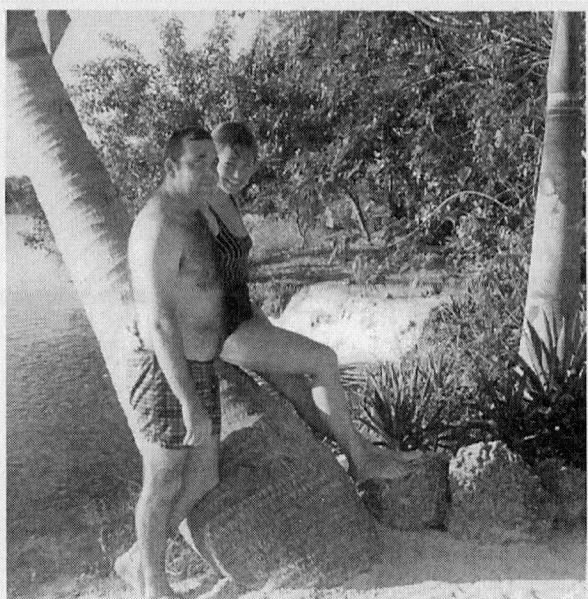

A 'honeymoon' in Florida with Dale in December of 1968, before the wedding on January 8, 1969.

Runaway bride walked down the aisle by my brother-in-law; my expression says it all.

First vows, then photos.

Chapter 13

1969: MY FIRST MARRIAGE; FLORIDA; LONDON

Before we left for Sarasota, we visited Dale's favorite aunt, Marie-Ange, in downtown Montreal, and she gave us her blessings though we had no thoughts of getting married at that stage of our re-acquaintance. We then drove to an address somewhere in the suburbs where Dale said he had to retrieve something. While waiting in the car, I observed Dale and a young woman having a short conversation at her front door. He came back with an item – not sure what it was. I heard her emotional voice saying "Good bye, good luck, all the best, and take care Dale." As we drove away, he said "I am not the father of her child." (That should have been a red flag).

Dale's parents had reserved a unit for us in the motel they were temporarily renting while in search of a permanent retirement location. We arrived shortly before Christmas, just in time for a cozy family Christmas dinner. They thanked me profusely for Dale's latest weight loss and improved appearance, and I appreciated the care I received regarding my eye infection and abscessed tooth (one tooth had already been pulled two months prior). I overheard Dale telling his parents, "She is so appreciative of absolutely everything she is given." We were tent camping in the Everglades when Dale proposed to me after our first attempt at intercourse, and I automatically answered with an obligatory "Yes" and decided to deal with my uncertainty about a life time commitment when we returned to Montreal.

~/~

As soon as we had returned to Montreal, Dale informed me that he had been offered a job in Istanbul, Turkey, for a long-term project with Western Electric. According to company policy, we had to be married if I was to come with him. The prospect of traveling was enticing since I had no reason to stay in Montreal. Marriage sounded like a practical plan, and it had to be executed immediately. I also thought I might have another opportunity to see Father. So much had transpired during the previous years, I had forgotten, or more likely suppressed the fact that I had already seen him two years earlier, as well at my sister's house a year prior to that, and that I was on the rebound from Fred. Mother gave us her blessing, saying, "Dale will never hurt you." Wedding arrangements were made for the next evening, and I ran away one hour before the wedding.

~/~

Hanne, Hermann, Brittney and Miles found me in Fred's car, having searched for me throughout the snowbound community. I had been pleading with Fred to take me away, but he suggested I approach Mother for help. They managed to persuade me to get out of Fred's car and go through with the ceremony. The minister, groom and guests in the church were assembling and waiting, and I didn't know that my mother-in-law was crying her eyes out in Florida because she couldn't be at her son's wedding, for which she would have no doubt liked to be involved in the planning. All she could do is to celebrate our marriage with her friends and send us a photo of her holding a cake decorated with, "Best Wishes Dale and Emily." So sad.

It was on January 8, 1969, seven p.m., and I walked down the aisle, as a seemingly beaming bride, with one eye partially closed due to a stubborn eye infection, in the church my brother-in-law had built on the corner lot next to his house. I was in my sister's wedding gown, and Dale was in my brother-in-law's tuxedo, both fitting us as if made to measure. We had a small reception in my brother-in-law's yacht club by the St. Lawrence River. Mother gave us a fifty-dollar bill, and asked us to give her and two lady friends a ride home before we returned to my sister's basement suite to pack for our trip (including a trunk full of American food staples not readily available in Turkey), then first thing in the morning, take a quick trip to Ottawa to pick up our passports and get a birth control prescription. The new doctor, for reasons I never did find out, had told Dale, "I think your wife may not be able to bear children." We had one night's stay in a nice old hotel in London, England, and we spent an afternoon in an expensive shopping district where Dale bought me a tweed suit with a matching cap, a piece of jewelry, and some perfume, and we settled on a traditional supper in a classic English pub.

~/~

ISTANBUL; AUSTRIA

Dale's company put us up at the Hilton International Hotel for a few days, and then we were transferred to a Turkish hotel downtown Istanbul, where I was asked to remain inside our room until Dale's return from an orientation to his new job and from checking out accommodations for the upcoming months. There had been sporadic rioting nearby. I did a lot of yoga while waiting for Dale, and that night, the head waiter at the hotel's restaurant didn't seem phased at all when I showed him a live worm in my salad.

~/~

It took six weeks until the installations of a sink and toilet had been completed to our fifth-floor walk-up apartment in the suburban community of Bebek. Meantime, we used the facilities through a hole in the floor. I heated buckets of water on the kitchen gas stove to fill the bathtub, ready for Dale's bath between 9 and 10 p.m., when he'd returned from work. While Dale worked full time, with plenty of overtime, I filled my time learning basic Turkish, sitting in on classes at the University, taking Turkish baths, doing yoga, and shopping in the bazaars. I availed myself of fabrics from an undercover bazaar to sew with German Burda patterns. I cooked with the aid of a great little cookbook compiled by American army wives in Istanbul, using ingredients readily available in Turkey.

I learned how to thwart off the advances of men in the Turkish custom of the time, by the clicking of "t"s. It worked. Being fluent in German and French also helped. If the "t"s had been "r"s, I would have loved to roll them to my heart's content, perfectly and effectively, thinking, "Now my high school friends, this is how it's done!"

Within several months, my birth control pills unexpectedly and suddenly forced my menstrual periods on, with excruciating abdominal pain, as if my insides had ripped apart. I had last menstruated in the summer of 1962, at the age of sixteen, six years earlier.

Dale had lost considerable weight due to chronic dysentery, and I had gained some weight (accessibility to a trunk full of canned, processed and instant foods and goodies didn't help). There was still no passion or affection expressed in our marriage. Dale knew I had problems, but as long as I played the good little wife and didn't allude to our shaky marriage, he treated me decently. I still wanted out, however, and I sent a pleading letter to Fred in Montreal, who replied in kind and included a key to his apartment, which Dale promptly confiscated.

Our social life consisted of occasional dinners with Dale's boss and his wife from Montreal, and some meals on the American army base. Oh, how much I would have loved to dance, but I had to sit there all evening. Dale didn't and wouldn't dance. One of the soldiers asked me for a dance but Dale got up and told him where to go. So, I obediently functioned as a new spouse, possibly a trophy wife. The climate in Istanbul at that time was much like the dreary and overcast winters in the Okanagan, only worse, because I could not use the lovely chaise lounge on my spacious corner balcony, and listen to the chants calling for prayer time at the mosques, due to either rain, snow, air pollution, or soot spewing from the chimney tops.

In Istanbul,
March 1969,
sporting new
pearls and
suede suit.

My balcony view of the Bosphorus Sea.

A sketch of me done by Turkish caricaturist, Faruk, while painting a skyline of Istanbul (below).

Dale's supervisor's wife told me that the artist of some of the beautiful paintings of Istanbul they had acquired also gave art lessons. The next day, and I found his studio on a narrow cobblestoned path in an old quarter of Istanbul. He told me that he had worked in Hollywood for several years in order to hone his skills as a professional movie star caricaturist. His studio seemed like a hole in the wall from the outside, but inside it opened up into a huge art gallery. I gave it my best effort on an oil painting of a skyline of Istanbul overlooking the Bosporus River, and he rewarded me by offering me fine Turkish coffee and chocolate, while he sketched a professional caricature of myself, depicting me as I paint that very same picture.

Around Easter time, I had a knock on the door by the wife of another Canadian Western Electric employee, urging me to come over right away. During the ten-minute walk, Lynn did not go into any details and I imagined the worst. I gingerly walked to the bathroom where her husband and a Turkish couple had pointed me towards. There he was, fully dressed and immersed up to his neck in a tub of cold water, with water dripping down from the faucet onto his face. I was too afraid to ask what and why he did what he had done. I had to get him out of the tub and onto the couch, which had been soiled by vomit. We let him sleep off whatever it was that he had taken. I fetched a change of clothes for him, and didn't dare bring up the subject again.

On Dale's only weekend off work, we decided to visit a popular ski resort located about one hundred kilometers out of Istanbul. I looked forward to doing a little skiing in Turkish fashion. It was a long weekend and the traffic out of Istanbul was heavy. It took hours to just get out of the city. The bus we were on was filled mostly with Turkish locals also getting away, but not to ski. They, with chickens and bags of food, dropped off at different villages to see their relatives. It turned into a 24 hour, stuffy and tiring ordeal, and we didn't arrive at our destination until the early morning hours. Our reservations had been canceled, and we were put up in a tiny room supplied with two cots. It was 6 a.m. and

Dale had come down with a fever. We took the next available flight back, and arrived in Istanbul within one hour. We'd had enough, filled the empty trunk with souvenirs such as patchwork leather shoulder bags, ivory, copper, and Turkish delight candy, and decided to return to Canada via Austria to take advantage of another opportunity to see Father again. It was in May of 1969, close to my 23rd birthday, when we left Istanbul for Vienna. My cousin Gildis met us at the airport, and we went for "BBQ Chicken and a glass of the season's latest wine" – "Backhendel und ein Heurigen", in Grinzing, a suburb of Vienna studded with wineries. And then we headed for Linz to see Father.

This time Father welcomed me as a married woman with a brand-new husband of five months. Dale, as designated chauffeur, drove us all around Linz, the Wachau Valley, and to a prominent Alpine peak in a rental car. He felt out of place and he hated having to follow traffic directions, such as *"rechts," "links,"* and *"gerade aus!"* – "right, left, and straight ahead!" He was totally out of his milieu and had a taste of culture shock. I didn't offer to relieve him by driving. I knew he would never allow me to take the steering wheel in his presence. I subconsciously wished I were alone with Father, and have his support in annulling the marriage and to start all over again in Austria. Father asked me if I loved Dale. *"Hast ihn doch gerne?"* – "Do you like him?" What could I say but *"Ja."* And though I pried again, Father didn't offer to speak about his own childhood, about Hanne, or about Mother.

An old acquaintance of Mother's asked us to take her and see her great grandmother in Grieskirchen, which was near Mother's birth town. There, we were greeted with the smells and sounds of a typical old European farm, with its own inner medieval courtyard. The lady had a separate entrance to her apartment, comprised of simple furnishings, with walls and credenzas laden with flowers, religious pictures, and icons. There she was standing, a little old lady as if straight out of the 18th century, with headscarf, apron, boots, layered long skirts and all. Her ivory, rosy cheeked face conveyed pure peace and love. Her eyes told me, as they kept trying to reach mine, that she may have known Mother and probably remembered me as a little girl as well. I doubted if she had ever stepped out of her village. She had it all right there where she was born: health, family, roots and nature. Now that's what I call independent retirement living in the grand style of God's creation. It had been this beautiful, forever smiling, memorable, great-grandmother's 100th birthday.

~/~

Aunt Mitzi, and with Father (below), May 1969.

At a 100th birthday celebration with Mother's old friends.

With Dale in Hallstadt, Austria, May 1969

Back in Montreal, we set up an apartment with my in-laws' stored furnishings they had no intentions of ever using again, since they had already been snowbirds for eight years. Their family heirlooms and antiques meant a lot to Dale, though I did not particularly fancy antiques, especially dark wood, rather depressing I thought. I tried hard to settle down and be a good housewife, but I was still emotionally attached to Fred. I felt hopelessly lost, but I enrolled in a few night courses at McGill University, and tried to keep my dreams alive of eventually acquiring a degree. I was also physically strong and conditioned enough to qualify for the Boston marathon run, a dream that never materialized.

I was hired for a secretarial position by a major pharmaceutical manufacturer. On the first day, I sat at my desk for hours until my new boss introduced himself. When he finally called me into his office the next day, we had a short chat, and asked me to familiarize myself with some literature on a bookshelf. On the third day I still just sat there and literally twiddled my thumbs. On the fourth day I quit because he hadn't given me any work. I was bored to tears, and he thought it was a shame and said, "Are you sure you want to leave?"

I then answered an advertisement looking for a fitness instructor. I was told, "You have to lose ten pounds right away, like in a week." I thought, "So much for that!" and I asked Dale to install a lock on the kitchen door to help control my eating disorder. I had a habit of nibbling on crackers or cookies during the night.

By August, we decided to have a housewarming party. I prepared an elaborate buffet supper. I didn't know most of our guests very well except an old high school girl friend of Dale's, whom he had sit on his lap for a while. The next day, while he was at work, I had a binge and purge episode with the left over pie I had made for the party.

Except for a patchwork leather shoulder bag I kept to store my knitting supplies, we doled out the trunk full of souvenirs we had brought back from Istanbul to friends and family – material evidence of our sojourn. We didn't have anything joyous to report otherwise.

~/~

I still couldn't get over my break-up with Fred, and I decided to contact Dr. Engle, the psychiatrist I had seen seven years earlier with regard to Mother's electroshock treatments at the Allan Memorial Hospital. The doctor consulted Fred first and then he told me, "Fred enjoyed you very much, but he would never commit himself to you." And Fred's last words to me had been, "You can do better than Dale," and I accepted that as my final verdict. I was beginning to feel quite defeated. I was still battling bulimia at times, and I was desperately lost and unhappy. So far nothing and no one had been able to fill this insidious void in my heart. I had stopped saying my prayers sometimes. The "evil one" seemed to have taken control. I wonder what my heavenly Father would have told me, if only I had prayed harder and asked him for divine guidance. I think I didn't want to be reminded that I had made a vow at the altar, to cherish and honor my spouse 'until death do us part'.

Mother had remained behind the scenes as a housekeeper for retired brothers who resided in an estate home on Mount Royal. One of the brothers was Senator Phillips. Mother loved being surrounded by old world money, prestige, two men, and a convenient walk over Mount Royal and downtown to shop at Eaton's. She was anxious to introduce us, so we dropped in to say hello. When I saw her at the door, my heart sank, as if a child, once more abandoned by her mother, this time for two men. Much to her chagrin, Mother developed chronic bronchitis and had to leave her dream job.

About six months after our return from Istanbul, I started to withdraw and stopped communicating with Dale entirely. After a day or two of silence, I checked to see if he was all right, because he remained in the bathroom for a conspicuously long time. I found him lying on the floor with his wrists cut and an empty pill bottle on the counter. It took some fast and hard talking on my part to convince him that he needed medical attention. My reprimanding comment, "Is this how you handle your problems?"

worked. Like a slap on the face, it shook him out of his stupor, permitting me take him to the hospital, where he had his wrist stitched and his stomach pumped. On our way home, he touchingly said "I was afraid of not being man enough to keep you." After that, I resigned myself to stay with him. A life, *his* life, depended on me. I convinced myself that he really did care for me and I had better appreciate that. Soon his parents, Alf and Mary Tinsley, would be back from Sarasota, and we focused on them and the alternating Sunday family dinners we were going to enjoy. Of course, it was a charade to cover up for our marital deficiencies. They had replaced the parents I didn't have and I am sorry for having disappointed them since they had been very kind to us. And they knew their daughter-in-law was very good for their son.

In the fall, Dale offered to take me to a Viennese concert at Place-des-Arts. During the second or third number, he excused himself and left me seated by myself for the rest of the concert. He was unable to pay even a token of appreciation for my culture, whereas I had to live and breathe his. I still wanted a separation, and this time he agreed to go away for a few weeks. He showed up three days later, looking quite dapper in a brand-new custom-made-looking suit, and he looked so trim. I wondered how he managed to lose so much weight in just a few days, but he quickly gained it back again because in his words, "It didn't make a difference." I continued to keep myself busy with courses, part-time work, housework, and I filled my time with a huge knitting project – a beautiful dress that would last a lifetime. At Christmas time, I built an elaborate gingerbread house project for Miles and Brittney (then around eight and eleven years old), fenced in with a barn, greenery, and animals.

Dale must have loved me very much to take up skiing again, since his first attempt at it had been a disaster when he had taken it up for me the first time, and had vouched never to ski again. But he'd remembered how much I loved the sport in high school, when he had volunteered to drive me to the ski slopes in his father's car and then wait for me in ski chalets while I skied enthusiastically all day. I think the best part for him, his anticipated reward, was when I allowed him to warm up my chilled toes under his backside, while he drove me back home.

I had to quit taking birth control pills because of an unusually painful episode which forced me to crouch down on the floor of a nickel-and-dime store in Roxboro in which Mother and I had been shopping. All she could do was stand by helplessly until my cramps subsided.

~/~

One Saturday morning in June of 1970, I did not know that I was pregnant when Dale had collided with a commuter train at the Roxboro station. He had been on his way to the laundromat with the radio speakers on high volume. His brand-new Honda had been dragged 50 yards down the tracks and it had been totaled, but he was not seriously hurt; just scrapes and bruises. I could possibly have ended up a widowed mother with a baby girl. I am ashamed of having welcomed that thought, or wishing someone other than Mother dead. I was not afraid of being a single mom. All I wanted was to be relatively happy and to get out of my trap. I wronged Dale in many ways, but I tried to be honest with him too. He knew that I was unhappy. I had pleaded with him to let me go, and I told him that he was deserving of someone who could truly love him, because I couldn't. I was not fully cognizant of the fact that I couldn't love anyone who did not acknowledge his creator or a higher power. I needed someone to model strong moral and spiritual values to calm my tormented soul.

~/~

I had to quit my job at a plastics factory because I was beginning to feel nauseous from fumes seeping from the plant into the office, and I soon found out that I was two months pregnant with Emma. That period of my life was a wonderful and perhaps the first stable period in my life. Though we had little, I felt complete, with something of my own flesh and blood to look forward to. I paid exceptional attention to my health and diet. My eating disorder disappeared forever. I never took as much as one aspirin during the entire pregnancy, and I knit and sewed baby outfits in great anticipation. Paid maternity leave and paternity benefits were non-existent in the early 70's, money was short, and Dale told me that he had a gun collection stored away somewhere to be sold for our new expenses, which I appreciated.

A happy-looking couple, north of Ottawa, 1970.

Chapter 14

1971: MY BELOVED CHILDREN–EMMA AND SHANE

Numerous blizzards left much of Montreal crippled and snow-bound in February and March of 1971, and we nearly entertained getting to the hospital via snowmobile from our upper duplex. Luckily, baby Emma decided to wait a few days until the snow had subsided and a pathway had been dug out.

Men were not included to witness the birth of their babies in the 70's. Some, like Emma's daddy, took off to the local tavern to wait for the news. I felt no pain since I had a spinal, which was routinely recommended at that time.

Emma was perfect in every way. Her beautiful hands in particular, captivated me, and the staff delighted in her as the "little darling" of the ward, already trying to lift her head and look around the other newcomers. As we were wheeled out of the birthing room into the hallway, Dale laid his eyes on the bouncy 8lb, 8oz pound baby girl, and said, "Oh, Emily, we have to do this again *soon!*" I was pleasantly surprised and felt rather proud of my heritage when I heard my doctor tell Dale that he had married into good stock.

The day we brought Emily home, Hanne, Hermann, Miles, and Brittney dropped in after a day of skiing. It was heart warming to see them absolutely thrilled with the new addition to the family. I can still see Brittney and Miles's beaming faces.

~/~

Yes, we did it again, and soon. Our feeble attempts at birth control did not work. I had two more pregnancies within one year. One was an early miscarriage, and the second gave us a baby boy, Shane. He weighed 8lb,2oz. I am not sure why a doctor came to check my toes for any abnormality or deformation, and he did not explain why or if he had noticed anything unusual with baby Shane's toes. He didn't see any defect with my toes, I didn't see anything wrong with Shane's toes either, and it didn't occur to me to check Dale's toes. He was healthy, except for a rash and some colic. According to my mother-in-law, who so generously paid for diaper service and a semi-weekly teenage helper, we were now a perfect family of four. I experienced perfect joy and fulfillment, despite post-partum depression and noticeable physical wear and tear. I didn't have to ask Dale to have a vasectomy. He practically ran to a clinic.

Motherhood kept me grounded, and I gladly sacrificed matrimonial bliss other couples apparently enjoyed. I held on to hope that someday, when my children were all grown up and had left their nest, God would somehow help me find my true self and my true mate. Meantime, I gladly endured and persevered with my marital duties, and all thoughts of leaving my husband vanished.

~/~

When Emma was three months old, we purchased a government subsidized townhouse on Spring Garden Road near Dollard-des-Ormeaux, for a about $12,000. We were thrilled with our babies, and we took great pride in our well-run, maintained and constantly upgraded new home.

Three years later, we sold the townhouse when the real estate market had taken a sudden upturn. Had we known and waited even a few days, we would have realized a substantially larger profit, but we wanted to purchase the reasonably priced duplex next to Mother's in Roxboro, for $25,000. The children were two and four years old at that time. Living next to my mother, the children's grandmother, Omi Fahrmann, sounded good. What were we thinking? Solidarity of course.

~/~

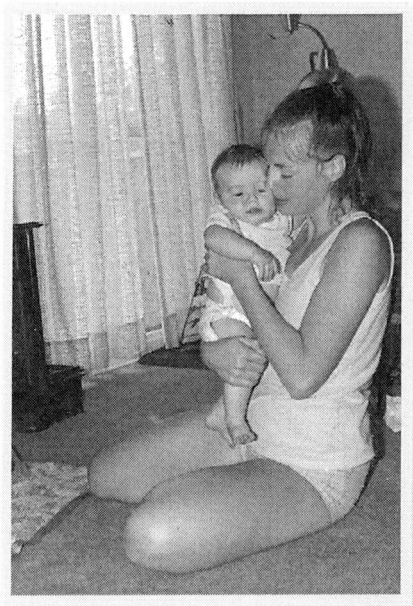

Me with baby Emma; Spring Garden Road; Montreal, 1971.

My lovely little Emma at 18 months.

Emma's second birthday.

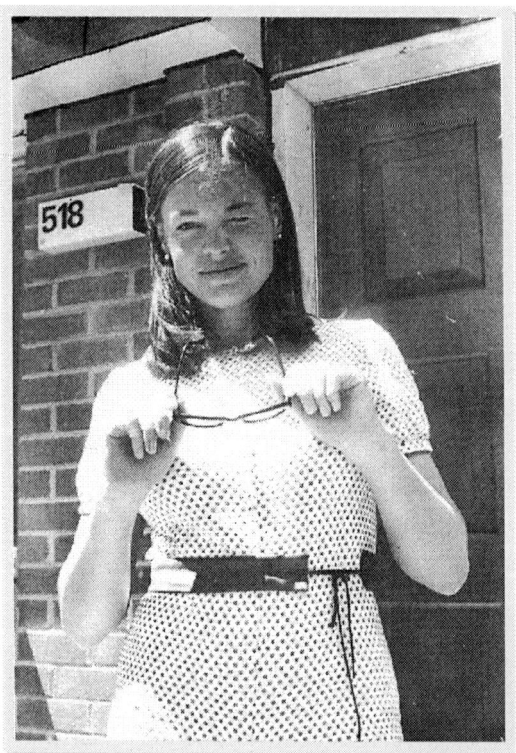

Pregnant with
Shane, outside our
first home on
Spring Garden
Road, 1972.

Bath time fun;
Shane (1) and
Emma (2).

With my little guy
Shane, 1973.

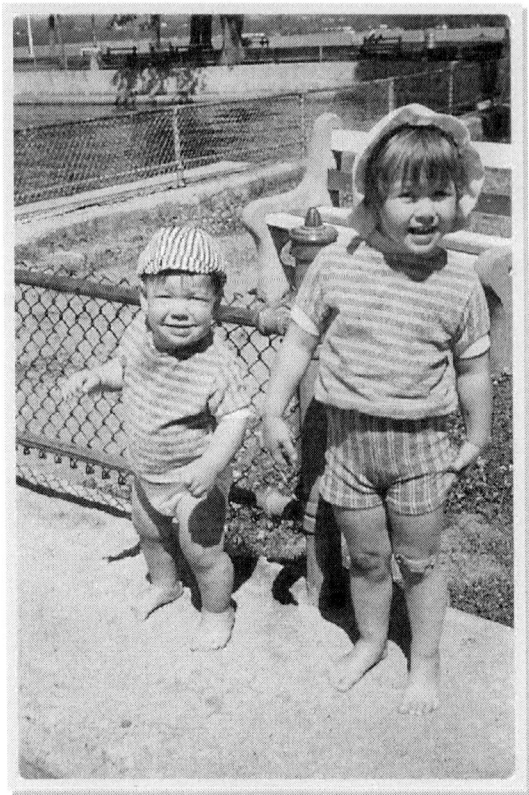

Shane and Emma; out exploring nature.

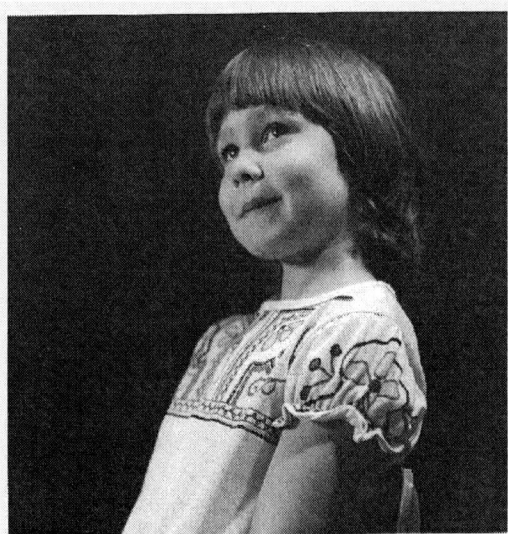

Emma at five.

All dressed up
in Mom's
hand-sewn
outfits;
Roxboro, 1974.

Dale's youngest nephew, Kevin, often came from Ottawa to Montreal, via rail, to spend weekends with us. Kevin was the youngest of three children and a much-favored grandson of the Tinsley's, and I trusted him implicitly with my children. I wanted to give him a connection with an extended family since his parents had recently divorced. He took the children to the park daily, enabling me to catch up with cooking, cleaning, sewing or whatever I needed to work on (rather obsessively and compulsively). I hardly ever used an opportunity to rest, or even read. A little voice in me said relaxation was *verboten*. I'd become a domestic workaholic.

I enrolled the children into the local Montessori pre-school program for several afternoons per week. I had provided the supervisor with some tips to improve the quality of the program and she immediately asked me to work there. She told me how impressed she had been with my children. She said, of my children, "Mrs. Tinsley, you have a lot to look forward to with your children." But after some serious consideration, I declined her job offer. I was busy enough, but I had complete faith in her compliments about my children.

The children had had their fair share of throat infections and colds, and their pediatrician recommended tonsillectomies. It was painful to witness their surgery related ordeals, while I had no one to share my concern. At that time I hadn't been able to connect their recurrent respiratory symptoms to their father's heavy smoking, because second hand smoke didn't bother me at all, having resilient athlete's lungs. Yet even I started to feel sick from the pervasive and toxic air pollution.

Meantime, Mother at the age of 60, had found a second husband, tall, blonde and good looking. Goodness, it was actually encouraging to see her acting like a giddy teenager with a new beau, originally from Northern Italy. They had a formal wedding and reception, at which little Shane, age three and a half, sang his favorite songs for the guests. The wedding was officiated by Pastor Bart Zentke, the minister who had married us in Dollard-des-Ormeaux five years earlier. I never had a word with the pastor. He seemed unapproachable, and judgmental about the circumstances around my own wedding, and of course I was still ashamed and embarrassed about having run away just before he solemnized my marriage, and I had made myself rather unapproachable.

Mother and Mr. Del Fabbrosi took their honeymoon at her investment property in Florida, but they didn't take to the Floridian social lifestyle very well together, and they divorced within a year. She kept his name, "Del Fabbrosi," because she thought it had a beautiful ring to it.

~/~

In 1975, I sought professional help. My nerves were beginning to unravel. In other words, I was a nervous wreck by the age of 29. I was referred to a psychiatrist at the Lakeshore General Hospital, who reassured me that I was a good mother and that the children were happy and healthy. From my personal history, he gathered that I was spiritually inclined. He had been the second doctor to recommend I get away from Mother, *as far as possible,* but I struggled with the idea of denying the children time with their Omi.

I attempted to confide my marital discontent to Mother, but it went on deaf ears. She knew what was to be a sole provider and in her opinion, *"Beklage Dich night. Du hast es doch gut."* – "Don't complain. You've got it pretty good."

Dale had wanted to leave Montreal due to the animosity he had held against the French population in general, and the FLQ separatists in particular. It didn't take us long to pursue a new adventure; another marital distraction. We sold the duplex in the spring of 1976 for about $34,000. Dale flew to Calgary to find accommodations, and I had our household goods crated and shipped to Calgary.

The children and I took a short detour to Boulder, Colorado, to visit my high school friend, Loa, then divorced. We all, including her eight-year-old daughter, Ingela, took a day in the Rocky Mountains, a memory that always brings John Denver's song 'Rocky Mountain High' to mind. As usual, I found Loa to be the kindest and mildest tempered person I had ever known.

When I saw my husband of seven years waiting to greet us at the Calgary Airport, I was shocked to find myself looking into the eyes of a stranger. If it hadn't been for the children, I would have turned around right there and then.

Mother's second marriage, to Mr. Del Fabrosi (1975).

All the girls except for Emma, at the family wedding.

Chapter 15

1976: MOVE TO CALGARY, AB; FAMILY LIFE

We checked into a motel near the future Canada Olympic Park, and waited for our crates to arrive from Montreal. We had a look at the home that Dale had rented. It was a new, not yet landscaped split-level in a remote and undeveloped area of Silver Springs, Calgary NW. That night, I realized why I had been avoiding intimacy in my marriage because I felt like I had been put through the wringer once more, and it took me a while to recover. I had never forgotten what he had told me early in our marriage: "You are the first and only woman who has been able to satisfy me." I'm embarrassed to say I may have taken it as a compliment.

~/~

The following year entailed an orientation to a new city, new schools, a different climate and a new culture. We took every opportunity to enjoy Banff and all that the Rocky Mountains had to offer, and we painted a glorious picture for all our friends back east of how happily settled we had been.

In the spring of 1977, I had a telephone call from the family services office asking if I would take a child into my care. A geophysicist with Suncor Oil urgently needed day care for his two-year-old boy, Michael. He proved to be a delight, and he got along beautifully with Emma and Shane. Actually, he cried when it was time to go home for the night, but after a few trial months with us, his family decided he could be with his mother again.

In the fall of 1977, Michael's dad returned to see if I would take his little boy into my care once more, because his mother had been under psychological duress again. He had been very impressed with me as a mother, and he desperately wanted his boy to come back into my care. In his opinion, he didn't think I was particularly suitable for the real estate career I was about to undertake. He was willing to assist us financially with a down payment for a house of our own, if I were to take Michael again. However, Dale convinced me that I could make big money in the booming city on my own, recoup the expenses we had incurred in our move, and purchase our own home. Michael's father was extremely disappointed with my decision. I kept his detailed letter of reference, in which he recommended me as an excellent child care worker.

When temperatures had dropped later that fall, I experienced tremendous discomfort in my hands while on one of our daily walks. I had contracted Raynauds syndrome and soon learned to always have a pair of gloves on hand (pardon the pun), just in case.

In my initial profile assessment from the Calgary Real Estate Board, I scored in the highest percentile academically, but it was also suggested I try a career choice more suitable to my personality, perhaps in office management. I went ahead with the original plan, against that which my heart was telling me, just to please my husband.

Dale bought me an expensive business case, washed the car, and sent me off as a rooky realtor. He willingly took over the household in the evenings and on weekends, and I had no reason to distrust him, except I did not approve of the Playboy Magazines left in the bathroom for the children to come across. I gently asked him to keep them out of sight. Other forms of pornographic material showed up just the same, and it had no doubt made an impression on my little girl, because when her concerned grade three teacher had called me in, I went into complete denial mode over some shockingly explicit notes written by one of her students. I demonstrated to her that it couldn't be Emma's writing, because there was a slight variance to her normal handwriting.

Helping Mommy do dishes in our new home in Calgary, 1976 (above); the joy of being a little girl (right).

Off to Banff with the Tinsleys.

The kids, age nine and ten, anxious to get going to their activities.

Mamma's boy (above); all ready for a boys' choir performance (below), 1978.

Emma loved playing with her Barbies (above); her 7th birthday Silversprings, Calgary, AB. (left).

Some serious carolling.

With Mother and Joe in the Okanagan Valley.

Happy
times!

Ready to ski near Banff.

Growing children in their Sunday best (above); visiting with Dale's parents in Sarasota, Florida (below).

Lovely Emma, age 13 (left); doing a beautiful back dive (above); me with a broken ankle (below).

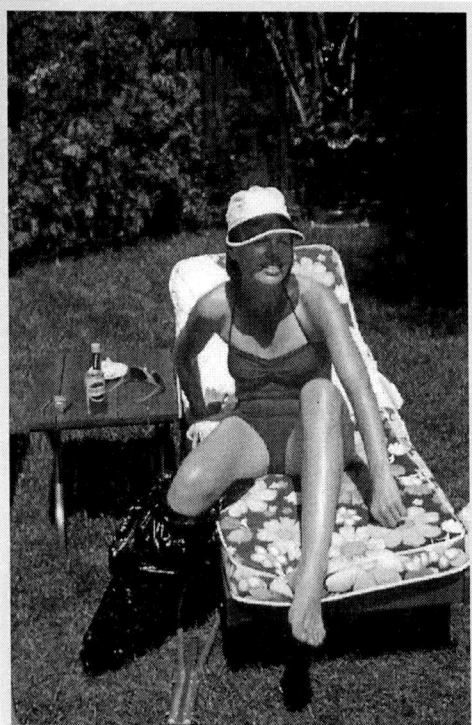

I was not thoroughly familiar with our new city. I had no established business ties and few social connections, and six months of hard, diligent work ended without a single profitable transaction. I resigned from a career in real estate against my manager's advice, but I continued testing the job market out of curiosity, and was offered a permanent job in the Dean's office of Mount Royal College, but l thought it best to be a stay-at-home-mom with my children, and resorted to childcare and house cleaning for extra income.

I enjoyed knitting Barbie doll outfits for Emma, I sewed Batman costumes for Shane and his friends, and it was nice to have time to play games and to bake all kinds of goodies. One of their favorites was *Linzer Gitter Kuchen*, a lattice topped square, filled with raspberry jam. The children couldn't wait until we were ready to begin their nightly routine. We usually started with the Dr. Seuss book series and other popular children's books of the 70's. Then we sang the songs I had taught them, with *"Alle meine Entchen," "Ticke-Tacke Tingleling,"* and *"Haenschen klein, ging allein."* Next we said a children's prayer in German, *Jesukindlein komm zu Mir* – Baby Jesus, Come to Me, followed by the Lord's Prayer in both languages. These are extra special memories of my beloved children.

I had needlework of all kinds on the go. I sewed and knitted all kinds of outfits and Afghans, I cultivated a vegetable plot, and at the end of the day I enjoyed long midnight strolls and jogs under the clear, starry skies of Alberta when none of the neighbors could see the uninhibited side of me.

~/~

I experienced my second childhood vicariously. I had just as much fun as the children had, with the mini gym I had set up in the basement, equipped with swings, tumble mats and skip ropes. Our house was always open to other children, and we included them in picnics, movies, and hikes. In the winter we enjoyed skating on the large lagoon in Bowness Park. While the kids were in school and the washing machine was going, I'd skip away the cobwebs of my brain like a professional light weight boxer.

Upstairs, we kept gerbils and a budgie bird. At the age of eight, Emma had taken the welfare and breeding of the gerbils very seriously, and she studied up on them with a book from the school library. She was absolutely delighted with little critters of all kinds, while Shane exhibited a real zest for life, and showed talent in his poetry and music. As a matter of fact, his grade two teacher was quite impressed with his reading ability and wanted to know how I managed to help my son attain reading skills to an exceptionally impressive level. All I had done was to read bedtime stories to my children, just like any other mother. Sad to say, I never heard their father read one story to them. Though he was very helpful around the house, I could have used a little support at Emma's and Shane's birthday parties. For some reason, he invariably abandoned us just before the little guests were about to arrive, so I barely managed by myself. The highlight at those parties was a piñata dangling from the ceiling of the converted playhouse, originally the shipping crates from Montreal.

We had portrayed a perfect family image over the years, but I had also developed an ulterior motive. I suffered with depression and came to the conclusion that the only place I would find relief would be in my home country. I loved my children so much that I included them in my secret plan. I tutored Emma in basic German, and I was going to take her on a visit first. She was almost eight years old, and her demeanor and maturity were outstanding for her age. Shane was still rambunctious and a little hyperactive and would have to wait a year or two.

I knew that Dale would refuse to share custody of the children, nor consent to a divorce. "I'd fight it tooth and nail" was one of his favorite expressions. Why should he? He had been the main breadwinner after all, but I had supplemented his income and I had cooked meals, prepared lunches, and budgeted wisely. Coupons were clipped, the house was spit and polished, shirts were ironed, vegetables were in the garden, the children were healthy and happy, and I kept myself in great shape. But then, how could I hurt my dear in-laws who had so much faith in our marriage?

Dale was predisposed to brute force from the pleasure he exhibited from violent domestic scenarios he had referred to. He gave me the impression that he wouldn't think twice about using a gun or resorting to a malicious plan to avert the breakup of our seemingly perfect family if things didn't go his way. He said, "You'll never make it on your own." He also said to me, "You love me, but you don't know it." And I kept putting Daddy on a pedestal for the children, just as I had put my own father on an imaginary pedestal. Our marriage had been build on a weak foundation, like the statue in Nebuchadnezzar's dream, with the head made of gold, but the foundation weak, and bound to collapse.

Emma and Shane had never wanted for food, clothes and love. I wanted my children to have so many things I had missed out on in my life, and I appreciated the fact that Dale had been a steady provider, that he was supportive around the house, and that he was an accomplished handyman. But I would have gladly sacrificed those conveniences for the support of a husband who knew when it was necessary to administer firm yet kind discipline, and guidance of our children, and relieve me of the pressure to fill both roles. I really had no one to lend me a compassionate ear. The general consensus seemed to be in his favor, since he was the breadwinner, and Mother reinforced it saying, "You should be happy. You've got it made." But bread does not fill a spiritual void.

Around 1979, I had enough money saved from domestic and part-time secretarial work, and I contacted my cousin Gildis in Vienna. She had also gotten married and had started a family of her own since the last time Dale and I saw her on our way back from Istanbul, some ten years prior. I sent Gildis the itinerary of our travel arrangements. Meantime, she sent me a letter in which she had changed her mind about accommodating us. She told me her strata council did not approve of Americans staying in their building, and she was looking for an alternative place. I felt insulted and rejected, and certainly did not want to give the impression we were rowdy American tourists, as she had implied. The thought of leaving Shane behind with his father seemed unconscionable, let alone to disappear with his sister forever some-where in Europe.

So, I used tight finances as an excuse to cancel the trip. Be-sides, Emma had just joined a swim club, and had immediately won first place in local swim competitions. But she had also shown talent in dancing and gymnastics. I had intended to give her an opportunity at synchronized swimming first, to see what she loved the best, but her father had quickly pushed her into competitive swimming. I did not want to feel responsible for keeping Emma out of the swim club, if that is what she was going to settle for, and I backed out of the trip because I was confused with so many conflicting messages, and I never saw or heard from my cousin Gildis again, though I searched for her many times.

~/~

My in-laws, as well as my sister visited us at our new location out west, and a year later, Hermann, my brother-in-law, passed through Calgary with a business associate. They were on their way to Las Vegas. Dale and our guests went out one night. I had an uneasy feel-ing about the situation because they hadn't returned by midnight. I decided to stay up and wait. Around 1 a.m., Hermann showed up and tried to make advances, which I quickly rebuffed. He respected my wishes, as he had always done since my college days, and he went to sleep in the guest room. I was sound asleep when Dale re-turned from his night out. In the morning, he told me that our other guest had taken a motel room because he was not welcome to stay with us for the rest of the visit. It didn't sound right, but who was I to question the powers that be in this world.

We always took our guests to Banff and to the hot springs, in-cluding one of our favorite visitors, Phil Knightly, who hailed from Australia. We also skied at Sunshine and Lake Louise. We liked to treat our guests, and we didn't save any money.

When Mother had decided to leave Montreal in 1978, she didn't mention if any squabbles with my sister had affected her decision to move away. A passenger next to her on the plane to Calgary had recommended the Okanagan Valley as an ideal place to retire in western Canada, so Mother asked me to fly to the Valley with her, and check it out.

We took a motel room near a local mall. We didn't bring any food with us, and it took hours until she conceded into going out for a meal. She was still religiously averse to spending money in a restaurant and she preferred to go hungry (and have me starve as well.) Deep in the recesses of her mind, I am sure that she was hoping to make connections with a friendly soul on the street and ingratiate herself into their home, and contribute to their groceries, just like she did in the good old days. I am happy to say that we did end up going out for once-in-a-life-time fish and chips that day.

I wasn't surprised to find Mother still in the habit of approaching random drivers for car rides in exchange for a little gas money. In other words, we were the only hitchhikers around town in search of apartments for rent. "Why wait for the bus or pay for a taxi when you can use your thumb?" It was a habit I had been accustomed to from a very early age. I had absolutely no choice as her fully grown and married daughter, to accept her rules exactly as she dictated.

At the end of the day, while Mother rearranged the contents of her purse, she gave me an opulent looking ring, the size of a small walnut. On close inspection, I saw five garnets interspersed on an intricately designed maze of little flowers serving as perches of gold for the stones. She told me that it was valuable (no doubt), and that it was one of several pieces of estate jewelry she had bought from a Russian lady whom she had befriended from the back balcony of her 5th Avenue duplex in Roxboro. I promised I would cherish it forever, and I have to this day. I only wish I had a special memory to cherish while we were living together in that duplex, in the summer of 1967, instead of the sudden outburst that drove me into a co-habitation situation with Fred. I also wish I knew if Emma, Shane, or a grandchild would want to inherit Mother's fine estate jewelry.

Mother returned to Montreal, sold her duplex and other investment properties, and with one suitcase in hand, flew back to us in Calgary. She had left her whole household contents for Hanne to pack and have shipped to the Okanagan.

After a few weeks with us, Dale asked Mother how long she was planning to stay. In other words, he told her she was no longer welcome. I heard Mother stay up all night. I could smell a roast of beef cooking in the oven. In the morning she asked the neighbors to take her to the airport. They refused, saying that we had been very good neighbors to them and they didn't want to get involved. She took a taxi to the airport, flew to the Okanagan Valley, and checked herself (and the roast of beef) into a motel, and was shortly hospitalized for a mental breakdown. The owners of the motel called me about her unpaid bill, because Mother didn't think it necessary to pay for her stay there, given she was sick and had given them our telephone number. When she was discharged from the hospital, she walked to the lakeside, took a seat on a bench, and wept. A gentleman by the name of Joe came along and took her under his wings. He contributed financially towards a new home, and they took occupancy of it upon arrival of the furniture and household effects which Hanne had had shipped from Montreal.

~/~

When school was out in June of 1980, the children attended day camps run by the City of Calgary, and I continued cleaning houses for the rest of June. Then Mother and Joe extended an enthusiastic invitation to come and visit them during the community's summer festival. She had discovered that many of her new friends and neighbors had already been enjoying their grandchildren in the sunny Okanagan, and she wanted to experience the same joy.

Dale decided that we were going to view the destruction of Mount St. Helen's massive volcanic eruption in Washington State before our vacation, so we ended up following a trail of spewed ashes that had been windblown all the way from its source to Calgary. On our way, we had taken a brief stop at Mother's to meet Joe, and then carried on for a long, extremely boring and uninterrupted drive straight to Mount St. Helen's devastated area, around it, and straight back to finally get to relax in the Okanagan. Mother didn't complain when we spent time at the beach that summer. Her life with Joe seemed to be going very well.

I was delighted with Mother's new partner, Joe, and with the home they had created for themselves. They had done a lot of work on it. It had been an original orchard house, with its front and back doors facing east and west. The house had a double lot with beautiful old pine trees, which Mother had us irrigate with bucket loads full of everyone's bath water.

The shelves in the basement cold storage room had been filled to the brim with canned fruits and vegetables, cherries, apricots, peaches, and pears, not to be touched, but kept for a rainy day, just in case of an emergency or war, and they had also cultivated and planted a vegetable garden and a few grape vines. We loved picking fruit directly from orchards, watching the festival parade, and basking on the beaches. I overheard a friend of Mother's saying of me, "She is such a good mother." It was very gratifying to receive a pat like that, and knowing that Mother was finally content and hopefully settled with a compatible partner for the rest of her life.

~/~

That fall, the children had to attend different schools due to the frequent re-zoning of the rapidly growing suburbs of Silver Springs and Bowness. Shane, outgoing and sociable, always took well to his new schools, but for reasons I will never truly understand, Emma refused to go to her new school for several days. With a little encouragement from a classmate and her mom, she then willingly attended school. She was fine after that episode, though her grade four teacher did mention she seemed depressed. This had been the fourth time Emma had to change schools since we had moved to Calgary. Perhaps she was afraid of giving an account of her vacation experiences in the Okanagan Valley with her grandmother, even if the last one went without incidence, but I may be projecting. I have been accused of projecting, but I don't think projecting is such a great sin, since by definition, it is a kernel of truth altered slightly to suit the projector.

Later in the fall, our landlord gave notice to our rented house in Silver Springs because his newly married son was about to take occupancy. When we told Mother about our situation, I was pleasantly surprised when she didn't hesitate to lend us $10,000 towards a three-bedroom row house in Ranchlands, a community adjacent to Silver Springs. It was listed at around $85,000. In ten years, prices had gone up significantly since we bought our first home in Montreal at $12,000.

The cleaning and unpacking on our new address on Ranchlands Drive, as well as keeping up a daily domestic routine, proved to be the most exhausting move I had experienced so far in my life. I hadn't learned to pace myself yet, and it would take decades to grant myself permission to take my time and know that everything would eventually fall into place. My sister and I had always been obsessive-compulsive about having everything looking perfectly spic-and-span. The children had to be orientated to a new school in mid-year, and Emma's gerbil seemed to have gone into hibernation during the move. Poor little Emma cried and grieved over it. I tried to comfort her and encouraged her to wait a few hours overnight, but it didn't come to life, and we made a special burial ceremony and plot for it in the garden.

Dales' nephew, Kevin, and his new bride, Deanna, had moved to Fort McMurray in northern Alberta for an entry level job with a major department store. For visits, they stayed in our developed basement, mostly on long weekends and holidays. When they were alone downstairs, I often heard Deanna not quite screaming, but shouting or whining loudly as if to say, "Quit bugging me all the time." I had entrusted Kevin with the children since they had been toddlers in Montreal, but I couldn't discern whether Emma was jealous because there was a new wife in his life, but my gut instinct told me something else was bothering her. I couldn't help but notice how Emma started looking at her cousin Kevin, as if to say, "What happened?" or "I don't like what you did to me." Again, I may have been projecting.

I had taken an evening course on Effective Parenting at Mount

Royal College to be sure I hadn't missed any basic parenting skills, considering my precarious upbringing. I thought it was probably okay that Dale had not expressed an interest in the parenting course. After all, he had a stable family as role models, and I didn't, so I developed a strong sense of family with the Tinsleys. By trying to make them into exemplary role model for my children to emulate, how could I possibly question this grand hierarchy I had established?

~/~

In the year of H.R.H., the Prince of Wales and Lady Diana Spencer's wedding of July 29, 1981, my in-laws from Florida joined their relatives from England on a trip out west to Calgary. I put my housecleaning jobs on hold to entertain, feed and chauffeur the five guests, consisting of my in-laws, a happily married couple celebrating their 30th wedding anniversary, their spinster cousin, in addition to my children, for the whole duration of that rained-out month of July, except for their short visit to see Kevin and Deanna in Fort McMurray. Dale conspicuously worked overtime all of that month. We never saw him except to eat and sleep. They asked if everything was all right in our marriage. All I could say was, "Oh, sure." I couldn't complain, because we needed the extra income from his overtime hours to help pay down the second mortgage he had taken out on the house. Our guests had brought me a set of commemorative stemware of the royal couple's wedding, with which I served Irish coffee while we watched the wedding on television.

Shortly after our guests had returned to England, I made preparations to take the children to the Okanagan to visit their 'Omi', when our old friend Phil Knightly (aka "Pa"), a globetrotter from Australia, had stopped over from England, after visiting his son, the author of the book, *Suffer the Children*. Mr. Knightly was always ready for a new adventure, and had always enjoyed our family and welcomed the opportunity to join us for a trip to the Okanagan Valley, and to meet Mother.

Pa Knightly, as his name suggests, hailed from British royalty. I think he reminded me of our beloved sponsor "Vati" in his refined demeanor and pleasant physical appearance. He told us many stories of his royal ancestry and how his manufacturing business of flags and souvenir items had prospered in Australia. His family had recently taken over, freeing him to explore the world in his retirement.

Pa Knightly inspired my interest in healthy foods. He gave me a recipe of his favorite breakfast dish cooked with a variety of nuts, grains and seeds which, unfortunately, Dale would never have touched. Dale was a bread, meat and potatoes, pop, chips and beer kind of guy. Pa had closely observed my family, and I think he liked the potential he saw in my children. He even tried to talk us into moving to Australia.

Pa Knightly joined us on our next trip to the Okanagan, and Mother was thrilled to meet him. She even did his laundry. All went well until one night she exploded for no apparent reason, as she had done in the past. Rather than argue, we packed up as we had before, and drove back through pouring rain, which forced us to take a stop over in Revelstoke. Pa said, "In all of my travels, I have never met anyone like your mother." That was his only comment on my mother. He had received more of an adventure than he had bargained for, and it took Pa some time to recuperate from the whole ordeal.

Mr. Knightly kept sending postcards from other parts of the world, as well as many letters and pictures of his family at their estate in Australia. He came around to our part of the world one more time several years later, and he was a little disconcerted because things had changed so drastically in our family. He noticed that Emma was not quite the happy little girl he'd remembered. He noticed changes in Shane too. I answered with an emphatic, "Yes, absolutely," when he asked me, "Do you have faith in your son?" He shook his head. I didn't know what he meant. My son had always been a happy, pleasant and co-operative boy, that I could see. Pa didn't elaborate and it didn't occur for me to ask. His letters and cards from Australia eventually indicated that his globetrotting days were over due to his failing eyesight and within a year, we received news from his family that he had passed away.

~/~

I had noticed that at age thirteen, Shane had been smoking during his early morning paper route, and my concern went unheeded by his father, and Shane blatantly told me, "Dad said I can smoke. There's nothing you can do about it, Mom." That was the first time my son had ever asserted himself to me in that manner, and a dark cloud started to hover about and refused to go away.

Within six months, the police asked us to meet at the home of one of Shane's friends. Shane had been getting into trouble in the neighborhood. There had been an angry exchange between parents, the police, and Dale, about some bullying. Dale sent a letter to the police in which he fervently defended his son. I kept a file of extensive reports exchanged between Dale and the police. Within a week, a policeman asked to see me personally. He seemed quite perturbed, but all he said was, "If I were his father, I know what I would do." I had not personally received any complaints about Shane, but I was aware that he had been seeing the school counselor on a regular basis. All he wished to share was, "Wherever there is trouble, Shane seems to find it." I didn't know what to make of all the vague insinuations.

~/~

We had adopted a stray tabby kitten whom we named Buster. He was my favorite of all of the cats we had fostered. I called and searched for Buster throughout Ranchlands for many days, and I was heartbroken when he didn't come home. One day a boy I didn't know stopped me in the alleyway to say, "I know what happened to Buster." All I could muster was to say "Oh?" It would have been too painful to ask for any details.

~/~

Emma was still heavily involved in the Swim Club, and Shane enjoyed singing with the Calgary Boys' Choir as the youngest boy ever admitted, at age seven. I took them to the Austrian Club, a beautiful new facility in Calgary, where Shane picked up *Schuhplattler* dancing quickly and naturally. He looked great in *Lederhosen* – short or knee length leather breeches. The demands of the choir, attending a bilingual school, as well as *schuhplattlering* – a traditional style of folk dance popular in the Alpine regions of Bavaria, proved to be too exhausting for him, so I let him drop the latter, and we continued to attend family occasions at the Club.

~/~

Within a year, Mother wrote me about some trouble she was having with Joe. She had set legal proceedings in motion for a separation. She complained how unfair and crude he had been, and he in turn wrote me to say that he had moved out because he couldn't tolerate life with Mother anymore, and he asked me for advice. I could not give him any legal advice, other than to suggest he resort to legal aid and consult his sister for support. He also confided in me that Mother had controlled all his pension income, that he had to practically beg her for his spending money, and that she had objected to his fishing with his buddies. He moved into a subsidized apartment, and understandably, this meek, mellow, and kind man had turned into a very bitter, vengeful and spiteful person towards Mother.

The following summer (1983), as if nothing had ever happened, Mother asked us to come out for our third consecutive visit to the Okanagan Valley, and as the obedient daughter, and budget conscious mother, I automatically said "Yes" to a vacation we couldn't really afford otherwise. Mother was still the consummate task master, harnessing everyone's time and energy, and still trying everyone's patience. We had done quite a bit of work inside and outside of her house and Mother still kept delegating and made our lives difficult again. She complained that I gave the children too much attention, and she made note that I had put on a pound or two. If she'd had her way, her patio set would have remained stored in her garage covered in plastic permanently. Not an inkling of leisure in her.

UNCHARTED WATERS | 199

I had always been proud of my children's excellent behavior, and I was really surprised how composed they remained, and never complained about their maternal grandmother's behavior, but then, neither did I (complain) at that time. They hadn't questioned her behavior since I had put her on a pedestal to show respect and keep the peace no matter what. Dale took time off work and joined us for two weeks, just in time to spare us from another possible disaster. In retrospect, family counseling would have been in order, but I doubt if Mother would have ever agreed to changes.

~/~

Later that autumn, Hanne and I complied with Mother's wishes to come and visit by ourselves, unencumbered with husbands and children, just like it used to be back in the good old times. The week passed relatively smoothly and without incident. However, a picture of us shows the faces of two grown up daughters who appear lost, sad, exhausted, and way too serious as we cower in our easy chairs. It had been a stressful time indeed, just like the good old days.

To compensate for our last misspent visit, Hanne and I decided to get some quality time together in Montreal, but it was Hermann who showed up at the airport. I was shocked at his appearance. He had gained weight and his face was swollen and red. He said in a matter-of-fact voice, "Hanne is in the Psych ward, so I'm taking you straight to my new restaurant. I could use another hand." I was indignant and insisted, "No, I have to see my sister first." At the hospital, Hanne refused to see Hermann, but I managed to get a short visit with her. She had just been admitted, and I found out that her mother-in-law had just arrived from Dusseldorf, Germany. Hermann put me to work as hostess near the front door of his restaurant to hand out red carnations for Valentine's day, until I got tired and took a taxi to their house. His sweet mother and I got along splendidly. I helped her with her hair and bath, but soon she broke out crying over her son and daughter-in-law's recent dilemma, and she actually wished that I could replace Hanne. Hermann had made his spare car available for my visits to the hospital, and I was about to find that it had not been insured when the police kindly told me to take it back home and leave it there. I had a little visit with the Jurman's, my daughter's godparents, and poured my heart out to them before they took me to the airport for Calgary, because Hermann had made himself scarce, and their teenage children were nowhere to be seen all week. I thought the Jurman's and the mother-in-law had made my visit worthwhile.

~/~

By Summer of 1984, I was determined I was going to get it right on our fourth family visit with Mother. We were going to have an enjoyable vacation in the sunny Okanagan with Omi, who, by then was a well established member of the German Canadian Club's choir and the ladies auxiliary. I had chosen to dismiss any upsetting memories, and I had also to learn much about conflict resolution skills, but I had forgiven and I had forgotten. Wasn't that what the Bible taught me?

So, there we were on our fourth visit with Mother. I was downstairs, getting the children ready for bed around nine o'clock one night when a young couple showed up to visit Mother. They had a lively time as they recalled the jolly times they had when they had boarded in the downstairs suite, but soon as they left, Mother went into a neurotic tantrum! A real fit! I took it that we had somehow gotten on her nerves, and I followed suit with an emotional outburst of my own. I packed up and took the children back to Calgary. According to Dale, it took me several weeks to recover emotionally (as usual).

Surely there had to be love somewhere in this all-pervasive confusion in my heart, my mind, and my soul. Surely the children had to feel love overriding this scenario, and I prayed to God to please help them understand my family, because I just did not know how to explain it to them. I hoped my deep love for them would override any friction they had witnessed. I believed that as long as they had me, just as I had believed as long as I had my own mother's support, everything would turn out all right.

~/~

I continued working around Emma's and Shane's school and extracurricular schedules by the usual cleaning of houses, giving childcare, doing alterations, and working for temporary secretarial services, but my health was beginning to decline in my midthirties, with chronic fatigue, depression, and excessively heavy periods. I went to the local walk-in clinic where the lady doctor had me wait for quite some time while she did some background research. She must have contacted Mother for some information since she alluded to something I had never heard before. She said, "You were very little when it happened." I instinctively knew what she meant, and I broke down sobbing. "Oh no! Not to me? This couldn't have happened to me!" I cried and started to feel an unfathonable sorrow. I had an instinctive and sudden flashback to our street Mattigstrasse in Braunau when the trauma happened. She then told me she was going to refer me to a psychiatrist, and that the wait period might be lengthy. I waited patiently for about three months and I was thrilled when I received a call to set up an appointment.

~/~

I started seeing Dr. Shoemaker on a weekly basis in springtime of 1984, and one of the first psychological insights I had gained with regard to my relationship with Mother, according to him, "She's one in a million. What a character!" He also painted an analogy in which Mother and I had been a pair of happy and well-adjusted clowns within the confines of our assigned roles in a circus, until separated, and all hell breaks loose.

I held on to every word Dr. Shoemaker said, including his opinion on children with religious upbringings. He said, "These people have an especially hard time in adulthood." He also told me that I had paid the price for all of my family's mistakes, that I had had to be as strong as a man to have survived, to "grab the bull by the horn", but also that I had a lot to give. I was taken off guard to hear, "Men have feelings too," and automatically answered "Really?" He also thought I had unrealistically high expectations, because as a little girl I'd had a taste of affluent life with my sponsors in Switzerland. He said I reminded him of a "waif". He also said, "You need a few relationships. There are many good guys out there." I think he already had someone in mind. I had had big meltdowns after every visit. As soon as I came home I broke down and wept. I simply adored Dr. Shoemaker for making me feel understood, and I couldn't wait for my weekly appointments. He also suggested I apply for a job at the University of Calgary.

Six months into psychotherapy, I enrolled into a government sponsored three-month word processing course at The Career College in down town Calgary. All had gone well for the first weeks, until my usual eight-day periods turned into a heavy flow which wouldn't stop. I had suffered with heavy menstrual bleeding for several years, but this time it would have been breakthrough bleeding for the whole duration of my course if my family doctor hadn't prescribed birth control pills half way through the course. Paradoxically, the birth control pill, which had originally forced my periods on twenty years earlier, this time, was prescribed to do the exact opposite. Dr. Shoemaker's theory on a cure leaned towards further psychotherapy, but as soon as I had earned my word processing diploma, I set up an appointment with a gynecologist for a hysterectomy.

Emma was now attending grade seven middle school in the adjacent community of Charleswood. She was thriving, and had obviously made a strong connection with her home room teacher, who fueled a passion for her study subjects. But, suddenly, Dale arranged to have her transferred to Queen Elizabeth High School downtown because of closer proximity to the other swimmers and to the training center. He left me with the task of taking our daughter out of her school, and it broke my heart to see her in tears, all packed up and ready to leave it and her beloved teacher, who asked "Are you sure this is what you want to do, Mrs. Tinsley?"

I should have told her that it was her father's decision. The memory still breaks my heart, because I could not take charge of the situation.

In the spring of 1985, I took a break from my therapy with Dr. Shoemaker, as well as from all the other responsibilities and pressures that came with taking care of the family, keeping up with the Swim Club demands, a part-time job while physically depleted from chronic blood loss, and waiting for an appointment date for my hysterectomy. I decided to see my old high school friend, Loa, her daughter Ingela, and her grandparents, in Sacramento, California. We had a lovely reunion and took trips to the ocean side and to redwood forests. Loa and her daughter had last visited us in Montreal in 1974 when Ingela was around eight years old, and now she was graduating from high school and competing in national horse jumping champions. But, I will never forget Emma's sudden scream in the background while I was on the phone with her father. He had momentarily put down the telephone, and hit or punched her for something she had tried to convey to me from the background. Lord, why didn't I cut my visit with Loa short, and return immediately to comfort my precious little girl? I was a coward and afraid of his acrimony if I had confronted him.

~/~

In July of 1985, Dale took us on our fifth road trip to the Okanagan Valley, and things had changed again. A highly decorated war veteran was living with Mother this time. His name was Bill. She had sent us pictures of them happily marching in a Veteran's Day parade. Mother was really proud of him, and he was totally captivated with her. Unfortunately his mental health had declined within a year of their co-habitation and he was hospitalized in an extended care unit for Alzheimer's. Apparently Bill played a heroic part in the Italian Alps by masterminding the defeat of German troops in WWII.

Emma refused to wear a swimsuit that summer when, or perhaps because, she had practically lived in racing swimsuits for the past six years. She reluctantly accompanied us to the beach, and she chose to sit on a log all huddled up beside her father, while

Shane and I took a swim. It pained me to see her so miserable. She had changed so much since she was made to switch schools. I think the stigma of knowing her mother had been under psychiatric care during the previous year had affected her as well, and it seemed to me that she was echoing her father's opinion when she said, "Mom, your brains are fried."

On the other hand, Emma was 14, and her body had changed. She may have been under the weather, so to speak, or she may have been suffering from depression. But I knew there was nothing I could do, and I hoped her extraordinary attachment to her father would get her through this phase. The fact that her new L.P. albums had melted from the heat of the sun coming through the car's rear window didn't help, though I had warned her this could happen if she didn't move them to a cooler spot under her seat. She didn't move them. It was as if my advice, as her mother, had suddenly become dismissable and worthless. Shane might also have been wondering what this next visit with Mother was going to be like.

Emma had been a strong swimmer, no doubt about it, but she also had strong artistic talents. She had taken first place at the Stampede City's 1976 Art Competition at the age of five, and everything she had created showed talent beyond her years. Oh, I just loved all of her artwork, but the swim club had dominated all of her time and energy, and her social, family and artistic life had gone to the wayside. Our family physician surprised me when he said, "It really isn't worth it, Mrs. Tinsley." because she had lost a good percentage of her school year to swim-related fatigue, bursitis, rashes, and ear infections. I could tell she wasn't her happy self, but I had to go along with the swim club's demands and with her father's Olympic expectations. She was Daddy's girl. She always was and always would be Daddy's girl.

After Shane's three year involvement with the Calgary Boys' Choir, he took private guitar lessons, and according to his teacher, he was extremely talented but had difficulty in applying himself. Shane was so good-natured, but I wonder if he had some Attention Deficit Disorder (ADD), but most likely he sensed that something was wrong in our family. And my psychological and medical problems seemed to have turned into a burden and a stigma my family could not handle. Subtle mixed messages were flying around everywhere, and they simmered and festered until the whole family eventually collapsed.

Mother with her dog "Girlie" at her Okanagan home; below, with husband Bill; I'm on the left, Shane and Emma are on the right.

Mother with our Australian friend Paul Knightly.

Hanne and I visited Mother — never a comfortable occasion.

Chapter 16

1985: LIFE-THREATENING SURGERY AT FOOTHILLS HOSPITAL
On the afternoon of Halloween, October 31, 1985, while Dale was at work, and Emma and Shane were at school, I took myself to Foothills Hospital on public transit in order to check myself in for my scheduled hysterectomy on the following morning. After my surgery, I heard Dr. Wintemute saying, "We nearly lost you on the operating table. You hemorrhaged." He kindly advised against a blood transfusion. "A blood transfusion would be too risky because, as of this month, the Red Cross is just at the beginning stages of screening for HIV infection." Instead, he prescribed mega vitamins to build up my strength.

The following morning, Dale came to my bedside. I heard, "Emily, you look terrible." And then I saw the shadows of Emma and Shane leaving with him. I don't remember seeing anyone again until Dale brought me home seven days later. Upon my discharge, a nurse forewarned, "You will have a major depressive episode. Your body will go into deep grief for a short while." I'd hoped that two Witnesses who had come to my door would lift my spirits. Instead, I felt utterly exhausted with Biblical indoctrination.

I was bedridden all of November, which happened to register a consistent and record breaking -30°C throughout the month. I could hardly eat. I had lost twenty pounds. I think Dale had convinced himself and the children that I was going to die, if not thinking I had lost my "womanhood" entirely at the age of 39. It felt like they were anticipating life without me. No one came to my bedside to say hello, nor to share what was going on in their lives. I do not remember a kind word or any moral support. For one month, I remember only catching quick glances into the bedroom, when I desperately needed to be nurtured and encouraged. The two fresh grapefruits my in-laws had sent from Florida didn't help very much either.

I had distinctly remembered the discharge nurse's warnings about going into deep grief, which helped me accept it when it happened. It did within two weeks, suddenly and unexpectedly I started to weep uncontrollably, and without inhibition. My wailing must have reverberated throughout the house. Emma stopped in the hallway and said, "It's okay, Mom. Everything will be all right." Her sweet words were very comforting and encouraging. By the third week of October, I had discovered I could eat a few things, mainly grapes and imported chocolates. Three weeks later, Dale took me for my first follow-up checkup with my doctor. I was still so weak that I needed to lie down in the waiting room. Dr. Wintemute was sympathetic towards me. He gave me an innocent kiss on the cheek. He liked me!

~/~

By mid-November of 1985, my sister, who had been separated from Hermann for some time, decided to fly out from Montreal for Christmas. She was still living in her matrimonial home, and she didn't know if she was going to be able to keep it. Her daughter Brittney had moved to Europe with her husband and baby boy, Cameron; and her son Miles lived in Texas with his wife and family, and unfortunately, the geographic distances, plus our combined personal problems, had kept us all estranged ever since we had moved away from Montreal in 1976.

Hanne looked spectacular in her white fur coat, and white poodle in her arms, but within hours of her arrival, she exhibited strange symptoms. She said she was bleeding. I took her to a walk-in clinic and to a general practitioner. We were told that she'd had a bipolar episode, and was admitted to the General Hospital. I took care of her poodle, Chico. I had barely recovered from my hysterectomy and I tried to bake and prepare for the kind of family Christmas we had become accustomed to, and I visited my sister every day, in hopes of creating a closer bond with her. Chico certainly had become attached to me.

Christmas was just days away, and as soon as Hanne's Lithium medication had been regulated, she was granted an overnight pass. When I took her back to the hospital, I realized one of our framed family photos had gone missing from our house. She had mounted it in her hospital room, all cut up into sections, rearranged and re-framed.

Dale asked me why I was so dedicated to Hanne. Well, I hoped to be an example of family solidarity. She was my sister, my only sibling, and I had to help her get through it. She had had a long history of psychotherapy and medications, whereas I had received psychotherapy relatively recently without any medication (so far), and I was determined to live up to my self-image as the little sister who had escaped the 'curse' and had remained strong for her. She was still so very pretty, and she reminded me of the blonde gymnast she had been in Austria. Apparently she lived up to her athletic prowess during volleyball matches in the hospital's gym.

On our next day trip to Banff, Hanne's overdrawn credit card had to be cut up in a souvenir shop. We then paid for her bills and medications because she refused to cash her alimony checks. It took four weeks until her medications had been fully adjusted and we had a family consultation with her psychiatrist before she flew back to Montreal, from where she wrote me a letter saying that she had been extremely disappointed in her Christmas with us.

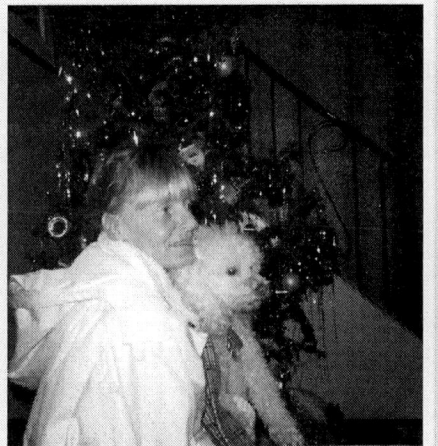

Hanne on her visit from Montreal with Coco; Calgary, 1985.

Chapter 17

1986: MY DREAM JOB AT THE UNIVERSITY OF CALGARY

Once I had recovered from my surgery and from Hanne's visit, I took a day job looking after a professional couple's children. I had made it clear to them that it was on condition to a job application I had submitted to the University of Calgary. They hated to see me go; the mother almost protested. I also needed reassurance that I was still female, and took my first ballet class ever, for adult ladies, and found myself quite challenged among some very accomplished adult prima ballerinas.

By mid-March of 1986, I heard some very exciting news from the University of Calgary's Human Resources department. I was offered a position at the Foothills Hospital. My dream job had finally come true, but Dale was not so thrilled with the news, however. He didn't think it would be worth it, because in his opinion, my income would have to be declared. He would have preferred if I had continued with what I had been doing for over ten years for an extra source of income: housecleaning and childminding for others (as well as my own). I sensed that he felt somewhat threatened and insecure at the idea of me realizing my potential and of being truly happy.

~/~

On my first day at work, I found a formal document at my desk, which was routinely provided on the first day of every new secretary's employment. It explicitly stated that fraternizing with the doctors was strictly forbidden. There had been some serious problems just before I was hired. The secretary who shared my office space had just recovered from a nervous breakdown on account of some inappropriate behavior of a brilliant researcher who had discovered a new remedy to treat cancer. He had just lost his license with the Canadian Medical Research Society, and had been ordered to return to his native country. I was still married, so I didn't have to worry about socializing with my bosses.

~/~

With his new doctorate from the University of Oslo, my new boss, Dr. Abel, had just embarked on a career as a neuroscientist at the University. He had set up his own research laboratory, and he trained me from scratch, as it were, to suit his personal academic style. He seemed tickled pink to have me. In my resume, my education, my experience and my languages had been adequate credentials to qualify me for work in the highly academic field. When he said, "You are going to be my backbone." I took it as a compliment, but eventually he literally did work me to the bone. His enthusiasm for work matched mine, but as per the university's policy, my time as a secretary had been allocated to several medical researchers, unless they were willing to pay out of their own pockets for a full-time secretary of their own. I worked very hard to keep up with the demands of a brand new career and welcomed all the challenges that came with it.

Dr. Abel's research papers rapidly amounted to over fifty internationally published articles. He was prolific indeed and his grants kept flowing in. He was a pleasure to work for because his instructions were so precise. His lovely new wife was working towards a medical degree, and she came by often to say hello. She had given birth to two babies during my tenure there, and I got to know the family quite well since I was given the task of filling the application forms for private schooling of their children, sending bills, typing personal letters and memos, and filing other personal forms, often in one of the three languages, over and above the regular job description.

During my six-month trial period at the University Hospital of Calgary, I met a very charming businessman at an Austrian Club's

National Holiday Celebration. His name was Wally. We seemed to have a lot in common, having lost our fathers at an early age in post-war Germany. One day, as we were having coffee at a Tim Horton's, I realized that he had taped our conversation when I saw him adjusting a little voice recorder inside the pocket of his jacket. Furthermore, he had stopped at Dr. Shoemaker's old home to drop off a little parcel. I didn't let on that I knew Dr. Shoemaker and his associate were still keeping a second practice in his old house, because that where I had taken Emma to see a specialist regarding her eating disorder. I wanted to believe that my employment at the U. of C. was part of an experiment as well as part of Emma's rehabilitation, and I was willing to go along with any research if it was going to help. If my new boyfriend Wally and my boss Dr. Abel had been fraternizing, and I had good reason to suspect so, I concluded that it had to be out of genuine concern. I thought my reasoning was logical, if not a little naive.

~/~

My mother-in-law's husband, Albert, had passed away earlier that year, and a family Christmas in Florida with the recently widowed lady was necessary, though it proved to be our very last attempt to save our marriage. I packed my royal blue dress for a New Year's Eve celebration. Unbeknownst to me, Dale's cousin Kevin and his wife Deanne caught up with us from Canada, and we ended up driving to various cafes. There was so much hush-hush in the air that I almost suspected they had to be dealing in something illicit.

I wonder if the children knew what was going on, or if they were forced to carry a big secret by their conspicuous silence, as if a foreshadow of future events. I made sure Emma and Shane were safe and secure in our motel room by having the motel owner to check on them, and make sure they were having a nice New Year's Eve together with takeout food and movies. Dale, Kevin, Deanne, and I ended up at a bar in Fort Lauderdale. I was way overdressed and bored to tears. No romantic New Year's Eve dance in my sparkly royal blue dress to save our marriage. I couldn't wait to get back to my job and to see Wally.

~/~

Soon after my return from Florida, Wally suggested we have sex, to which I agreed, because we had been seeing each other for over six months, and I wanted to find out if I could feel like a real woman with a man. I knew this went against my Christian principles. I was toying with the idea of adultery, but I needed to find out if I was okay in that department. We decided to meet at his house one day in March, when his mother had planned to go away for a weekend. I never met Wally's mother, but I did know that she raised him by herself after his father had died in Germany during the war.

I was supposedly going to the gym (and I did for a little while) one early Saturday morning. I drove across town, parked the car at a shopping center across the highway and walked to Wally's house. After coffee and cake, we decided to carry on with our plan. He still had his boyhood bedroom set up exactly the way it had been. When he saw me undress, I could tell he liked what he saw, and he said, "You have a beautiful body, athletic, like a swimmer's." He excused himself for a while, and I was beginning to feel a bit suspicious that he was up to more than just getting a condom. I felt like we were under video surveillance. "Maybe," I told myself, "Maybe, I am a part of an experiment to help get me through this stage of my life." The act seemed a little too hurried for me, but l liked it and would have liked more. I felt like a real woman after all. "You are very sensuous." he concluded. Feeling reassured, yet slightly disappointed with his lack of expressed feelings, I dressed, drove home and carried on as usual.

~/~

Dale usually brought Emma home around 9 p.m from her daily training at the newly constructed Calgary Sportsplex downtown. I tried to give them a warm welcome and have a hot meal ready, but all I got was nasty sneers with her father's nod of approval. Emma ignored the healthy meals I had kept warm for her, and she fixed herself Kraft Dinners, which seemed to turn into a daily ritual. One of our senior billets may have noticed the discrepancy, and I was delighted when she made it a point to ask for plenty of vegetables with her meals (as a good example for Emma). The cravings for the thousands of calories Emma expended training in the pool every morning and night were being replenished at the expense of nutritionally balanced meals. I was getting concerned about her health, and I worried about her spending most of her free time downtown with her new friends from Queen Elizabeth High School. I had seen a drastic change in the girl who had been so happy at Charleswood community middle school.

~/~

So far, I had no reason to distrust leaving my son with Kevin, though I had always wondered about him having had "upset" Emma when she was younger, but after a day of skiing with Kevin and his business partner, Shane walked in the front door and he wouldn't stop to say hello, but hurried straight up the stairs to his room, saying, "Mom, my bum is so sore." This did not sound like an ordinary bruising due to a fall on the slopes, and Shane did not join us for the rest of the evening. After dinner, Kevin and his business partner agreed that Shane had been excessively difficult to handle, and I felt badly because I was not able to persuade Shane to talk to me about his *accident*. Of course, Dale hadn't noticed anything unusual, and if I had expressed my concern, it would have gone on deaf ears.

~/~

A MOTHER'S LAMENT
Emma missed a great deal of school due to colds and swim related injuries. I knew she was missing out on a normal, healthy, life, and she had developed a nasty and condescending attitude toward her mother, right in front of her father's chuckling demeanor. During the last two years of her swim career, I had to go along with some questionable behavior on the part of one coach in particular (an Olympic medal winner) and of some swimmers. I wouldn't dare complain in case I be accused of being jealous or, heaven forbid, jeopardizing her father's Olympic dream for her. Shane was ignored

by his father, while my instincts as a mother were disregarded, if not made a mockery of entirely.

Emma quit competitive swimming voluntarily several times. The last time she quit, she became severely depressed at her rapid weight gain, and with boyfriend issues, and within several months she looked disturbingly pale and thin. She had developed the same problem I'd had when I was her age, except our circumstances were entirely different. Still, I felt as if my old secret had leaked out somehow and had lodged itself inside my daughter. I felt like a contagious disease, and I fell into a desperate fight/flight mode. My attempts to "fight" it by consulting a specialist in the field of eating disorders and happened to be a colleague of Dr. Shoemaker, resulted in my being told there was nothing that could be done for Emma for at least four years. He took one hundred dollars in cash for the visit, and Dale thought there was nothing to worry about, but I was very aware of the life-long repercussions of an untreated eating disorder, having researched the subject in depth, and I was terrified of this happening to my daughter. My ardent pleas to get Dale to take my concern seriously continued to be ignored, and I was sliding into an emotional nightmare. In the extreme, I related closely to a movie called 'Orphan', in which the father does not respect the mother's instincts about their orphan girl. He naively sides with the girl and in the end, she kills him and almost kills the mother and their son. The story's theme is about an undermined woman, rather, the undermined instincts of a mother.

Then Dale brought a chainsaw into the basement utility room and sawed off the padlocks I had installed on our chest freezers in order to control the volumes of baking and meals from disappearing, and I was beginning to feel utterly defeated. I found myself going into "flight" mode, in which I was prepared to disintegrate if it meant sparing Emma from the unwarranted hell I had to go through because it hadn't been dealt with. All it took was a push from a disgruntled husband to make me leave. It may look like I deserted Emma and her brother, but I think it actually was in a valiant attempt to save them from the effects of my past afflictions.

The pain of knowing that my departure didn't protect them very well is almost unbearable to this day, and I look back wondering if there was a better option.

Shane was also out of control, and I could do nothing to stop the impending nightmare. I am crying my eyes out as I am writing this. Yet, I am also so very thankful to God for his grace in allowing me to write this down and for the promise of a restoration of the bond between a mother and her children. All I could do was pray, "Lord, I come to you in humble prayer for Emma and Shane, since only you can make such miracles possible." But God seemed to say, "You did commit adultery and you did desert your children, and for the rest of your life you will have a difficult time with struggles upstream and against the tides, in uncharted waters. Just the same, I always have, and always will grant you the ability to work hard, and hold on to your dreams."

~/~

Dale and I were prepared for the inevitable. We had both been seeing someone else, though we acted as if we didn't know about each other's infidelity. The house went up for sale, our teenagers, going on 15 and 16 seemed to carry on as usual and we never, in eighteen years, had had an open, honest, transparent family discussion. Nevertheless, it seemed that Dale had developed a strong father/daughter relationship with Emma. They were obviously very close, and they had unusually long and inaudible chats at her bedside. I liked to think that he was trying to make up for my deficiencies and that she was receiving the reassurance of a caring daddy.

The love for my children, the vacations, the ski trips, the jewelry, and the help from the in-laws had been bonuses for an attempt to do a good job, and had sweetened my marriage enough to sustain it, and in a way, had been bribes that kept me going for almost twenty years. In a letter from Grandma Tinsley in Florida, she commented, "You didn't love Dale the way you should have. But if it will help, maybe we can assist you towards a trip to Austria next year." But it was too late to accept another bribe to save the marriage. And they dropped me like a hot potato.

~/~

Our silent rift had widened by early June, and Dale pressured me to move out right after he had put the house up for sale. He started walking around the house with a clenched fist, while the children had been completely silenced, but his voice had remained typically soft as usual. He was a smooth talker. I refused to leave before Shane's fifteenth birthday, which was coming up on the tenth of June. I remember having some difficulty finding a pair of running shoes to fit his foot, which was already a size 13. On June 14, 1987, four days after Shane's birthday, I found my personal things strewn in a heap on the bedroom floor. I felt threatened, I feared violence, I was afraid, and I knew I had to get out. With everyone quietly waiting out of sight, the children most likely having been ordered, "Stay in your rooms until she is gone," I started packing and checking for available apartments close to the university. And then they left the house, and I was by myself.

At the stroke of 12 noon, an alarm had gone off from a seemingly rigged and hidden contraption (possibly from telephone wiring) near the kitchen window. It shrieked as loud as a police siren, and I bolted out of the house until it stopped. Then Dale's realtor showed up and pointed to my replacement car which Dale had provided for my use, and which coincidentally looked identical in color and make to our family car. I returned back inside to finish packing. I did not have enough time to check for any responses regarding advertised apartments. Around 5 p.m., I drove off from my beautifully decorated, spotlessly clean and well maintained three bedroom Ranchlands Drive home (including a developed basement and garden), with my bicycle strapped to the back of the car. At this point, I was still hoping an Austrian prince, or my imaginary hero Arnold Schwarzenegger would come to my rescue.

Everything can be taken from a man but one thing;
The last of human freedoms – to choose one's own way.
– Victor Frankl

I drove down McLeod Trail. It was a very hot day and I stopped at a McDonald's to change into shorts, and then I headed back towards downtown. I checked myself into the YWCA for the first night. In the morning, I went straight to work and acted as if nothing had happened. My adrenalin and other hormone levels must have kicked in from all the excitement, also from the considerable relief I had suddenly experienced at the thought of my new found freedom, and I felt exceptionally sexy. Of course it went against my better judgment and Christian principles to seek male companionship in a bar or at work. The next evening, I settled into a motel room near Canada Olympic Park, and in the morning, I returned to the house to check up on the children and retrieve the rest of my clothes. Shane informed me that his father's girlfriend had been at the house the day after I had been evicted.

During this period of upheaval, I thought Shane and Emma would benefit from spending time in a neutral environment in Ottawa with their grandparents, but within two weeks, Emma wrote me a letter complaining how critical Dale's family had been of me, no doubt believing their son's likely version that I had voluntarily deserted my family. Emma said that she salvaged the torn-up pieces of a letter I had sent Grandma Tinsley. "Grandma tore it up, and threw the pieces in a waste basket, and she never even read it." Emma added that she managed to decipher it after she had put the pieces together that night, and she confided that my letter had made a lot of sense to her. I will never forget the empathy Emma displayed at the tender age of sixteen, and at such a trying time. And then, within two weeks, Dale informed me that she had been hospitalized for dehydration and anorexia.

Then I heard from Mother, and automatically assumed she had heard about the scenario and that she wanted to see me out of concern, so I took up on her invitation and flew to the Okanagan for the weekend. The first thing she had me do was to reorganize her disheveled bedroom drawers and closets, then I lost her at the supermarket (she had gone home ahead of me), and when I had caught up with her, she picked up on my frustration, and we both 'lost it' once more. I broke down and cried like a baby, she screamed at me and called her friend, who took me to the airport for the next flight to Calgary, shook up and sobbing all the way back. At work the next day, my boss came by my desk and said, "Our computers were smoking like crazy this weekend."

The life I had envisioned for myself and the future of my family seemed to be disintegrating in front of my eyes. But I was not alone. The lives of many Biblical characters like Joseph and Job had taken tragic turns too, and I had to believed that there was a reason for everything and that God would reveal himself with preordained justice, at his appointed time, and I carried on the best way I knew how and with what was at hand. Trials are presented to strengthen and prepare for a greater destiny.

> *"If you are irritated by every rub,*
> *how will you be polished?"*
> – Rumi

~/~

Dale asked me to meet Emma at the Calgary International Airport upon her return from Ottawa, and assumed he had granted me an extra precious visitation opportunity, a sign that he had relinquished some control over her, but I could not believe how emaciated she looked upon her arrival. On the way home, she told me plans had been set up for therapy.

Again, at Dale's request several weeks later, I agreed to pick Shane up at the airport, but he had been delayed by airport customs inspectors for quite some time. He was finally released around 4:30 a.m. with no explanation; just a three hour "routine" inspection of a fifteen-year-old boy? When he came out of the interrogation room, he seemed happy-go-lucky as usual, and I felt unqualified to question the authorities, who may have spoken to his father and agreed to keep me out of the whole scenario. Dale most likely would have told me, "It's just a phase he's going through."

~/~

I had rented a furnished basement suite in a little old house located not too far from the children or from the university. I tried to see Shane and Emma often, though their father made it difficult for me, because he insisted I leave when he was about to arrive or that I leave whenever he was there. I brought food whenever the cupboards were bare. Dale had complained that he had trouble controlling the volumes of groceries from disappearing and that he had installed a padlock on their chest freezer. I was tempted to remind him that when we were still living together, he had brought a chainsaw into the house to defiantly cut off the padlocks I had installed to our deep freezers.

In September of 1987, Dale had sold the house. My share of the proceeds was $4,817.61, a substantial part of which I contributed toward Emma's extensive dental work apparently not covered by Dale's coverage with his company. While on the topic of money, I kept an itemized list of financial assistance to Emma and Shane over the following four years, amounting to $11,938.

Meanwhile, a bouquet of exquisite flowers had been delivered to my office weekly, and anonymously for eight weeks. I assumed they came from a secret admirer, maybe my boyfriend Wally, the president of the university, or perhaps even my imaginary rescuer, Arnold Schwarzenegger. It never occurred to me that it could have been Dale going to such a lavish expense, when, according to the children, he was having serious struggles with having to budget for the first time since our marriage of almost twenty years, though he did write me a touching letter saying he still loved me and missed me, that the children needed me, and he even suggested we remarry, and in a card, he wrote, "Emily, to know you is to love you and I didn't mean to frighten you." It was too late. My husband had terrified me when he forced me out of our home into uncharted waters, with nowhere to go, and it seemed he had turned my children against me. The best thing I could do for my children was to retrieve my identity so I could be strong for them.

I was asked to meet a gentleman for coffee at the university's cafeteria, and I assumed that he was someone from the human resources department to assess my job progress. We had a short conversation because he was about to visit a patient in the hospital, and he told me that he would keep me on his mailing list and left me a note with his name on it. I didn't know that he was a well-known politician, and I never did receive any mail from him.

There were times of utter desperation and panic. One time, I jumped out of bed and into my car in the middle of the night, drove west toward the Rocky Mountains, took a turn left onto a forestry road in Kananaskis Country, and had a rude wake-up call when I found my car dangling at the edge of a lake. I had come perilously close to being literally submerged in "uncharted waters" permanently. I gingerly backed up and slowly drove back home.

~/~

Wally, my boyfriend, had kept his distance during my separation and had not been around to help or get involved in any way. He had consistently determined when and where we were to go. When I called him with a suggestion of my own, he was usually unavailable, or at least hesitant. At Christmas and holidays he was always tied up with his children for whom he had joint custody. My hopes in him had faded, and I was beginning to have the painful realization he was not the committing type.

In December of 1988, Dale asked me to keep an eye on Shane and Emma while he vacationed in Florida with his girlfriend. Everything seemed to be in order whenever I checked, but by the weekend, their place had been trashed during a party which I had not been made aware of, and items had gone missing. Dale subtly blamed me for the vandalism and theft. He also told me that his mother was pleased with his choice of a new woman, who apparently didn't play "head games." I was invited on Christmas day, but not until after they'd had a traditional turkey dinner. The pain of having been so cruelly cut off and alienated from my children made me break down and weep all the way back to my apartment.

I hadn't heard from Wally over Christmas, nor about plans for New Year's Eve, and I was alone in my basement suite, while the rumbling activity between the upstairs executive and his prostitute kept me awake for hours. A few months later, I was surprised to see

Wally a bit perturbed when I told him that I had met someone new at the German Club. I must have meant something to him, but it was clear to me that he had been womanizing, and I fell into a depression serious enough for Emma and Shane to have noticed and have Dr. Shoemaker, my long-term psychiatrist, contact me. He noted that my experience with Wally had been a typical reaction to the first separation anniversary from a spouse, and that it should serve as a lesson to make me appreciate a "good" man.

Sadly, I had lost another opportunity to return to Austria when a researcher from a remote area of the medical research complex had befriended me. She was going to move to Austria on a sabbatical and run an art exhibition and hoped I would join her and her mother. They sent me endearing letters and photos with glowing reports of all the concerts and art shows they had been attending, and they urged me to join them in Vienna. As tempted as I was, I was too concerned about the children's welfare so short of our separation, and with keeping my job, and I allowed another golden chance to return to my homeland slip through my fingers. I have to admit I had also been somewhat paranoid and suspicious, since Wendy and her mother were Jewish, and the thought of a contrived retribution for Hitler's anti-Semitism had entered my mind.

I could not understand what had deterred Emma to see me on her own, but I was hoping that she was happy with her boyfriend and enjoying her interest in some of my old recipes, one of which was *Linzer Gitter Kuchen*. But I was really delighted when Shane visited me in my office. He seemed happy doing what he loved: entertaining at festivals. He also played a song for me over the telephone, by The Cult, from their Sonic Temple Rock Band album. The song was "Edie, Ciao Baby." I found the melody and the lyrics quite beautiful. There is also a video of the song with a glamorous young woman depicting artist Andy Warhol's girlfriend, Edie Sedgwick, who unfortunately succumbed to drug use or suicide. It is a beautiful song. The lyrics touched a sensitive nerve in me because I could have gotten perilously close to her own demise. God knew I was vulnerable and at risk, but with his grace, and my efforts to hold on to the strong values I was raised with, I hadn't and never would fall into street life, drug use, alcoholism, or prostitution.

I allowed Shane to use my car to practice for his driver's license. It had taken some beating and ended up in his school's automobile shop, but that was minor if everything was going to work out just fine in the end. Much to my surprise, Shane and Emma took me to a German restaurant for Mother's Day brunch. On our way home, my heart swelled when Shane promised to take me to Austria someday.

One night, Shane asked me to come and get him at the end station of the east Calgary Transit line. He had run away from home and wanted to move in with me. He complained, "Dad is being such a jerk." We searched for a suitable place, but he suddenly decided to remain with his father after all. I suspected that Dale would never, under any circumstance, relinquish any control of "his" children, control that would have weakened, had they accepted an opportunity I had made available to them through the University of Calgary's scholarship funding plan.

Happy to see my children on Christmas Eve, after the separation; 1987.

Chapter 18

GOING ON DISABILITY AND MORE PSYCHOTHERAPY

Dr. Abel finally took the opportunity to subsidize me as his full-time secretary, when my other bosses had relocated; one doctor had moved to a remote part of the building and managed to do his own paperwork, the others, as married partners in research, had returned to the United States. Dr. Abel had extremely productive years without any complaints about my secretarial performance, when suddenly, after three years, he started to complain. For example, while I was going through my routine of filing away daily correspondence in his office, I had always forwarded all incoming calls from my office to his office, as usual, when one of the calls was from Wolfgang, the German gentleman I had met at the German Club. Just then, Dr. Abel overheard me speaking on his telephone as he was about to enter his office. He immediately walked away and filed a formal complaint about a personal call I had taken in his office. He sent the dean a memo saying that his telephone had been used for "romantic purposes" and "in German at that." He also complained that he was tired of being used as a guinea pig with the numerous unqualified secretaries previously assigned to him, none of whom he had been satisfied with. (I was under the impression that I had been his first secretary at the University). He feared his job was at stake, though he had found me quite "personable." Some of his complaints were not only addressed to the dean, but to other department heads I was not familiar with. At this point, I had to defend myself with a lengthy memo to the dean and to the relevant department heads. I applied for a transfer anywhere else in the university. When my boss heard about it, he took me aside and asked me to stop writing memos to those concerned. Things simmered down for a while, but on the annual secretaries' social night out, he continued to keep me late to work on urgent documents. I received extra heavy workloads after the last incident. He left a Post-It note on my desk saying, "After all, my wife is pregnant," as if he owned me. I crumpled it up and threw it in the waste basket as if reading it had been a great sin in itself.

I loved working at the U. of C., and I did not have any complaints from any of the doctors I had been assigned to whenever Dr. Abel was away at conferences. I thrived working in an academic atmosphere. I used my breaks and any opportunity to do extra research in the library. I worked through lunch hours and took work home, if I felt it necessary. I attended seminars conducted for medical students and doctors. I took part in the noon hour exercise classes in the hospital's gym, and in the summer I enjoyed picnic lunches on the beautiful campus grounds. The regular pay check was adequate and the medical and dental coverages were nice fringe benefits.

Suddenly I had trouble deciphering Dr. Abel's handwriting, which had been consistently clear and easy to read. It had become impossible to make it out and I told him so. He didn't take it kindly, and he took his work to someone else. We had formally filed our grievances, but there was no response to my application for a transfer. I could not believe it when the administration manager, Barb Wieber, indignantly barged into my office and belligerently said, "You cannot do the job, and you are out!" She also mentioned that speaking with the doctor who had a laboratory next door to my office, wouldn't serve me well. "He has no influence here. He's a nobody," she said. This doctor and his team had always included me in their social gatherings because it was well known that my boss didn't have social skills for his department. He was too cheap. I had a feeling that Dr. Sharma would have stood up for me. The whole scenario seemed like a real joke.

I was too stunned to go the union, even when a union representative tried to reach out to me by passing me her home phone

number on a small piece of paper. I was paranoid by then, and I
was even suspicious of the union. To me, using the union's service
meant disloyalty to the U. of C. and to my ex-boss, and I feared repercussions for confronting my employer.

~/~

I had broken up with Wolfgang for a serious violation. My eight-
month co-habitation lease with my landlady had run out. My job
had been suspended for a temporary leave, and I found myself in
uncharted waters again, just like the day I drove away from my
nuptial family home four years earlier. My son hadn't shown up
with his pick-up truck as promised, so at the last moment I rented a U-Haul and moved my belongings into a storage locker by
myself.

Having driven around town at random that evening, I decided
to park in the parking lot next to the professional building where
Dr. Shoemaker had his practice, conveniently located next to
Westview Village Mall (as if my psychiatrist's proximity were my
last refuge). I slept in a sleeping bag in the back of my car. During
the night, my eyes detected the momentary glare of a flashlight. It
was security or the police, so I felt safe. I had breakfast at McDon-
alds, washed and changed in the washroom, and checked the classifieds for a live-in-job. There were quite a few domestic jobs
listed in the Calgary Herald and I settled for the first job available,
and I was on my way across Calgary to my new position as a nanny. This job led to three additional temporary live-in nanny positions over a period of eight months.

I may sound paranoid, but Shane always showed up to
transport me from one family to another. How did he come to
know them, I wondered. Every time I witnessed child abuse, the
parents asked me to leave. I had called Family Services to report
my concern. I had no response. I feared I'd be followed, even
killed, had I reported them in person, and I thought, "Oh my God!
Organized crime! Pedophiles!"

I was convinced that I was only on temporary "lay-off" from the
university and that I would eventually be reinstated, and I truly be-

lieved that meantime I had been sent on a mission to save those unfortunate children I tried to nurture.

I had nowhere to go but to a motel, but Shane showed up just in time to recommend me to another family. He must have been prompted by someone else. He was only nineteen years old. I didn't hear from Social Services, and I felt my personal mission to try and save these children was complete.

At one point, Emma's principal at Queen Elizabeth High School told me in a consultation that she was going to have a career in the food industry, and that she was going to go a long way in her life. He also commented that she had been seen passionately smooching with a boy, and that she made a 'mighty fine' figure in her swimsuit. I felt like the high school principal had taken control of my daughter, and I considered a nobody; a disrespectful, absent, incompetent parent.

I had expressed my concern over my son and daughter to Dr. Shoemaker once more, because it was clear that they were not doing as well as they should have under their father's care. "Well," he said, "They are after all, Emily's children too." I'm not sure if he was insinuating a genetically inherited defect on my side of the family. He also alluded that I was jealous of Emma. I thought that was laughable because, as difficult as my teen years were, I would not have wanted to be in her shoes, and all I wanted was to see Emily happy and thriving. During our last sessions, he attacked me with random comments such as, "What do you want! You can't move to Austria! We went over your losses so often and I tried so hard with you in 1984-1985. Don't blame your mother! You remind me of a wench. You have a car, and you moved, and you are still not happy. There is much of your mother in you. Your age is definitely showing. Why don't you go back to Dale? Are you sorry for what you did? Most women would kill to have had a job like you had. You know you'll never work again. You need to get back into your mold." He didn't elaborate what my 'mold' was, but he obviously alluded to the circumstances of my precarious upbringing as an "Austrian landlady's daughter'. He added, "I once conducted an experiment with a patient, and it went terribly wrong. We don't want anything to happen to Emily now, do we?" He was obviously belligerent, aggravated and critical. Considering my unsettled situation, he had me admitted to the Psychiatric Ward in the Foothills Hospital.

A psychiatric nurse at the hospital advised me that Dr. Shoemaker had actually lost hospital practice privilege, but somehow he managed to have me admitted after the hospital's day program didn't seem to work. My official diagnosis: mental illness with a succession of antidepressant prescriptions: Prozac, Zoloft, Desirel, Paxil, Citalopram and more. Originally, Prozac had been used as an appetite suppressant. It worked well for me as an antidepressant for a short time, and the doctor thought I looked great, though I didn't need to loose any weight.

As I was walking into a therapy class one day, I overheard a staff member say to another, while glancing at me, "Here comes the soap opera!" I thought to myself, "Oh well. It's really not so far from my reality, but little do they know." While I was institutionalized, I found some relief from my normal everyday stressors and from getting a break from trying to meet ends on a limited disability pension. It enabled me to float in my own little dream world for a while: dreaming of my home country and of having my children back in my life, as well as being able to save some of my disability income for a car I purchased from some well-to-do people in Bonavista Estates for $400, only to have it break down within a week and having it scrapped.

When I was deemed ready to move on, I availed myself of the services of the hospital's Housing Department because my last attempt at living in an affordable basement suite proved to be a disaster. I hadn't been fully aware that I was claustrophobic and suffered with Seasonal Affective Disorder (SAD). Another dingy basement suite had not been a good prescription for my condition.

The Housing Department recommended me and another patient to an old hotel in downtown Calgary, which repulsed us both as an "establishment of ill repute." I was then referred to a home a rural community thirty-five minutes west of Calgary. Staff had raved about the beautifully custom-built home I was about to see, and bragged about the wonderful European owners I was about to meet. I was feeling optimistic and anticipating country living at its best. During the 30-mile drive there, they also hinted that I might be fond of the husband, who was temporarily in Europe, if I didn't mind the "touchy-feely type." This struck me as questionable coming out of the mouths of professionals. It was a forewarning to proceed with caution. The lady of the house greeted my drivers and then looked at me and said, "I can see you are used to having everything done for you." and I thought, "What else have they written on my medical chart I don't know about?" We then toured the spacious house. It did not strike me as anything close to the picture that had been painted for me, but rather sinister and lacking warmth. It was built into a densely wooded forest which could have conjured up a vision of the wicked witch's house in the scary childhood fable, "Hansel and Gretel."

A visiting sister from Europe would have to vacate the room I was to occupy (next door to another boarder's room), and she was going to be relocated to the foot of her sister and brother-in-law's bed in the master bedroom. I met the sister when she returned from an outing with the severely handicapped boarder. He was not able to sit at the same dining table since he needed the whole kitchen table to occupy himself by shredding newspaper to keep him busy. He drooled heavily into a towel wrapped around his neck while waiting for his spoon-fed dinner. Over a cold and skimpy supper, I found out I was expected to help with his care, including diapering him at night. We agreed I should try it out for one night. I opted to settle for the living room couch to avoid a temporary upheaval of the upstairs bedrooms. There was not one reading lamp in this huge space, nor any television reception. The next morning, I decided to take that "ten minute" trek to the local village. Thirty minutes later, in -20 degree temperatures, there had been no village in sight. To me this was beginning to feel like a nightmare, and after the sister's return to Europe, I would have found myself alone with a severely handicapped person, in the middle of nowhere, with our own caregivers away all day to take care of other clients in Calgary.

The wife gave me a ride back to the hospital on her way to work the next day. When I walked into my ward, I exploded with a rage I never thought I had in me. This ended my fifth experience under the auspices of psychiatric care. What seems so outrageous in this scenario is my sense of overly ambitious immigrants taking advantage of less fortunate immigrants under the guise of psychiatric care giving to speedily pay down their own mortgages.

Life at the psychiatric ward in Calgary had been particularly frustrating, when, five years earlier, I had been employed at the other end of the hospital as a medical research secretary, processing research papers and managing a doctor's office in the Faculty of Medicine, and no process had been initiated for a review or a referral of any kind through the University, and still believing a job was waiting for me. Even if I had reached out for support, I didn't think anyone in my family, including my old work associates wanted anything to do with me in my seemingly embarrassing and disgraceful circumstances. I had lost complete control of my life this time and didn't know that I was going to drift in and out of part-time jobs, hospitals, residences, and unstable relationships for the rest of my life. I asked God. He answered, "There is a reason. Don't give up."

Someone had set up an appointment for an independent assessment with a Dr. Kuhn in the hospital's Psychiatric Department, who, on his initial observation, determined, quite justifiably, that I had a persecution complex. He said *Verfolgungswahn* in German, and he thought I was steering myself in a direction I did not want to go. So true! I noticed that Dr. Kuhn's and Dr. Abel's theories had clashed. It seemed the former had become a threat to the latter. According to Dr. Shoemaker, "Dr. Kuhn has to learn his lesson and he needs to change." I thought he made many unprofessional comments, and I had the impression he wanted to get rid of Dr. Kuhn in order to carry on with his own agenda. And then I heard that Dr. Kuhn actually had passed away! I thought it suspicious, but then I was considered paranoid, no matter what I said.

~/~

Mother asked me to visit her again, and "This time," I thought as always, "This time, we will reconcile our differences. She will understand, because, after all, she has gone through two divorces, and many relationships and break downs herself." I had no objections to obtain a temporary leave from the hospital.

Shortly after I arrived in her Okanagan community, Martha Landstone, a part-time realtor and friend of Mother's dropped by and invited us for traditional German style coffee and cake. Her extremely large and beautiful home was situated in a small nearby community, and Martha thought I might like to live there and she invited me to come back and stay with her for a while, and see if I would like to live in the spacious mother-in-law suite attached to her spectacular home overlooking Okanagan Lake. A few months later I took her up on the invitation.

Mother flew into a rage when she found out about our plan. "What would the neighbors think? No! You have to stay with me!" We solved the problem. Martha would meet me at Mother's house right after my arrival from Calgary. We promised to visit her every day. The next day, Mother started badgering me to come back to her place in town. Her relentless pleas brought Martha to tears. Mother tried to persuade her friend Gunther, president of the German Club, to bring me back. For the first time in my life, it seems, I had asserted myself with Mother. I reminded her that she never wanted me there in the first place. Martha and I were very upset with the whole scenario, so we decided to put the whole idea on the shelf for the time being and I shortened my visit. I had tried to help Martha around her home and I gave her a large box of fancy chocolates. When she dropped me off at the bus station in town, she rolled down the window of her Mercedes and said, "*Das hat Gasoline Geld gekostet.*" – "This cost me gas money." She also said something to the effect that Hitler got rid of people like myself who lived on disability pensions and robbed government coffers. I thanked God I still had my bed at the Foothills Hospital.

Unfortunately, both Shane and Emma had dropped out of High School. Shane seemed to have found his niche in the entertainment industry, and I was happy knowing Emma was studying art at SAIT while earning money as a waitress. Everything still looked promising for my son and daughter. They were going to pull through their difficulties, cross that bridge, and have a wonderful, lasting relationship for the rest of their lives.

On one of Hanne's trips to the Okanagan, she took a layover in Calgary with Dale, Emma, and Shane. She visited me in the hospital, and I obtained leave to join her for coffee at the Chinook Shopping Centre. She told me that Dale was going to take her to Banff and surroundings, and then fly on to see Mother. Rumors were no doubt flying.

My sister Hanne, with her son Miles and daughter Brittney, on a visit with Father and his family in Linz, Austria, 1978.

Chapter 19

1991: CLARESHOLM CARE CENTRE
The sixth plan for psychiatric therapy, all else having failed according to the system, was a referral by Dr. Shoemaker to have me transferred to the Claresholm Care Centre, one hour's drive south of Calgary. On the eve of my transfer from the hospital, one of the psychiatric nurses came by my room to say, "The doctors owe each other a big favor by admitting you there." I don't know exactly what he meant, except to suspect that my psychiatrist feared repercussions.

My last appointment took place in Dr. Shoemaker's private office when he brought up the subject of my retroactive disability check of roughly $10,000 issued from Great West Life Insurance Company, and I believed him when he said, "This money is actually intended for my corporation." I either signed the check over to him or I issued a new check for the specified amount.

Twenty-three years later, I felt empowered enough to check it out with my insurance company, but it could not help me because the check was originally issued to myself, and my bank said that too much time had elapsed to trace it back to 1991. Dr. Shoemaker had washed his hands of me, and I suspect he took me to the cleaners too. His sympathetic statement, "Emily, you paid the price for all of your family's mistakes." should possibly have been, "Emily, you helped me pay down a few monthly mortgage installments for my castle up on Eagle Hill Estates." He also boasted that it had been his idea to have me sent to the Claresholm Care Centre, and said, "You have vegetated in the hospital and you prefer to be sick, but you'll like it at the center. They even pay for part time work."

With my suitcases in hand, I arrived at the beautiful, new, state-of-the-art Claresholm Care Center (CCC). My first appointment was at the grueling hour of 7 a.m. on Monday morning. The head of the CCC, Dr. Farnsworth, greeted me with "And you committed adultery?" I took a big breath and all I could respond with was, "But... but... so did he." Dr. Farnsworth didn't want to hear about the child abuse I had witnessed in Calgary and he literally told me to mind my own business. He said I was highly paranoid, implying that I had been projecting and making up stories.

I was extremely satisfied with the CCC program, other than to have another authority tell me, "It's best you have no contact with your children." Who would say something like that except to a convicted child abuser? I think if I had been guilty of anything, it would been for having doted upon and pampered my children, and for having treated them with too much reverence, and I am truly sorry for having overcompensated for the deprivations I had suffered in my own childhood.

A very pretty and sweet first nations girl had noticed my love of nature when I had hung a bird feeder outside of my room, and she invited me to attended a sweat lodge ceremony about which an administrator had asked me to write a report. Soon the young girl gave me enticing invitations to join her upon her return to her native home. With a most beautiful and heartwarming smile, she kept extending those invitations, and I was a fool not to break out of my trap and explore a brand new world I might possibly have fit in.

~/~

At Christmas of 1992, Dale telephoned to inform me that he was about to take Emma to Florida for an abortion. I was shocked and upset not because she was pregnant, but because he didn't give me any details about it and because I could not be there for her. As a result, I needed to be hospitalized, medicated, and placed into group therapy once more. As soon as I was alone, I fell to the ground and begged for mercy, and cried out, "Oh, my God, what have I done to deserve this? What is happening to my baby? Have you really abandoned me?"

~/~

I don't know who had given Mother all the details about my divorce, about my unemployment, my hospitalizations, and my affairs, and she expressed absolutely no sympathy for me, but she had definitely come to the realization of a possible connection between my early sexual abuse and my mid-life depression. In a letter, she confessed that I had been sexually assaulted when I was very young: *"Du warst vergewaltigt"* – "You were assaulted" and she blamed my sister for having refused to look after me. She added, as if whispering an afterthought, "They got you more than once." I thanked her for her honesty, and wrote both Mother and Hannelore letters with the intent of enlightening them on the subject. I stressed that Hanne should not have been blamed for a horrendous assault on me, but I had no response from either. All I wished for was to be loved and accepted by my family just as I was, but they were only comfortable with the old version on the topic.

While my new reality took the mystery out of my past, a great weight of awareness had altered my self-image, like Adam and Eve in the Garden of Eden who covered themselves up when they had been shamed with the knowledge of the good and evil sides of their lives. I wished my repressed childhood trauma had not resurfaced again, because it really did rob me of the sense of innocence and pride I had about myself, as if a healthy part of my self-image had been mutilated. On the other hand, it would most likely have to be dealt with sooner or later. But I was approaching my late 40's, and I was going through the aftermath of divorce, the loss of my children, the loss of my job, and a breakdown, and I didn't know about hormonal replacement therapy for my menacing post-menopausal symptoms.

Mother reprimanded, *"Vergiss den Unsinn"* – "Forget the nonsense", and *"Du bist tief niedergefallen"* – "You have fallen from grace." She also said "You belong in Claresholm. What goes around comes around." That was not very encouraging. Everyone seemed to be watching at a distance, and I thought, "Hmm, God must think

I can handle this by myself too. He must think a lot of me, so I'll keep forging ahead. Thank God for testing me."

I refused to let go of the unusually close bond I had developed with Mother since I was a child, and I held on to my hopes of taking care of her in her old age. I also dreamed of picking and canning Okanagan fruit, enjoying the beaches, going south in the winter, and of guided tours and getaways. I was looking forward to skiing on the beautiful Okanagan Valley ski slopes, just like we used to ski in Banff, being involved in the community, and having family and grandchildren visit just like everyone else. But I needed to stay at the Care Center and finish my three months of therapy, first.

And then came:

A CHRISTMAS FROM HELL

On the morning of December 23, 1993, I received a call from my son, Shane, then twenty years old, inviting me to join them for Christmas. It would be our first Christmas together as a family since our separation in 1987. I obtained permission to leave the Center, and I arrived in Calgary around five p.m. on Christmas Eve. I was full of anticipation for a pleasant family get-together, but as soon as I arrived, Shane and Emma were preparing to leave for the evening. They had made plans. Since their father and I were not on speaking terms, he promptly stumbled upstairs to his bedroom and shut the door. I ended up pacing the main floor, wondering what to make of it. I couldn't sleep. There was no evidence of the beautiful Christmas tree and decorations I'd left behind for them. I waited up all night, but they had not yet returned by five a.m., so I left a long explanatory letter and arrived in Claresholm by breakfast time.

I wish I could have turned into Mrs. Santa Claus that night, because I think they had missed all of their past fifteen Christmases with their Mom, when she had gone all out by celebrating in both the traditional and Austrian versions, or heavens forbid, hoped to see Mom and Dad magically reunited. I have a feeling their father contacted the CCC and complained profusely that I had spoiled *their* Christmas. After that, I told myself that sacred music, candles, and a peaceful meditative atmosphere is sufficient, and that the presence of others only serves to remind me of my losses. I can only dream of an ideal Christmas where family and friends gather by a blazing hearth, surrounded by a winter wonderland of sleigh bells ringing, horses neighing, and carolers singing *"Stille Nacht"* on Christmas Eve. I am a dreamer.

~/~

After my discharge from the CCC, I remained in Claresholm and took an apartment. I became a volunteer horticulturist at two dollars per hour. I had access to the CCC workshop with all the horticultural supplies one would need to run a regular indoor plant and landscaping business. It had turned into a passion, as I experimented with fertilizers and grafting, and happily transported plants and supplies on carts with wheels from one building to another.

I got around the town very well via bicycle. I found a church family which took me under their wings. I volunteered with a blind gentleman for two years, and accompanied him to his monthly CNIB meetings in Lethbridge until he was transferred to a senior's facility near Fort McLeod. I also assisted a deaconess on her weekly visits with dementia patients at the new rural Hospital.

I hoped for a regular job again, but I was forty-seven years old and I had developed low self-esteem and a new self-image: "mental patient on disability." My imaginary ID label said *Depressed, Outcast, and Medicated for Life.* My pride in my native heritage had eroded. My identity as the proud landlady's daughter was gone. Gone were my student years. Most of my family kept their distance. Gone was my prestigious job. Gone was my role as a wife and mother. My doctor's perception of me did not seem to match my self-image either. The words "mental illness" repulsed me. I would have preferred to be diagnosed as *Seelenkrank,* which loosely translated means "brokenhearted."

Shane was well on his way to a career journalism, or so I thought. He was about to fly to Europe on a business trip with a senior journalist, making it one of my biggest morale boosters at that time. I drove to Calgary and helped him get ready with all the supplies and necessities he would need for his new adventure.

Two weeks later, he called me from France, saying that his father suggested I wire him his return airfare. Apparently he was living on the streets of Paris with nowhere to go. I asked him where his partner was. He didn't tell me what had happened. I didn't have any extra funds, and I contacted his father. When I saw Shane shortly after he returned from France, I could hardly recognize him. He looked like he had aged ten years, and I felt like I had aged just as much in one moment.

Emma had dedicated time to writing me beautiful letters, all of which I have cherished and kept the wooden box she had sent me with special writing paper in it. Inside the lid she had inscribed:

*"What lies behind us and what lies before us
are tiny matters compared to what lies within us."*
– Ralph Waldo Emerson

And I prayed that God would help her get through her struggles, and hoped that she would thrive with her art courses at the Southern Alberta Institute of Technology (SAIT) and realize her true talents. She may have had a fear of inheriting my psychological problems, and I understood why my she may have avoided me, having to harbor secrets or feelings she was unable to express, but it didn't stop Shane, who had been the only one to visit me throughout my ordeals, and I gladly helped him out when he asked. He painted a glowing picture of a career opportunity in the entertainment industry, and he had done some acting in Fringe Festival side-shows, but it never occurred to me that he had been getting into drugs.

~/~

DIVORCE PROCEEDINGS
Almost eight years had passed since our separation. I needed to close that chapter in my life, and I filed for a divorce in the winter

of 1995. As we were waiting for our hearing in the Calgary court house's cafeteria, I happened to sit across the room, but I was close enough that I could overhear a little bit of Dale and Shane's conversation. I heard Dale telling our twenty-three-year-old son all kinds of defamatory information about me, and I clearly heard him say, "She even left just before your 15th birthday. (Good thing I kept a diary to prove him wrong.)

At the hearing of the Court of Queen's Bench of Alberta in the city of Calgary, I represented myself. Dale had hired his own lawyer. The questions were straight-forward and nothing out of the ordinary. After I had taken the stand, Dale's lawyer called for Shane, who had been asked to wait in the hallway just in case he had to take the stand, and she asked him what kind of a mother I had been. He testified that I had been a good mother and he was given permission to leave the courtroom. Then, Judge Janeczek deliberated that I was not entitled to alimony because too much time had elapsed since our separation. I was satisfied with his statement, but, just before his final dismissal, he made a remark that still resonates to this day. He said, "Did you know that your relatives were Nazi conspirators?" I was too numbed and shocked to say anything. On my way out of the courtroom, Dale's lawyer approached me and asked "Are you all right?" I nodded in the affirmative and returned to Claresholm. My Certificate of Divorce was issued on July 20 of 1995 by the Clerk of the Court of Queen's Bench of Alberta.

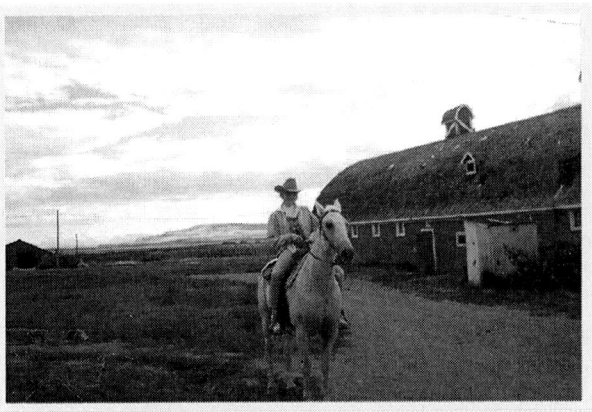

Me, riding a horse at a Hutterite colony; 1994.

Chapter 20

1995: A HAPPY TIME IN MY SHACK AFTER LIFE WITH MURRAY
I met my neighbor, Murray, one year after I had settled into my
Claresholm apartment. He had noticed me from his house next
door to my apartment building as I was coming and going to and
from my various volunteer activities, and he asked me over for
coffee one day. He told me that he was about to have minor abdominal surgery after which he was planning to quit consuming
alcohol entirely. I offered to help him with his household chores
until he felt better. At the hospital in Lethbridge, I met Murray's
brother, an executive who gave me an official Calgary Flames
hockey jersey.

Within six months, Murray convinced me that we should live
together. We had gotten along really well, and his family was
thrilled with the idea. We attended his niece's wedding in High
River. I learned that Murray's birth father had been a provincial
politician, and that he had been adopted into a prominent Albertan family. I met his appreciative and very beautiful daughters and
their families, and I broke into tears as I leafed through his family
albums, as if I had just found my own long lost family. We enjoyed
house and yard work, picnics, cooking and redecorating, and it
was so nice to be living in a regular house again. He wrote glowing
letters about me (which I still have, the fastidious record keeper
that I am) to friends and family. His daughters had enjoyed a so-
ber father again, I was happy for them, and I loved nothing more
than to see a family reunited, especially when his younger daughter's lovely young family came all the way from Idaho, USA for
Easter to enjoy a multi-course dinner with crafts and decorations

to entertain the children. This is how I visualized future grand-children, delighted to leave 'grandma's' house with cuddly stuffed animal in their arms.

I had volunteered to walk my neighbors' puppy, Kooter, so many times, that they offered her to me due their mobility issues, and I soon changed her name to Polly, because 'Kooter' just didn't seem to fit her personality. She would prove to be my best com-panion and a great source of comfort in my ensuing trials, until I tragically lost her in my next big move.

Soon, my son Shane and his girlfriend, Monique, drove up from Calgary, and spent the weekend with us. He had recovered from his ordeal in France and he was his normal happy self again. We had a great barbeque and lots of fun. We were all thinking that our lives had finally settled, and the future seemed rosy.

Murray had close friends at a Hutterite colony who enjoyed coming into town to shop, and drop in for a visit. We and Polly were also welcome to visit them, and pick vegetables from their gardens. We admired the young girls' sewing and domestic skills, the abundant crops in the fields, and watched a sheep shearing contest. Murray asked me to do the driving back home after a so-cial, when I was feeling slightly dizzy behind the wheel and I nev-er found out what they had put into their 'specialty' tea.

One day, Murray arranged for a horseback ride with one of his friends at the colony. I donned a beautiful blue cowboy hat and boots I had already purchased in Calgary. The horse was slow for a few rounds in the pasture, but on the homeward stretch, the owner of the horse whistled from the barn. The horse took off so fast and so suddenly, I would have fallen off if I hadn't hung on for dear life. What they won't think of to get their kicks, but they were quite im-pressed with my tenacity.

Murray eventually convinced me to have my old jewelry, in-cluding my wedding ring designed into a new custom designed ring by his jeweler in Lethbridge. I was very satisfied with the product, evaluated at about one thousand dollars. Then, when I came home from church service one Sunday morning, his buddy tried to pressure me into trading my car for his car. Both men were slightly inebriated, and I was beginning to see red flags popping up all over the place.

After eight months of sobriety, Murray expressed a desire to meet Mother and to announce our engagement. We never made it. He had abruptly turned to the bottle again. How and when and where he drank all that beer is still beyond me. The only evidence I saw were dozens of empty beer cases stacked at the back of the house. He started with violent, verbal outbursts and eventually resorted to physical aggression. I had to run for protection several times.

The first episode occurred one evening for no apparent reason. It escalated and terrified me to the point I had to escape. As I was walking down the street in the middle of the night, clad in a housecoat, barefoot and carrying Polly, I tried to flag down a policeman who was on night patrol. He had been speaking with a motorist down the street, and he ignored my waving for him, and proceeded to drive off when I shouted for his attention. He finally stopped and said, "Aren't you a mental patient from the Care Center?" I talked him into taking me to a motel, where I received a call from Murray's brother in Calgary, who then put his mother on the line to persuade me to return to him. They had spoken to Murray and they assured me it wouldn't happen again. Within five days, it did!

This time, I had been hiding under a desk until the police arrived. "We can't come to every family squabble you know," the constable said, but he took me and my puppy Polly to a motel. Murray apologized profusely, and I returned to the house. It happened again within a week. He broke down a door, wrecked furnishings, and attacked me with beer cans. "I want that hockey shirt!" he demanded, referring to the Flames shirt his brother had given me. As he yelled at me in a drunken stupor, he spilled his beer on the floor, which made me slip and fall. He would have come down on me with a kitchen chair if I had not treaded hard with my legs up in the air and pushed him against the edge of an appliance. I took refuge with a neighbor, who in turn also tried to assault me. According to the police, the neighbor had a record for assault. By then, Murray showed up and apologized and took me home.

The next day, I received a call from the same neighbor asking me to come for Murray, because he was inebriated and could barely walk. While I unlocked the door to our house, he fell and cut his forehead. As ambulance personnel took him away on a stretcher, he blurted, "She attacked me."

A week later, during another rampage, he injured a female visitor, a long-term resident of Claresholm. We ran for our lives. The police took us to the hospital for hyperventilation, trauma and bruising. The police had to press charges. Her arm had been fractured, and this time there had been a witness. While packing my things that night, I noticed a tiny slip of paper on Murray's dresser with my ex-husband's telephone number written on it. At that moment, I suspected that my ex husband and Murray had not only had a clandestine alliance, but had likely been in cahoots with the jeweler in order to reclaim the jewelry Dale had given me over our married years, and I feared that he had and would sabotage other scenarios.

Murray was temporarily jailed for assault, and then he took a room in a small-town hotel until he went to trial. He was prosecuted, and never returned to his house. I had heard that the house was actually still in his ex-wife's name.

Someone had also managed to make a sizable withdrawal from my bank account. Two lines had been x'd out in my bank book, and I had come to the conclusion my bankers as well as the whole system were plotting against me, and I didn't follow up on it for another twenty years.

~/~

Polly and I proceeded with our brand-new life in a rented turn-of-the-century shack. It turned it into a quaint little dollhouse using donated items from the owners of the Bluebird Motel, where I had been staying with Polly for a month, and from the Salvation Army which was conveniently located right around the corner. I became the adopted grandma to the boys next door, Andrew and Ben, with whom I shared Polly and my cats, Moxie and Smokey.

I bonded with the Ganslins, a church family with an artistically gifted little girl, Rosalynn, who loved to draw pictures for me. I enjoyed life again. My little shack was non-claustrophobic, with plenty of windows in all directions and a huge yard. Rent was $350 per month, including heat. Murray showed up twice, pleading as usual, and I didn't fall for a fabricated invitation to his daughter's wedding that very weekend. This time I took my stand. I had seen enough red flags, and had become immune to his voluminous love letters, which kept coming just the same.

I could not find the written evaluation of the ring which Murray's jeweler had made out of my old rings, so I returned to Lethbridge to obtain a duplicate. I could not find his store, so I walked up and down the block several times and I inquired in another jewelry shop nearby. I was told that the store upstairs had been shut down and that its owner was imprisoned for dealing in stolen jewelry. I had a satisfactory evaluation made by another jeweler. My new ring may not have been made with the original gold (which I suspect is in my ex's possession), but it was made of genuine gems just the same.

~/~

I was still determined to pull up my stakes and follow through on my dreams of retiring in the Okanagan Valley. I knew I could easily find work as a social worker or caregiver, and Mother would surely put me up temporarily, since she had a five-bedroom house, a townhouse, as well as a condo that was up for rent. But she suddenly expressed a desire to move to a different Okanagan community, or even to Claresholm of all places, for a brand-new start for herself.

Mother still had control over me and I didn't dare make that move without her approval, and I honored her wish when she abruptly wrote, "Stay in Claresholm. You belong back there! What would the neighbors think if you moved here to the Okanagan Valley? *Jetzt hast Du genug Manner glucklich gemacht. Gebe es doch auf.* – Stop making men happy. Give it up finally!" I suspected someone had influenced her. I kept a letter in which Hannelore tried to convince Mother to cut me out of her will. She states that I didn't need anything since I had a better education, and in it, she asks Mother to sign her whole estate over to her, if she were to leave Montreal and take care of her.

I still had three safety nets: first, a monthly disability pension and second, knowing psychiatric hospitalization was always an option. I'd never starve or go without a roof over my head. The love of my pets, my interest in fitness, nutrition, needlework, sewing, and the recording of all genres of music from Radio CBC, would keep me happily engaged. My third safety net was knowing God was always with me, even if I didn't say my prayers in the old conventional way at bedtime, as I had learned in my childhood. Rather, I tried to rely on my heavenly Father in a steady undertone of prayer for comfort and support on my designated journey.

I don't speak of my faith as much as I should, and I have been hesitant to share an extraordinary spiritual experience when I was in my mid-forties. I was on an outing with my therapy group, and I separated myself from the group to be alone, and as I was watching billowing white clouds go by under the deep blue Albertan skies, I had a clear vision of Jesus sitting at the right hand of God the Father. Instantly, the Biblical verse came to mind in Acts 7:55,56, in which disciple Stephen gazed into the heavens and caught sight of Jesus standing at God's right hand, and he said: "Look! I see the heavens opened up and the Son of man standing at God's right hand."

In a flash, any doubt of an Almighty Creator of the Universe had vanished from my mind. He had made himself apparent to my person in his own unique way, and I knew then that I could "let go and let God" for the rest of my life, but I was a little too presumptuous to take this as a sign of an impending miracle in my life. I evidently had much to learn for another epiphany. Had it only been an illusion of Jesus sitting on the right hand of God up in the clear blue yonder, my faith had been strengthened regardless. However, I had to learn to honor God not only when I felt his presence or when I needed him, but at all times, whether favorable or not.

My beloved Maltipoo, Polly.

Chapter 21

1996: MY SECOND MARRIAGE; MOTHER'S FUNERAL; HAWAII

When I was well settled in my shack, I met a very nice and kind looking man behind the counter of the Claresholm Vac Shack, a vacuum cleaner repair shop. We caught each other's eyes. There was an immediate connection. In contrast to Murray, Eugene seemed mellow and stable. He didn't drink or smoke, and he frowned on my occasional smoking (which helped me give it up eventually.) However, his business was going bankrupt and his grant had run out. He had already moved himself and his German Shepherd-cross into the back of his shop, having had received notice to his apartment. I had heard enough about Eugene's family background to know that he had come from a good family and I let him stay with me to help him get back on his feet. He was raised in British Columbia, had lost his father at an early age, and was raised by his mother, a nurse, and by his older sister who was a teacher. He was supportive, helpful, strong, and capable handyman. Since our dogs did not get along very well, he took his dog to friends in Calgary. I was a little perturbed about how easily he had given up his endearing fully grown German Shepherd who liked to nudge Polly off my lap so he could come up and be petted too.

Several months later, an inebriated Murray showed up at my door. He cried and pleaded incessantly for me to come back to him, even with Eugene at my side. We gently persuaded him to leave. It was a pathetic sight as he stumbled back to his waiting driver.

Eugene became dependent on me. He seemed to love everything about me and my lifestyle. He was not sexually inclined, but he was very romantic. One day I found reams of printed out pages, covering every wall of my little shack, saying "I Love You!" in big letters. It was an exaggeration I could not really appreciate, because in my subconscious mind that kind aggrandization can only be reserved for the most Holy.

~/~

In March of 1997, Eugene took me to Reno on the funds he had received from a fire insurance policy on a house he'd had under construction in Red Deer. We had never discussed marriage before, but we simply went ahead and tied the knot. It was on the *Ides of March*, the 15th. Like going for a convenient joy ride, it felt like a wild adventure to compensate for my first and forced marriage to Dale in 1969. Or, perhaps it was to ease my pain for all the lost years with my daughter, who had just turned 26 on the 14th of March.

Our Claresholm friends, neighbors, and church family were elated with the news of our marriage, and they took us for a lovely dinner. I had 'respectable' social status again, and hopes of living happily ever after, in wedded bliss.

~/~

Three months after our wedding, I was informed that Mother had been permanently hospitalized, and it was suggested I come as soon as possible. As soon as we were at her bedside, Mother told us that she still wanted to move to the smaller nearby community, and she still introduced me to the hospital staff as, "This is Emily, my baby and popular teenager, but she had it too good when she was young. She had too much freedom. Please, pray God, make her the way she used to be." She paused, took a quick look at me, turned to the others with pleading eyes, and as if an afterthought, she said in her broken English, "But Emily came under bad influence." The patient lying next to Mother seemed quite perturbed with what she had heard and interrupted Mother, saying, "Your daughter is really very nice." Of course, the "bad influence" Mother had referred to had been Satan's attempt to destroy me, but he would not succeed, and I was prepared for further attacks knowing from the book Revelation 12:12, that Satan is very angry since he has only a short period of time on this earth, and that he is doomed!

Within days of our arrival, the executor, Howard, advised us that the house was going on the market shortly and that we should consider vacating it as quickly as possible. We ignored that, but we itemized and stored her personal and special things in a rental locker just in case we did have to vacate the house.

Mother was still concerned about her unclaimed lotto tickets, and she still had an eye for men. She scrutinized Eugene's walk as not quite all man. He had wide hips. But she was no longer antagonistic towards me, which was a relief. I may have fallen from grace, but I was married again, leaving her relatively satisfied with me as a lesser level of disappointment. The doctor and staff were not as satisfied with her behavior, however. They took me aside to let me know they had to chastise her. She still wanted to be transferred to the hospital in the other community, and she was quite belligerent about it, keeping the other patients awake at night. She had also had clandestine talks with Hanne before she left Montreal for the Okanagan, and while she was on her way, Mother said, *"Du kannst jetzt zuruck nach Claresholm gehen."* – "You can return to Claresholm now." Those were Mother's last words to me, and I wondered what had happened to the deep faith and love of Jesus which she had demonstrated in my childhood, as well as the faith she demonstrated at 'Vati's deathbed, but hadn't mentioned it at all on her deathbed.

The day after Mother's passing, the attending doctor stopped me in the hallway for a quick consultation. He asked, "Do you know where your mother is?" On impulse, I said, "Yes, she's a mummy in her chosen town." That exchange brought lots of chuckles. Then he said, "Did you know you were brought up by an insane mother? You should write a book. People wouldn't be able to put it down until the very end, just like a Steven Spielberg novel." So far in my life, three doctors have suggested I write a book. No, I didn't know that I was brought up by an insane mother. All I knew was that my upbringing was difficult, that I hated Mother at times, but that I also loved her dearly. It was a love/hate relationship.

When the hospital's Social Services provided me with the keys to Mother's house, we started sorting papers and did yard work between visits. Almost all of the canned fruits and vegetable she and Joe had canned and stored in the cold storage room in 1980 (for a rainy day or in case of war) had gone bad after almost twenty years. I also came across an old get well card filled with signatures of friends from the German Canadian Club, in which Mother had added a remark in its margins. It read, "Hannelore let me down because I would not sign the house over to her."

~/~

Hannelore had arrived from Montreal within a few days, and Emma flew in from Calgary. I made it clear to Hanne that we were not going to be relocated to the basement suite, so she could take the bedroom upstairs which I and Eugene had already settled into, and that a box of Mother's assorted photos was to be returned from the basement to the kitchen table for all to agree upon. I hoped to set some standards of decency, and I did for a while. Hanne didn't approve of the outfit I had just acquired at the Salvation Army – too cheap, and she lent me a finely tailored suit to wear at the funeral.

Mother was buried at the Lakeside Cemetery with a traditional funeral service through the Mormon Church. Two elders and I agreed to give eulogies. I tried to emphasize Mother's strengths, referring to her writings and poetry, and I thanked the Mormon family for the many years of support they had lovingly extended to her. After the service, Emma told me that my talk had brought tears to her eyes.

At two o'clock a.m., Eugene started harassing me for attention. I was exhausted from the previous day's funeral, and I insisted he let me go to sleep. When he continued complaining, I lost my temper. Exasperated, I shouted, "You are going back home to Claresholm!" He left that morning. That must have convinced the rest of the family I was crazy, or at least nasty indeed, because Eugene had been pleasant and co-operative, and I pushed him away, too engrossed in my own self-pity to care about his needs.

The friction picked up. Hanne had been going out with the executor every night all week long, leaving me on my own to cook and clean. They didn't return for the meals I had prepared, as if she was still in her childhood mode of avoiding me. One evening, I intended to slightly trim my shoulder length hair. When finished, I was sporting a pixie cut which, if permed, could have come perilously close to the "little Miss Piggy" look, which I had acquired at age 13 with my long hair cut and permed into tight, short, curls.

The next day, Hannelore accused me of having had a "big mouth" when I was younger, and that she wouldn't be having any trouble if she had arrived earlier. Then the executor told me he was terribly disappointed with us as sisters. Then, "Here, for your birthday!" Hanne snapped, as she handed me an airplane ticket back to Alberta. I didn't touch it, but I had to get out of there, so I checked myself into a motel. Perhaps I should have told her that I wished she'd had a "big mouth" too, so we would all have known where we stood. I was prepared for some disagreements, but I still had this naive notion about Mother's death finally drawing us closer. However, God said, "No, I have other plans, and I shall reveal them at an appointed time, perhaps in two or three decades, when Hanne's son, as well as her grandson, and eventually her great great grandsons will have an opportunity to read their great aunt's memoir to help them dispel the clouds of chaos and despair that have cast such a heavy shadow on some of our lives." Thank you Lord!

Shane and Emma somehow got wind that trouble was brewing, and their father flew them both to the Okanagan this time, likely because he feared their inheritances ($10,000 each, plus the contents of the house) being at stake. They had already set up an appointment with a lawyer before they checked themselves into the same motel I had been occupying. Hannelore had remained in Mother's house. Eugene had returned from Claresholm, and unbeknownst to me, had also checked himself into the same motel.

None of us was speaking, but the lawyer promptly made it clear that Howard could not act as executor and realtor simultaneously. I wish my dear niece Brittney had been there. She had passed away several years earlier, and I am still sorry for not having flewn to Montreal for her funeral. Perhaps a lame excuse, I was terribly ashamed of poor mental health, but I will never forget her comment, "Emily, you are the black sheep of the family." She hadn't meant it maliciously, I am sure. Rather, I took it as a truly candid and compassionate observation.

I had given in to Eugene's attempts to see me, but I made it clear that I wanted a separation. He agreed. We returned to Claresholm with the two boxes of fine Alfred Meighen china (origin-ally from my Vati, Otto Protzki, our sponsor), which had been willed to Emma by her 'Omi'. This was the china I had washed, dried, put away, and set the table with, hundreds of times during my first years in Canada. I could not understand how it could mean so much to Emma for us to end up squabbling over it, with a lawyer to boot. This didn't sound like Emma at all. It was worth its value of approximately one thousand dollars in legal fees to keep my Vati's china. Sadly, his china is still packed away. It has en-dured many moves, and Vati will someday rejoice when his china will grace a china cabinet again, hopefully with Emma, if she will ever forgive me.

~/~

I give Mother credit for her faith, her indomitable will, and ruthless determination to have made it for herself, considering all that life had dealt her. She could have been a business tycoon with an iron will when it came to money, or a politician like Margaret Thatcher if she had had a stable upbringing and a university education, in which she would no doubt have excelled. And to quote her grand-daughter, "Omi certainly wasn't perfect, but what she wore defi-nitely reflected her as being both strong and bold, yet feminine and unique." Well said, Emma! Posthumously, Omi got credit where credit was due, and I am impressed with my daughter's ability to help me see my mother in a new light. I wonder what kind of an epitaph I will have, because I have had visions of being thrown into a common grave, like Mozart had been, before he finished his requiem mass.

Quite frankly, Mother's passing was a relief and has made my life a little easier, but it certainly did not resolve my problems instantly, as I had imagined. My Father in heaven knew I had tests, trials and tribulations to face yet, that I needed to deal with flaws and shortcomings of my own making, and last but not least, he knew that it would take time (almost twenty years) to accept the fact that I possibly had a mental illness, including post-traumatic-stress disorder, paranoia, dysthymia, and whatever else I had been or rightfully or wrongfully diagnosed with over the years.

~/~

Eugene had rented an apartment in Claresholm, and I filed for divorce in the fall of 1997. My counselor had mentioned there was a reason why Eugene had originally moved to Claresholm, a farming community surrounding the CCC, which is a facility for the mentally ill and for drug rehabilitation. I had to deduce that Eugene had mental issues and hadn't been honest about it, because at one point, he did confide that he was inclined to self-destruct, and I felt compassion for him.

Eugene kept showing up everywhere. I now call that kind of behavior stalking, but his persistence paid off. He cried rivers, and I took pity on him again. I had received proceeds from Mother's estate in increments, and since one of my lifetime dreams was to see Hawaii, I invited him along for companionship. This was five months after I had filed for a divorce. What was I thinking? I was most likely hoping we could still be friends.

I did not have enough time to join Emma and her long-term partner Qiáng (whom I hadn't met yet or ever would) for a rushed trip back to the Okanagan to help sort through the contents of Mother's house (Emma's and Shane's inheritance), so I asked the rental management there to give them a duplicate key to the storage locker I had rented for Mother's personal items. Emma said, "Mom, do you know what this will do to our relationship?" I felt sad, controlled, and subtly threatened by my estranged daughter, just because I hadn't been prepared to go away on such short notice. I hadn't realized that I had just possibly missed the only opportunity to reconcile with my daughter, and I deeply regret having disappointed her so profoundly. I am not sure if we were in some kind of delayed battle of wills or in a power struggle. I just wanted to be treated with some respect.

I heard through the grapevine that they had had a very successful garage sale and enjoyed their time at Mother's house. Of all things, I wondered whatever happened to the crates Mother had kept in her basement storage area for over forty years, covered with 1956 travel stickers from Austria.

~/~

One year after Mother's passing, I finally made that long-desired move to the Okanagan a reality, and Mother could not stop me this time. It was also an attempt to revive my marriage with Eugene, as well as to vindicate myself of perceived rumors as the wayward, depressed, unsuccessful and disgraced daughter of Mrs. Margarete Del Fabrosi of the Okanagan Valley. When Mother had a penny, she invariably stretched it to ten. I had not inherited her penny pinching genes. I had fallen into Mother's pattern by taking a series of live-in jobs, but I didn't get ahead and watch my earnings grow. I ran a car, helped with the kids, enjoyed decent clothes, owned pets, took out gym memberships, took self-improvement courses, flew to the Okanagan for visits, paid divorce lawyers, and supported Eugene.

Once Mother's estate had been settled, my lawyer wanted to know if I was satisfied with my share. He thought I was entitled to more, but I waived it. I didn't need any more aggravation, but I wondered what happened to Mother's other properties (a townhouse and a condominium). Hanne's boyfriend, the executor, declined to provide me with a copy to show how Mother's estate had been distributed. A bit of wisdom from Friedrich Nietzsche: "Whoever fights monsters should see to it that in the process he does not become a monster."

Funds from Mother's estate were deposited into my bank account in increments, and I was thrilled to have received a respectable windfall for the first time in my life. I paid for a vacation in Hawaii, the move to the Okanagan, a new car, a mobile home, new appliances, trips and gifts for Eugene and his family, and all our living expenses. I hope Mother hasn't turned over in her grave in disgust over how I spent my inheritance, but I confess I actually did harbor that wish for her at one time, having been threatened once too often about her intentions of disinheriting both of her girls. This is a confession, and I pray for her forgiveness.

One of my last visits with Mother; I thought her hairdo was very spiffy. Probably our last kiss, and then, good-bye at her grave site.

Chapter 22

1998: MOVE TO OKANAGAN VALLEY

At 8 a.m. on July 1, 1998, Eugene had pulled our fully loaded rental moving van, with my beautiful cats, tabby Smokey and calico Moxie inside the cab, and an additional trailer hitched up behind it, out of the driveway, and headed for BC's beautiful sunny Okanagan Valley. By 9 a.m. I had pulled out of my driveway with my cherished white Maltipoo pup, Polly, on my lap, and the remaining household goods packed tight in the back of the van, including Polly's flight cage. I hadn't had much sleep. I drove south to catch my 2 p.m. Flight out of Calgary. I was to park the van at the airport, and have Eugene bring it back to our new home community at a later date, when he was to return to Claresholm to sell his second vehicle which he had kept in storage.

By 10 a.m., I was beginning to feel woozy behind the wheel, and I caught myself from veering into the oncoming traffic. Moments later I passed out. I knew that I had been in a serious collision when I realized that I was bouncing upside-down inside my van, while it rolled over. Fortunately, it landed upright. The seat belt was jammed, but I was able to squeeze myself through it and get myself out of the car.

As I looked up, I saw dozens of vehicles stopped in both directions. A lady ran up in complete disbelief, crying, "Oh my God, are you ever lucky to be alive. Are you all right?" I said, "Yes," and I started walking around the van in a daze, only to find that Polly had been thrown through the windshield and had landed about ten feet away in a pool of blood. The ambulance took us to the High River hospital, myself on a stretcher, and the driver of the pick-up truck my van had struck was seated right behind me. By then I was sobbing uncontrollably, and I was so relieved to hear that the other driver and his dog were not injured. I thanked God that the driver wasn't angry at me, and that I had been spared from a terrible burden of guilt if I had been responsible for serious harm or even death of another human being, or of an animal. My van was a total write-off.

Eugene immediately returned to Claresholm from the Okanagan via Greyhound bus, and my church family, the Ganslins, kindly took us in for two nights. I had suffered considerable bruising and a stubborn, painful lump on the periphery of my chest, for which my new family doctor prescribed aqua therapy which helped regain my mobility, but that tender lump is still there as a reminder. I was in a considerable amount of pain for about a year due to tissue damage in my right shoulder.

Pastor Dempsey, the pastor of my church in Claresholm had told me, "God is not finished with you yet." From his choice of words, I had to take it that he had had a little chat with God, and that God had not been entirely satisfied with me, though I had literally fallen this time and He picked me up again! And I surmised that he would see me through other challenges, difficulties and accidents, until satisfied that I had found my true calling in life, which I believe is to repent for my transgressions and give him the honor for enabling me to break my silence in a memoir.

We stayed at a campground in our new Okanagan community in which Eugene had set up his motor home, and we remained there until August 1st, which was the occupancy date of the mobile home I had purchased earlier that year. I had discovered how much I enjoyed camping out of a spacious motor home. I regret not having done more of RV camping.

In the months of August, September, and October, we were busy with minor renovations to the mobile home, gardening, canning, and even receiving guests from Alberta. By November, I became severely depressed. The sunny Okanagan Valley was suddenly plugged up with dark overcast wintry skies. The proximity

of the surrounding mountains and lakes loomed like a black claustrophobic trap all around me. I complained to Eugene about everything looking so depressingly dark. He thought there was a
problem with my eyesight. Funny, when my ex-husband thought
there was something wrong with my hearing, I went for a hearing
test which came out perfect. I hadn't heard about the Okanagan's
lack of sunshine in the winter months, and it hit me like a ton of
bricks. To move again so soon was inconceivable.

I remembered that Dr. Razi had been Mother's psychiatrist,
and that we had already exchanged correspondence out of Calgary. I decided to contact him, thinking that we had a solid foundation to work with. He said, "Your mother used to come by my office at closing time, and I gave her rides back to her house, and
she treated me, but I gave up on her a long time ago because she
kept crying inconsolably." He stared at me with big eyes implying
more than just the hospitable images I had conjured up of Mother
pampering him with *Leberknodel Suppe und Apfelstrudel* – Liver
dumpling soup and apple strudel.

Dr. Razi decided to admit me to the local hospital's psychiatric ward on January 1, 1998. I was confident that he was best
qualified to treat my depression, though it was apparent to me
that the doctor and I were both suffering from a mild case of
"Katzenjammer" – "Hangover" from our previous night's respective new years eve celebrations. He gave me his home phone
number, which I never used.

On our first consultation, Dr. Razi described Eugene as a "big
baby" and (in his words) he recommended I give Eugene "the
boot." During my three-month long day-program at the hospital, it
become evident to me that Eugene had no intentions of finding a
job and contributing financially, and I foresaw financial ruin or
even bankruptcy and I asked him for a separation, just as my doctor had recommended. He didn't respond to my offer to help him
get established, and when he was about to leave with his motor
home, he insisted on taking Sandy, the replacement puppy for Polly. I had to let him take Sandy because he was about to yank the

telephone line out of the wall when I reached for the phone to call 911 for assistance.

Several weeks later, someone poured sugar into the gasoline tank of my car. It took a full month and $1,500 to get it running again. I was told by a mental health worker it was best not to try to find out what happened to Eugene or to Sandy, and I did not know that the RCMP had been involved until my health care worker told me that Eugene had written threatening letters.

I wasn't aware of Eugene's whereabouts, until Suzanne, a patient I had met in the psychiatric ward's day program, and whom I had supported emotionally, told me she had taken a road trip to visit my best high school friend, Loa, in Sacramento, California, with Eugene! He had taken her address out of my personal address book. He also used my credit card. The charges were reversed when I called my credit company. Suzanne told me that she hadn't particularly enjoyed Eugene's company, and unfortunately, Suzanne committed suicide later that year. My friend Loa hadn't been very impressed with her visitors either. Being the true friend she was, she had not been swayed against me. In our retirement years, Loa and I were going to travel to our respective native countries of Iceland and Austria, and I was going to escape the dreary Okanagan winters at her horse ranch in sunny California. Sadly, Loa unexpectedly died from cancer before she had a chance to retire.

My social life soon centered around a clubhouse for people suffering with mental illness. It had bright open spaces and windows facing south and north where I could sit and watch the world go by for hours without feeling claustrophobic. The clubhouse was shut down after several years, the building was occupied by a local company, and the club was relocated to a site at the other end of town. I couldn't tolerate spending time in the new, dark, claustrophobic club without clear windows for a view to the outside world. I missed the old clubhouse. I had sold my mobile home for $20,000, five thousand dollars above the original purchase price, and invested the proceeds, and I temporarily rented a mobile home from snowbirds who spent the winter months in Yuma, Arizona.

By November of 1999, Dr. Razi admitted me to a local respite facility for severe depression. My snowbird landlords in Arizona sued me for breaking the lease (even with a doctor's note). The case was thrown out on the basis that they should have returned to the Okanagan and start legal actions themselves.

Since then, I have moved around my Okanagan hometown from one apartment to another, and I am quite sure Seasonal Affective Disorder (SAD), Post-Traumatic Stress (PTS) and claustrophobia in equal measure, have been at the root of my problems causing disorientation, but ultimately, I believe I was still homesick for my home country, and yearning for the father I never had, with a void in my heart much bigger than I'd ever realized.

I saw Dr. Razi on a regular basis for the next ten years, without need for hospitalization.

~/~

Dr. Razi's lovely secretary told me how vividly she had remembered Mother's visits some twenty years earlier, when she dropped into his office after her shopping trips, and then get rides back to her house from the doctor. Regarding Hannelore, the doctor disclosed "Your sister wronged you." Pretty strong words, I thought. "Hmm, I never thought of Hanne in that light." Only the words "rejection" or "resentment" came to my mind.

My stay at the respite facility was very pleasant; much like a bright group home and better than any psychiatric ward I had been in, other than the CCC in Claresholm. It was conveniently located near a pet facility where I could do volunteer dog walking, and I had the freedom to do my latest craft, lacy ornamental angels which I sold for fifteen dollars (and well worth it). I gave most of them away as presents. They called me the 'angel lady', because pedestrians walking by could see me through the windows as I was working under the bright light of my day lamp.

On a more serious note, I remember two interviews in particular. One counselor said it was a good thing I had left my family because I wouldn't be alive if I hadn't left. I didn't want to know exactly how to interpret that, and I didn't ask. He reminded me that Eugene had been bad news. He also hinted about a grandchild who might want to see her grandmother Emily someday. Oh my goodness, I have a granddaughter out there somewhere! On speaking about my children with another counselor, all I could to was break down and weep.

I really appreciated Dr. Razi's attempts to reconnect me with Emma, but apparently she had given him an earful of confidential resentment, and all he would convey to me was, "She is a very confused lady. All you can expect from your daughter is a few crumbs thrown your way." Now that was a bitter pill to swallow, when I had always regarded Emma as strong willed and confident in her choices. With regard to Shane, he said, "A reunion could be extremely problematic."

By February of 2000, I was deemed ready to move into the community again, and I automatically assumed a normal lifestyle. I busied myself making an attractive and cozy nest out of my new apartment, and I looked forward to enjoying the spacious south facing balcony, on which I installed two venetian blinds (the consummate handy woman that I am) for privacy and shade, only to have some powerful Okanagan windstorms, twice loosen the ties and flip them up and over the rooftop. The plants on the balcony seemed to fade as fast as I watered them, and then I realized that the uphill incline of the street below caused every car passing by was accelerating and emitting excess exhaust gas and noise, causing headaches.

I finally gave up on my vision of tropical outdoor living on my balcony. I also escaped my confines too often by exhausting myself with daily hikes, and by climbing up and down creek-side paths and stairways leading to the upper bench vineyards for a glorious open view of the Okanagan Valley, wondering if it was true that I had come from a school of hard knocks, according to Dr. Razi. I was beginning to question my life, and wondered why I hadn't had the courage to opt for a meditative Buddhist retreat in India, take a real risk, do some improvised globetrotting in a converted van, and find my niche in this world. I hadn't yet been able to distinguish the folk wisdom conveyed by the Chinese philosopher Confucius (551-479BC), "He who chases two rabbits catches neither!" – from the biblical message to the effect that one can serve God's as well your fellow neighbors' needs simultaneously, just not two masters at one time; rather confusing theories, but I was soon side tracked by someone who promised to open a window to new vistas, and I could not resist the temptation of another misguided pursuit of pleasure and adventure.

~ / ~

MEETING JOHN
I had attended seniors' dances, I took advantage of gym and pool memberships (then subsidized by BC Mental Health), I enjoyed the clubhouse, I took a temporary cleaning job, and I took regular Bible studies with a wonderful German girl from the Jehovah's Witnesses. I volunteered at the SPCA, and with other community organizations until a gentleman named John approached me at the community pool and asked me out to lunch at Wendy's. His beautiful, resonating voice and imposing physique led me to believe he was a lawyer, a policeman, or a professor. Actually, he had been an extremely successful farmer, and businessman, with a grade three education.

We got along very well, considering our age difference of twenty-one years. We were compatible in our languages, food choices, recreational preferences, and in our similar fatherless and impoverished post-World War II European psychological makeup, except on religious orientation. I had considerable objection from the convener of my primary bible study group, and John threatened to break up our relationship unless I discontinued my other bible studies with the Witnesses, and I gave in to his wishes, since he was Catholic and I was Protestant, assuming we would, in time, find common ground on our religious orientation. I gradually gave up volunteering at the SPCA and with Bible studies with my primary church affiliation. It amazed me at how well he was able to keep up with me hiking, biking, and on the dance floor, and he seemed smitten with me. We loved having our photos taken. We looked great together. When I told Dr. Razi about my relationship with John, he commented that in his opinion, John was somewhat like an octopus in nature. I found it rather amusing how the doctor liked to label people. He had called Eugene a "big baby," and he had referred to me as a "dangerous woman."

John soon wanted to live with me, whether in my apartment or in his mansion up on the hill, and I would have loved to rent his bright and spacious mother-in-law suite on the main floor of his impressive home, but he decided against it and rented it to someone else. He introduced me to his three daughters who lived in major cities elsewhere. They were delighted with their father's new found happiness. However, it turned into a stormy relationship because I panicked at his unexpected verbal outbursts and mechanical sexual demands. I had broken it up several times, and I decided I had waited long enough to visit my home country once more.

~/~

My father had long passed away, Mother had recently passed away, and I felt alienated from the rest of my family. I had suffered with clinical depression, and I had been living on disability pension for almost ten years. I needed to see my beloved home country again, if it meant backpacking and staying in hostels. I was determined not to touch what was left of Mother's inheritance because I needed to know I had funds available for future necessities and emergencies, such as dental work or a motorized wheel chair.

My scheduled flight to Austria had been booked for September 11, 2001, and unfortunately, it had to be canceled that fateful morning since the NY towers had just gone down in an attack by the Islamic terrorist group al-Quaeda, and this time I really felt jinxed. I had just lost my fourth opportunity to visit my home country, and I gave up plans of going back. Co-incidentally, I heard that John and his daughter vacationed in Europe at that time.

Then, I took a two-week directory assistance training course. I enjoyed working in telecommunications until pressure was on to keep even complicated calls down to below twenty seconds from the thirty-second-time period I had already achieved, from the initial sixty-second time limit per call. The stress was intolerable and I had to quit, just like others who walked away from their computer stations. That was such a relief, and it was nice to enjoy time with my elderly lady friend Hazel, take her shopping, to dances, and walk her puppy again. Besides, my disability insurance company had claimed half of my part-time income, and I hardly found it worth working at all.

When I focused on my son and daughter, I realized that their rejection of me was the most difficult and painful of my issues, but I also realized that I was not the perfect mother I thought I was. I had tried to avoid the pitfalls of my own upbringing. I had taken a course on effective parenting when they were in elementary school, and I had read up on child development and psychology, just to be on the safe side. However, my concern, love and prayers weren't enough and the tides had gone against me. I think God was trying to tell me that nothing would change until I was willing to give up my worldly ways and rely exclusively on His guidance.

~/~

While John and I had gone our ways, he sold his mansion on the hill and had relocated to a smaller home closer to town, and I had been busy writing my memoir, having been inspired from a book I had read by Ursula Hegi. I had seen John dating other women, and he had seen me dancing regularly with Roger, a ballroom dance instructor. But we realized we missed each other, and we decided to get together again. The news was received with strong objections from my best friends, and it would be an understatement to say that they abhorred his intrusiveness, though I was blind to it and actually found it quite alluring.

John was about to have major surgery, a triple bi-pass. He gave me the keys to his new home to do some cleaning while he was gone. He still had the wall above his desk covered with professional photographs of us together. He had made it a point to tell his daughters that I was his angel. On his return from the Vancouver General Hospital, he walked into the condominium with his daughters flanked by his side, and a red heart-shaped pillow held up to his chest. He seemed like a brand-new man, so mellow and calm. I welcomed them with a sparkling clean house and hallways decorated with bright welcoming banners.

By the end of July, John proposed a trip to Germany and Austria to celebrate his successful surgery, and to give me an opportunity to see my home country again. He also wanted to celebrate what he had read so far in my original manuscript. He was convinced my memoir should be published someday.

I was flying high already, but I was fully aware of John's need to recuperate fully. He would require a cane and walker, weekly blood work, the occasional wheelchair, possible emergency treatments due to falls, possible treatment for lung infection as his daughter told me he was susceptible to pneumonia, and help with keeping track of his blister pack. In other words, he had a caregiver in me, and I was willing to do anything in order to see my home country again. A minimum of sixty re-locations on this planet had already taken a toll on me physically, and on my pocketbook. My nest egg from Mother's inheritance had already been depleted with my short-lived marriage to Eugene, car repairs and health related expenses, and I didn't mind accompanying John as an unpaid tour guide and caregiver.

One could say he was a bit of a sugar daddy and I cannot deny I liked that. At his best self he reminded me of a charismatic Donald Trump. We joked about me being his Austrian princess, and he being my Prussian prince. It was supposed to be forever, and somehow I still believed in fairy tales.

~/~

As soon as we entered our hotel room for our stay-over in Frankfurt, John immediately demanded intercourse and threatened to divorce me (out of wedlock) if I wasn't going to cooperate. I was exhausted from the long flight and from towing our luggage around the old town in search of the cheapest hotel, and I threatened to split up right there and then. "If this is how our vacation is going to be, you should go to your home country, and we'll meet in Frankfurt for our return flight at the end of the month." John did not want to go and see his relatives again. He had already done that numerous times. Things settled down after that incident.

We took an interesting open double-decker bus tour of the old city of Frankfurt, but I couldn't wait to get away from the pervasive tobacco smoke which had irritated my sensitive nasal passages from the instant we had entered the city's airport, to finally breathe pure Austrian mountain air. I knew I was closer to my homeland when I found myself enjoying my first of many delightful European-style continental breakfasts in our cozy little hotel in Frankfurt.

Chapter 23

2005: MY SECOND VISIT TO AUSTRIA, MY FOUNTAIN OF YOUTH
For sentimental reasons, I chose Bad Schallerbach in the
Saltzkammergut, the summer spa choice of emperors past, as our
first destination in Austria, because that is where I had met Father
thirty-eight years earlier, at the age of twenty. We found a charming bed and breakfast, from which we woke up to a view through
a large window into an inner courtyard, laden with gorgeous
flowers. I thanked John profusely for the joy I felt that morning. I
already felt truly at home and John enjoyed his introduction to my
home country as well. I was about to guide him through the major
cities in Upper Austria.

Our next destination was Innsbruck, in Tyrol. While we oriented ourselves to its charming surroundings, I looked up Mother's maiden name, Wilflingsmann and found Guenther, a distant
cousin. Guenther and his wife met us at an outdoor restaurant
near the historic Golden Roof, *Das Goldene Dacherl*. Guenther's
grandfather was Mother's father out of wedlock, and Guenther
had a hard time wrapping his head around that concept, just like I
had for a long time. From all accounts, Guenther used to be bit of a
ladies' man too, and he noticed the same trait in John. He confided
to me, *"Dein Johann ist ein gans gefahrlicher Casanova."* – "I see
your John is a dangerous Casanova." John had been making eyes at
gorgeous waitresses clad in revealing dirndls, and I had never
even noticed. I should say I chose not to notice.

Coincidentally, Guenther had a white Persian cat which looked
identical to my sister's Persian cat in Montreal. Not only that,
Guenther and his distant cousin Hanne could have passed for

identical twins themselves in photos showing them lovingly cradling their beloved felines. Neither cats or cousins (I am assuming) ever having met and living thousands of miles apart,

That night, we watched a spectacular Tyrolean Musical and Dance Extravaganza. The following day, Guenther's new Parisian bride, Gaby, had us over for lovely French style cooking comprised of numerous specialties. She served it on the massive veranda of their modern east side condominium overlooking Innsbruck from where, up the hill on the west side of the valley, one could see old chalet-style homes dotting sprawling alpine landscape one of was now occupied by his ex-wife.

Their reaction to my memoir, "*Was ein verrucktes Leben*," – "What a crazy life," was rather disappointing feedback. I had hoped to develop a meaningful relationship with distant family from the old country. Instead, I seem to have impressed them as a crazy distant relative in Canada. I gave up the misguided notion of finding sympathetic relatives. Any relations of mine will have to want to take the initiative first this time, if they happen to be interested in a distant North American cousin.

We then took a day trip via rail, north from Linz to Freistadt, which is just a few miles away from the hamlet of Rainbach im Muhlkreis (my birth town), near the border of the Czech Republic. I was surprised to find Freistadt's train station isolated in the middle of wide-open countryside. The small city in the distance was visible over acres of expansive fields. No fences, no boundaries, just miles of rolling green fields and patches of trees. Since we had been the only passengers to get off, the station master informed us that transportation to the town was available via taxi only, unless we opted to take a little hike with our luggage in tow. We took a taxi.

As soon as we were in the city center, I found myself whisked into another world not far removed from the imaginary Brothers Grimm fairy-tale settings. I was amazed at the disproportionately vast area of its city center, the *Hauptplatz*. *As* a toddler, I remembered briskly walking over the huge cobble-stoned square, while holding onto Mother's hand. It was a demanding hike even for a sturdy three-year-old. In the grandiose old Gothic church, I spotted our regular old seats by the location of the pillars. I saw the hospital where I had spent Christmas for a broken arm. I recognized the building which housed kindergarten, and the tower-bridge to get to it. I remembered touching the wheat stalks, poppies, cornflowers, and daisies, and cooing at Mother Nature in wonderment while Mother pushed me in my stroller through the rolling hills and fields. It was almost mystical to be near my birthplace again.

Then we took the train to Vienna for all of its glorious highlights, but we wasted a lot of time finding our own way around the city from an affordable youth hostel, where we were transferred around from one room to another, and had to transport our luggage to a common storage room every day.

We did a quick tour of Braunau, where I lived between the ages of four and ten, before we left for Canada. The city seemed stuck in time. Nothing seemed to have changed except a brand new water-slide park constructed on the outskirts. While John rested at an outdoor café, I walked the distance of the entire city center, the *Hauptplatz,* from the drawbridge near Hitler's birthplace and the nearby apartment where Mother's last lover had resided, past the bakery, and the flower shop I used to walk by on my way to Kindergarten, then all the way across to the other end, at least one mile where an expansive bridge crosses over the river Inn to Simbach, Germany, from where Mother had hoped to move back to Wasserburg in 1949, (and where she had smuggled margarine, underwear, and an alarm clock).

We then took a cab to my old street, Mattigstrasse. I tried to identify the house with the scary landlord. I had to strain myself to see the river Mattig across the street, and I was surprised to find a shallow and tame stream when it had been a roaring torrent back in 1954, flooding the whole area and taking with it a row of houses. I would have liked to wander to my favorite childhood meadow that used to greet me at the end of Mattigstrasse,

270 | EDITHA FLOSSMANN

and reminisce, but I was getting negative flashbacks and I couldn't wait to get out of the city fast enough. Even a modern water slide park couldn't tempt me to stay overnight. Besides, John wanted to save the extra night's hotel charges, so we asked the driver to take us straight to the train station. When I returned from the station's washroom, I noticed that John had been enjoying himself with three lively teenagers. The girl was particularly pretty. I had asked John to hold on to the special bag lunches I had ordered at the local butcher and delicatessen for us to enjoy on our way to Salzburg. However, somehow the bag lunches never made it onto the train with us.

In an old dream I walk down Mattigstrasse, and when I approach the house, it disappears and turns into an empty lot. I had forgotten the house number (#18) in that dream, just like in the real-life moment when I could not find the courage to knock on a neighbor's door and ask if they had remembered the three Fahrmann girls: Margarete, Hannelore and Emily.

~/~

One of the German immigrants, as depicted in Ursula Hegi's book, *Tearing the Silence: On Being German in America*, returned back to Germany with a cultural heritage group to visit World War II sites, including Dachau and Braunau. He had a need to see where Hitler was born, curious to see the environment this tyrant had been born into. He found that the locals hadn't made *Braunau am Inn* a landmark at all. It was not a tourist spot, just a spot in the middle of nowhere in Austria. Now I myself understand how severely the knowledge of having lived there has impacted me. I had avoided using the name *Braunau* for most of my life. Thank God I was not born there, but born in Rainbach by Freistadt, Upper Austria. *"Lobe den Herrn"* – "Praise the Lord." Talk about collective guilt and a persecution complex.

In Salzburg, we occupied a room in a lovely old hotel for three nights, at Hotel-Hofwirt, run by Familie A. Schrockenfuchs, on Schallmooser Hauptstr. 1. (details printed and taken off a souvenir napkin). We enjoyed a short version of the *The Sound of Music* at a dinner theater, and we visited the site where the musical had been filmed. We definitely felt the onset of chilly weather toward the end of September, and we were glad we had the matching his/her winter jackets we had purchased at Wal-Mart before our departure (they looked great on us with the red and white Canadian flags I had appliquéd on them).

That evening, fully aware of the risk involved, John insisted on taking a bath instead of a shower, and we ended up exhausting all means to lift him out with bath towels tied together, wrapped around him, and attached to plumbing under the sink, and by draining the tub and filling it again for buoyancy. Then he had a brainstorm. "Bring a chair and submerge it under my legs." That method finally worked, and I managed to pull him out with the extra leverage of an antique chair propped under his legs.

On our way back to Canada, we stopped in Heidelberg, Germany, to visit the granddaughter of John's highly regarded ex-World War II employer. Ursula went all out for four days by chauffeuring us to different relatives in neighboring towns for a grand welcome every day, with wine tasting and great food. I was amazed with their high standard of living. I was able to speak my mother tongue with great ease, and John's spoken German was surprisingly intact. Ursula liked and seemed to understand me, and she gave me a personal invitation to come back and visit her and her family. Unfortunately a house doctor had to be summoned. John had been up all night with a nasty cough. He had come down with pneumonia.

The food, the gondolas, the quaint villages, spas, and rail travel anywhere in Austria had left me feeling satisfied and complete. The distinctive dialects peculiar to their regions particularly impressed me, more so because I was informed that speaking in dialect was an educational prerequisite. For the whole duration of my visit, I dreaded having to leave my home country for the adoptive country I had struggled in for so long.

John had a very heavy cough on the flight back to Vancouver, and we went straight to the General Hospital. We then spent one night at his daughter's place, and one night at Harrison Hot Springs to rest for the rest up for the remainder of our drive back to the Okanagan. I was already plunging into a deep depression, and I don't think John quite believed me when I told him what I was going to have to do upon our return.

~/~

I immediately gave notice to my apartment upon our arrival, and I spent the rest of October packing and storing its contents. I had decided to take a bus to Arizona. My immediate thoughts were on avoiding SAD (Seasonally Affective Disorder), depression, and the discomfort of Raynaud's syndrome. My plan was to spend the winter in a southern climate, settle my affairs, and ultimately move back to Austria. No doubt, John was somewhat astounded, but somehow I thought he would, in time, fit into the plan. Dr. Razi had told me that my mental health was too fragile to undertake such a plan all by myself, and then I was side tracked with a last minute call from one of John's acquaintances to inform me about a suite in a nearby community, rent free, in exchange for some companionship for an ailing gentleman named Walter. This community, I thought, just might agree with me, since it is more alpine like, and possibly brighter. Coincidentally, Mother's last wish had been to move there, and I rationalized that this was my ultimate destiny, instead of Austria. Unfortunately, I ended up in a series of local shelters and motels.

Walter was a pleasant man. He was interested in medical research, and he had a cornucopia of pharmaceuticals and supplements in his kitchen cupboards, the use of which had actually extended his life far beyond those of his co-workers who had all passed away from the side effects of their careers in the trades. Walter had weekly housecleaning services, and I was only responsible for my own space, which was nice. He had large vegetable plots I intended to tend to in the Springtime, he smoked his own sausage on his back balcony, and he had an elder from his church visit regularly. To pass the time, I volunteered at a cat sanctuary.

I decided to get away from the basement suite in Walter's

house and attend the New Year's Day 2006 dance, and as soon as I walked into the dance hall, it was John, of all people, who greeted me with his big smile and wide open arms. He was expecting me! We had last seen each other at the end of September, three months after our return from Austria, and it seemed like a lifetime since we had parted. In the middle of our first dance, he proposed a three-month vacation to Australia and New Zealand, which he had already checked out with reputable tour company. "A real good deal!" he exclaimed. We could still catch the third wave of scheduled departures. How could I refuse? I had totally forgotten why I left him in the first place. We knew we were fairly good travel partners and we had been swept up once more, but the framed pictures of us, which had filled the wall above his desk, had since all been replaced with photos of his adoring baby boomer daughters who told him it was they who had been his real angels all along.

When I told Dr. Razi that I was thinking of setting up an agreement regarding a basic standard of decorum for our upcoming trip, he reacted as if it had been an affront on himself personally. He looked shocked, grabbed the phone, handed it to me, and told me to dial John's number and let him know exactly what I had just mentioned. I refused under such pressure, and reassured him I would speak to John in person and deal with any difficulties if and when they arose.

Dressed up in my dirndl for the first time since I had tailored it in Calgary, twenty years earlier.

Chapter 24

2006: A GLORIOUS WINTER IN AUSTRALIA

We flew out of the Okanagan in the third week of January, scheduled to return at the end of April. John had hoped to treat his three daughters to the same vacation simultaneously, but they declined the gift of an expensive three-month vacation package. Hypothetically, it is fair to say that if John spent 10% of his annual income towards our trip, then the roughly three thousand dollars he had insisted I contribute while we were traveling, represented well over 10% of my yearly income.

Our home base on the Sunshine Coast of Australia was in the lovely city of Caloundra, about 100 km north of Brisbane. We had a breezy suite with a panoramic view of the ocean, just minutes away from the beach. On our orientation tour, John was disappointed at the lack of wild kangaroos hopping about in the city, but we did see a few sprawling around the university campus, and we fed some very tame ones at the Australia Zoo. Those were really small compared to the images we had from documentaries and magazines of full sized kangaroos carrying babies in their pouches.

We were blessed with sunshine every day as we frolicked by the ocean side and lingered by the poolside. We went to a fancy horse race organized by the tour company. We attended a Mayor's welcoming luncheon at the city hall. We had lunch at our tour guide's dream home near Mooloolaba. I loved how her house was completely surrounded with a lap pool. The farmer's market was just up the street. The produce was cheap and abundant with tropical fruit and vegetables. I watched experts surfing the waves with ease and I tried it too. Little did I anticipate the ferocious power of tidal undercurrents. After a few attempts at the age sixty, I proudly sported a few nasty bruises from the impact of the surfboard's edge, having clung on in a sportsman-like fashion.

John was not interested in exploring the Sunshine Coast much beyond the immediate vicinity of Caloundra, except for an hour's bus ride to Brisbane. Much of our time was taken up with shopping, cooking, and regular doctor's appointments to monitor his health. Most tourists from our group took side excursions to Sydney, Alice Springs, Melbourne or Ayers Rock. One irate passenger shouted from the back of our bus heading for the local Australia Zoo, "You can't afford it, if you have to keep asking what everything costs." John had a habit of haggling with local bus drivers and shopkeepers in an imposing and bellowing voice, and sometimes it just made me and others want to cringe. I told myself nothing is perfect, and to remain loyal and supportive, for better or worse, like a marriage vow.

John took a second side trip into Brisbane without me the next time, and when he came back to Caloundra, he flashed pictures of himself standing next to a beautiful blonde. Silly, but extremely annoying. I paid the price for living in sin. I had already sold my soul the previous year for the opportunity of seeing my home country again, and now I was paying the price for basking in blue skies, azure oceans, and sandy beaches. I had sold my soul for the two of the three things I wanted most in my life, except for my children, and still I don't know if God will ever, in my lifetime, find it in his power to facilitate my reconciliation with them. Various scriptures read, *"For the moment, all discipline seems painful rather than pleasant, but later it yields the peaceful fruit of righteousness to those who have been trained by it."* – *"Discipline your son and daughter, for there is hope; do not set your heart on putting them to death"* – *"Honor your father and your mother, as the Lord your God commanded you, that your days may be long, and that it may go well with you in the land that the Lord your God is giving you."*

I know I have digressed and gotten carried away from my accounts on Australia, but all I wanted to express how abysmally sorry I am for not having raised my children according to the Bible's principles. Night time prayers alone were not enough.

John paid that seal $5 to kiss me; Australia Zoo, 2006.

Chapter 25

2006: MOUNT MANGANUI, NEW ZEALAND
The last month of our vacation was at the base of Mount Maunganui, in the Bay of Plenty, which is on the north island of New Zealand. We were the only couple remaining from the very last of the three tour excursions, and the weather had changed quite dramatically from the hot temperatures we had just enjoyed in Australia. Autumn had arrived in the tropics, and I needed to buy a heavy sweater. It was too cold to swim in the ocean, but the climate was perfect for hikes up and around the calibrated trails of beautiful Mount Maunganui, which was studded with sheep. Quite lovely. I loved hiking around the extinct volcano. John managed to walk half of its circumference, and he enjoyed the outdoor hot springs pool at its base.

Within days of our arrival, a Maori woman showed up at our door unannounced. He had called her because he had gotten into a huff and puff because I was not prepared to write our new set of post cards "Pronto!" I had promised him that I would do it by the end of the week, because I had just finished writing a stack of post cards before we left Caloundra. As she was writing them up while he dictated, she was obviously frustrated trying to understand his thick broken English. She later took me aside in the convenience store she managed, to ask if everything was all right. She wondered if there had been any sexual abuse, and she left me her contact number.

We took some day trips to Tauranga, and we enjoyed a traditional Maori barbeque. At a jazz festival in the town of Mount Maunganui, John suddenly disappeared into a crowd, and after a lengthy search throughout the festival, I returned to our condo. He gave me no explanation, just a grin.

John refused to travel to any other parts of the two islands, which I think one would expect to visit when having flown all the way from to New Zealand from Canada via Australia for a once in a lifetime adventure. I sometimes thought it would have been just as well if we had vacationed in Mexico or Hawaii, at a fraction of the cost. Quite frankly, we were getting quite bored with each other and the monotony of our daily routine. We had a tour guide show us around the beautiful city of Auckland for two days (at my expense). Our guide pushed John around the historical Auckland Maori museum in a wheelchair, but he had to get out and climb several stairs to take in a live Maori musical performance. On our way out, John tripped and took a hard fall down those stone steps, so suddenly, that neither the guide nor I were able to catch him. Fortunately John knew how to take falls very well by channeling the impact of his burly body into a somersault, and we made it back to Vancouver in one piece.

I could not settle down after either of our trips. I had seen my home country and I had spent a winter in balmy tropical weather, and I was still homeless. All my furnishings, household and personal items were stored away in two lockers. I was beginning to wonder what the rest of my life was going to look like. I was afraid I was painting myself into a corner, as Dr. Razi had mentioned, and never be able to get out of it.

I had become acutely aware that I was slightly claustrophobic and I had come to the realization that I needed at least one door leading straight to the outside, and an open balcony, if I was going to be able to live with someone else, let alone with myself. Not long ago, I'd had such an unencumbered and liberated feeling at a lovely bed and breakfast resort, on our first day in Austria!

I found myself in the same predicament I had been in after our trip to Austria, and I dreaded having to celebrate my upcoming sixtieth birthday in June, feeling so badly about myself. I needed my own place again, and not a lavish birthday party at a local

Club. The more I pleaded with John to refrain from wasting money on a big party, the more determined he became with his project. He liked putting on lavish parties. He had already so kindly thrown my first ever birthday party when he was still living in his mansion on the hill.

So, my birthday had arrived. I was in my everyday attire, and John practically dragged me to the designated venue where his guests had been waiting. I sat beside my friend Maureen at the other end of the table from John and his friends. There was live music, a buffet, and some obligatory toasts. The festive spirit was not there of course, and the owner took me aside as if I were a child, and tried to chastise me. "John went to a lot of trouble for this, you know, and you should be having a better attitude," she quipped, and I said to myself, "Only God knows what is really happening here."

As soon as we came home, he conspicuously shifted his eyes towards a stack of newspapers, under which I could see the edge of a little tape recorder. He started arguing over the immediate sex he was expecting for the trouble he had gone to and complained profusely about having spent one thousand dollars on my party. I withdrew to the guest room, and I was relieved that he left me alone, but I knew trouble was brewing.

Chapter 26

2007: Homelessness – Shelters and Motels
Within days of my disastrous birthday party, John and one of his fishing buddies left for his annual fishing trip to Vancouver Island. And I left him with the help of my friend Maureen, who accompanied me to the women's shelter, and a yellow alert had been posted because John (after he had returned from his trip) contravened shelter rules by trespassing. John thought he was generally exempt from rules and regulations, especially where women were concerned.

From the shelter, I attended a bible convention with three lady friends from my old neighborhood, and then one of them helped me check out an advertisement in the classifieds, which read, "House sitter needed. I am away to visit family out of town most of the time." The homeowner, named Joe, refused to let me unpack my things in my designated room, and then he was held up with a long, subdued telephone conversation inside of his garage. After supper, he told me to leave unless I slept with him. I could not believe it, and I had to avail myself of the shelter again, but they could only put me up for one night.

In the morning, I answered a message on the shelter's noticeboard, signed by a "George Baird," which read, "Room in bright house available." I learned that the shelter rules strictly enforced the rule about all males, including male friends and relatives, not trespassing within one block, but George came right up to the door of the shelter to pick me up, and I assumed that this person was a Good Samaritan, well connected with the shelter.

He had three tenants living in the basement of his house, and he gave me the spare room upstairs. The next day, when George took me for coffee, I saw John and someone else spying on us out of his white truck from across the shopping center's parking lot. They knew each other!

Mother's favorite mantra, *"Furs Alter sparen!"* – "Save for your old age!" had still been ringing in my ears. I was sixty, and keenly aware of a much overdue plan for my retirement. After a few weeks' stay at George's boarding house, I answered an advertisement written by a lady who was looking for a live-in companion for her aging mother who was hoping to remain in her beloved family home as long as possible. She was visually impaired and fragile looking, but she had the sweetest disposition. I was told all she needed was someone to cook and to shop for groceries in exchange for free room and board, which would enable me to build up savings for a rainy day.

Before I left George's house, I sent a letter of appreciation to the editor of a local newspaper in praise of my Good Samaritan George, for having opened his home to me under difficult circumstances. A reporter asked to come over and do an article on my experience. He did. However, George did not want to be around for it, and took off in a hurry before the reporter showed up. An article about my ordeal, cautionary comments by the RCMP, and a photo of myself with George's happy looking dogs flanked at my side, was published in the local paper.

I had not been informed that the lady was incontinent, nor that she had been secretly hiding her soiled diapers under and in between the clothes in her drawers and closets, and that she had been falling out of her bed at night. Within two months, her daughter, a professional in the medical field, flew from Vancouver to assess her mother's condition, and decided to place her into a retirement residence near her home in West Vancouver. George had frequently brought his dogs to roam on her spacious estate. He was also determined to take me back to his house. "I really want to be married," he said. My room was still available.

George was obviously very good at rescuing damsels in distress. I loved having kitchen access, and I baked, cooked, and cleaned to my heart's content. I had become extremely attached to his pets, two dogs, who in my estimation were in need of grooming, walking, and tender loving care.

Eventually, I noticed a tenant had come up from her basement room to visit him at night, sometimes drunk. I also saw him abusing the dogs. When I had seen him kick the little poodle hard, several times, with his boots on, another tenant and I anonymously reported him. A representative from the SPCA came to the home and determined everything was just fine with the dogs, and soon George and his future wife gave me notice. Someone had tattled on me. I was all packed up with nowhere to go. Both dogs, looking inside from the screened-in window to the backyard, barked and literally bounced up and down on their hind legs, in unison, as they watched me leave. I was heartbroken for them. They had witnessed the loss of too many friends.

And off I went, cruising around my Okanagan community, wondering where I was going to sleep that night. As usual, I thought it was in God's hands, and I thought someone would come to my rescue. Since motels were too expensive, I knocked at the women's shelter again. Months later, John told me, "You know you deserted those dogs." George and John had certainly been in touch throughout my whole ordeal. Some men!

Another lady from the shelter and I were sent to a safe cottage in the middle of an orchard in another Okanagan community. I was shocked when she suggested we have John and her own abusive mate visit us there. After one week in the orchard, we were transferred back to the shelter. I was beginning to feel exasperated and I left the shelter. I drove all the way to the far end of the valley, was tempted to drive off a cliff, but when I remembered that I had forgotten my address book at the shelter, I decided to turn around to retrieve it. I needed the names and numbers of people to whom I was going to say goodbye.

From there, I was sent to a women's shelter outside of the city. I loved the fresh country air there, and I came to love a beautiful baby boy staying there with his mom and her alcoholic/epileptic mother. I felt so privileged to hold him up as he took his first steps. He also enjoyed my singing of German children's folk songs to him. I was asked to leave the shelter on a rather bitter note because I had reason to suspect the baby had been given alcohol to sedate him from his teething discomfort, and I had reported it to the authorities. He was then kept away from me but he kept searching for me. It was heartbreaking. Sadly my songs and my complaint were taken as a cultural threat. One of the ladies said, "He has his own traditions to resort to," when I believed that we had created a beautiful multicultural bond. My allegation was in no uncertain terms firmly denied by the powers that be, claiming that they had used a natural remedy from a health food store. From there, I took a room in a local motel for two months, and then in another motel for the winter. I came across the above-mentioned grandmother in question several years later. According to her, her daughter and her son had moved to Surrey, and she received a no contact order to her darling grandson.

~/~

No matter which direction I gazed, the view from my first motel was mesmerizing. The front entrance to my unit faced expansive parkland near tourist attractions by Lake Okanagan. The back door opened to a view of the blue waters of a swimming pool, beckoning the sunrise every morning: very bright and non-claustrophobic. I found myself in an ideal time and location to savor autumn, meditate, catch up on my Bible studies, and pray for a residence of my own. I took advantage of pole walking lessons. I also had a little adventure:

WHO'S WHO IN LEAVENWORTH

My life, as my new counselor saw it, reminded her as that of a bumblebee carrying around a huge weight on its shoulders, yet always managing to get up and carry on, and she emphatically recommended a trip to Leavenworth, Washington, for some relief of my burdens. I instantly remembered the glowing account

Mother had given me about the trip she had taken to that Bavarian-themed village with her church group, back in the eighties. Apparently she yodeled out of the back seat all the way there, and I wanted to experience the same exhilaration of my home country too, and now was my chance. "Emily, you will just love it! I have been there so many times myself. Please go! You will feel like you are in Austria again," she urged.

I was the only single passenger on a bus of approximately twelve couples. One couple was seated separately but they visited each other back and forth. At the various stops, most of the passengers quickly disappeared into local taverns. I preferred to inhale fresh mountain air, frequent souvenir shops, and dream about seeing the next best thing to my homeland again.

Before we settled down for our first night in Leavenworth, the bus driver advised us of the inclusive Bavarian style dinner and entertainment included in our travel package. He also reminded us that a local bus ran into the village in the morning. I am not an early bird. Everyone else apparently was, and had already gone ahead. How they all made it into town is still a mystery to me. I waited patiently at the bus stop, only to find out from the convenience store clerk that bus service was not available on weekends. So I walked. I did not anticipate this to turn into a hike, and by the time I arrived in the village, my feet were aching enough to have to search for a shoe store.

I found a sporting goods store tucked away upstairs from the Bavarian souvenir shops below, and I bought the only pair that fit. It was a men's make and very expensive. By then, I was a little deflated as my budget had already been seriously compromised. Two classy shops did catch my eye though. One carried authentic and very expensive Dirndl dresses. The other had gorgeous handcrafted cuckoo clocks. I window shopped all afternoon in hopes that the Beer Fest later that night would cheer me up.

At the Beer Fest, I found myself sitting with the odd couple from the bus. Over a beer or two, we watched mostly university students drinking and dancing the evening away. After a while, the considerably taller member of the couple excused herself. When she did not return for some time, her partner was getting anxious, so I took it upon myself to look for her throughout the enormous beer hall. When I stepped into the lady's facilities, I noticed some exceptionally large runners and a heavy European-style tweed suit clad person coming out of a stall. It was her! I immediately got the impression that this towering statuesque person was actually a man. I ducked and disappeared unnoticed, and returned to sit with the couple as if nothing had happened.

A short while later, her short "husband" then took off, and we ended up doing an exhaustive search for him throughout the whole facility, until we called it a day. We took the shuttle back to the motel, hoping he had found his way back by then. Before I unlocked the door to my motel room, I noticed he had not yet opened their door. He repeatedly knocked, peeked through a window, and knocked again, but there was no answer. He called over to me, "She may have gone to sleep or she may be in the shower." So I waited a while. His demeanor was conspicuously nonchalant and unperturbed as he added, "She may be out all night, and I have no keys." More unspoken moments passed by, until we finally heard sounds from their unit. She came to the door after all and ushered her partner in. Knowing they were finally safe and sound together inside their room was a real relief.

Next day, we were shuttled to our special Bavarian style dinner. It turned out to be in a business meeting/dining hall with no decor, no music, no German fare; just a choice of two American style menus, and a couple who kept arguing the whole evening long.

The return trip was uneventful, except the driver forgot about me at the customs duty-free store and drove off to the border check point without me. I ran after the bus for dear life, and was I mad by then! I cursed under my tongue, and hissed between my teeth all the way back to the Okanagan. The driver had noticed my agitation from his rear-view mirror as I kept throwing darting glances at those two guys and anyone else who dared to look at me.

It was raining by the time my suitcase and I was dropped off in the parking lot across from the motel I'd been staying at. The driver made a fast U-turn around my luggage and almost knocked it over. I had to step back to avoid the same fate. He was in an awful hurry to get back to his headquarters.

~/~

I sent a letter to the Editor of the local paper titled "Disgruntled Tourist," because my complaint to the tour bus company was not well received. They did not offer to compensate, let alone lend a sympathetic word or apologize, and when I relayed my adventure to my therapist, she became really excited when I came to describe the scene outside of our motel doors on the night of the Beer Fest. She took a big breath and pronounced, "And Emily, you didn't, did you?" meaning she actually expected me to say that I had joined them for the night. Feeling demeaned and insulted, I retorted, "No! Of course not!" I think I spoiled her vicarious, anticipatory thrill. And thus ends another episode in my adventures.

Needless to say, this trip was neither therapeutic nor beneficial for my mental health, nor did I have the exhilarated feeling my mother had experienced in Leavenworth. However, I had another unusual story to write about. Those runners are now eight years old, and are still the best hiking shoes I have ever had.

~/~

I noticed that the occupant of the motel unit next to mine was a young lady I had already met at the community center pool some time ago. She had some of her most prized artwork with her; beautiful, classic Renaissance paintings, and her name was Samantha. Since her unit had been reserved for winter snowbirds, she found temporary accommodations.

My own unit had been reserved for snowbirds from the prairies as well, and it was time to move on again. Assessed as well-qualified, quiet, clean, and responsible, B.C. Housing recommended me to a motel near a lake. I enjoyed living in a motel just like a snowbird. The furnishings and service were of high calibre, I felt safe and created my own little community with some of the other guests, my favorite being two ladies with three dogs. I joined them on their daily walks, and I liked to chat with the front door manager while grooming and detangling the badly matted fur of her Himalayan cat. I tried to coax her timid Shi-Tzu into walks, but it hated to go out. I found out that she had rescued the traumatized puppy from a puppy mill. Of course, I always had my bicycle with me no matter where I happened to be, being my preferred mode of transportation, weather permitting – faster than driving to get around town for anything, even with full grocery bags dangling from both handlebars.

288 | EITHA FLOSSMANN

Chapter 27

2007: BC HOUSING

By the end of May 2008, I discovered that John had followed my trail again. He started showing up at my new motel regularly, with his van parked next to the booking office. Somehow he had found out that I had to move by the end of May (due to the approaching summer tourist season). John obviously wanted to get together again but I tried hard not get into another situation I would regret.

The vacancy rate for affordable apartments was exceptionally low that year, and I had to make up my mind quickly, because B.C. Housing had only two apartments available. The agency informed me that its clients' files are closed permanently when a prospective applicant does not accept one of the first two or three options offered. I was pretty much at its mercy.

Meantime, the managers of the motel recommended me to a pensioner who was looking for a live-in helper. I thought I'd check it out. His first words to me were, "Hello. Do you want to join me in bed?" I ignored him as I looked around, and then I noticed a strong, pungent urine odor emanating out of every chair I tried to sit in. They all reeked. He was on dialysis. He then told me that he had a girlfriend who showed up shortly thereafter. We had coffee and I went back to the motel.

The next day, the same managers invited me and the pensioner for coffee at their state-of-the-art estate home on an acreage. I was very impressed with their home and I was not too intimidated with their very scary guard dogs, but I was disappointed with their unprofessional match-making judgment.

B.C. Housing representatives then expected me to take an apartment, sight unseen, in a building that is located near its administrative offices. The current occupant denied access to his apartment, which was filled with cigarette smoke billowing out through the crevices around his door, and I opted to take the alternative choice.

John used his van to help me clear my belongings out of my storage lockers. My new apartment had no window coverings anywhere, so I initially used bed sheets for privacy. I purchased the necessary hardware, curtains, and venetian blinds for every window, including the sliding doors to the balcony, and John had a friend install them for me. After a while I found that I could unpack and decorate only in spurts of an hour or two at a time, because something was making me ill. I suspected it was the noxious fumes emanating from the freshly and unprofessionally varathaned floors. The uneven layers of varathane would not dry out, even with the use of industrial size boxes of baking soda, vinegar, and two rented air purifiers. I was having to stay away overnight. I was getting violent reactions with severe crying spells. I also received a warning by the landlord, "You are responsible for your boyfriend's behavior." which added to my stress. He was referring to the drunken scene John had made in the parking lot because I would not invite him in to my apartment for the night.

When I notified B.C. Housing about the problems I was experiencing, my agent thought I might be interested in a place a few kilometers up the valley, which she herself had not yet seen. Would I like to come along for a ride? Well, it was a long and slow 45-minute ride to an abandoned house at the very end of a road, in the middle of wilderness country, with not another house in view. Just as we were about to leave, a car with several male occupants pulled into the driveway. I was scared because they did not look like they were expecting anyone, and my agent's communication with them was conspicuously short. We never got to view the inside of the house, and we made haste for our departure.

Somehow, through God's grace, I had the pleasure of reconnecting with Samantha (whom I had last seen at the motel). She came around to my new apartment every day to offer support in my increasingly despondent situation. She had found herself living in an unacceptable, unsafe, and run down suite on a busy downtown street, and I am sorry I didn't take her up on her suggestion to look for accommodations together, because I still hadn't gotten to know her well enough to appreciate the fine person she was, and the loyal friend she would eventually prove to be.

The landlady had befriended me when we crossed paths on our way to our respective apartments, and confided about her health issues, that her husband was giving her problems, and that she felt a special spiritual kinship with me. But when she handed me several photos she had taken depicting the images of guardian angels in front of my door, rather than feel protected, I felt spooked and threatened, since I couldn't decipher whether they were angels, or ghosts shrouded in a foggy mist. I hesitantly tucked the surreal photos away and eventually disposed of them because they were unsettling.

Over the next three months I found myself increasingly staying at John's overnight, commuting back and forth in hopes of the noxious fumes having finally evaporated. After three months of aggravation, I gave notice. Absolutely delighted, John said, "See, you should have moved in with me in the first place."

I had received several telephone calls from my lovely ex-landlady promising me fresh salmon caught by her relatives, and promised to keep me updated. Several months later, I saw an incident on television about a shooting at my former apartment block. My beautiful ex-landlady had taken her life with a shotgun.

~/~

John and I no longer had access to the community swimming pool and gym we had frequented regularly for almost ten years, and quite frankly, I think we were a bit lost without our favorite ritual. The facility was under renovations, as if a forewarning of things to come.

We tried to enjoy the rest of the summer, and decided to break the monotony and cheer up by going to the beach, and as we were walking along the beautiful walkway, I had to stop when I found myself looking around in a numbed daze. I was momentarily frozen in time. I started sobbing with a sudden grief that gripped my heart, body, and soul. The future looked so bleak. I was not in a familiar landscape at all. My heart was yearning for the countryside of my homeland. I tried to tell myself, "I am here! This is here! This is as good as it is going to get. Pull yourself together, Emily." When John noticed my tears, he begged, "Emily, don't do this." My will had been broken, as if forced to accept a life-time sentence to a life-and-death struggle in foreign waters.

John asked me to accompany him to Vancouver Island for his yearly fishing ritual with another senior gentleman to help defray the cost. We stayed at the shabby, dirty fishing lodge he had gone to for many years, and I nearly froze to death in the fishing boat at five a.m., but I did catch two good-sized sockeye salmon I managed to turn into a tasty supper that evening. We returned with a plentiful salmon catch, had most of it smoked or frozen, and then prepared huge platters, loaded with special salmon sandwiches made with John's secret seafood mayonnaise, and distributed them to his business associates, doctor's homes, and offices, as we had done in the past.

~/~

Hannelore and I had telephoned each other regularly that summer, and in-between calls, my emotions sometimes boiled over when alone and found myself crying. Typically, our conversations centered around the miserable childhood she had endured under Mother's harsh tactics (which I took as an indirect apology for her past intolerance of me), and when I added, "I was there you know, and I had a difficult time too," she took a big breath and hesitated as if to say, "Nah, you! You had it much better than I did."

That fall, John quite abruptly decided that I needed to visit Hannelore in Montreal – at his expense! When he spoke to her on the telephone, I noticed that they had been a little too familiar with each other. I overheard him say, "Hannelore, do you still love me?" and I cringed in disbelief. When I inquired about their relationship, he said, "When you were staying at the motel last winter, we had planned a trip to the Bahamas, but I backed out because I wouldn't take her to the islands sight unseen, especially on her insistence for a four-star hotel, without meeting each other in person first." Then Hanne's boyfriend, Peter, called to say it wasn't really a good time to visit due to her back problem and other issues. Regardless, John staunchly insisted I go.

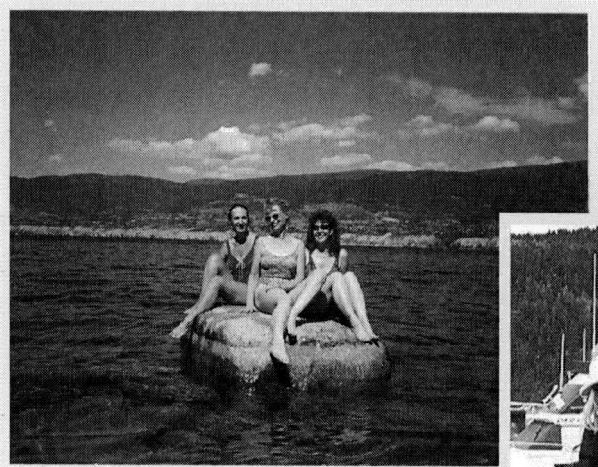

Good times relaxing with friends on Okanagan Lake.

After a successful day of fishing at Port Alberni with John.

Chapter 28

2009: VISIT WITH MY SISTER HANNELORE; MONTREAL
Hannelore kept her bachelor suite in immaculate condition with weekly assistance of home care workers. She'd always had exquisite taste in her contemporary style and décor, as well as in fashion, and it didn't feel like a small space at all with a spacious fifth floor balcony offering a panoramic view of Montreal's metropolis, where St. Joseph's Cathedral in the distance conjured up vivid memories of all the Sunday outings we'd enjoyed with family and friends, and the exercise we had benefited from by climbing up and down it's multitude of steps, sometimes sporting the two-piece pastel suit I had acquired with my babysitting earnings.

John had sent us a big bouquet of geraniums right away, and he followed up with a telephone call, "Did you find a boyfriend yet?" I was shocked and hurt by his audacity, and hung up on him, and then called back to apologize for *my* rudeness.

The following morning, Hanne telephoned her home-care worker to cancel her current week's services. I overheard a friendly and melodious voice with a strong French accent coming through on her receiver, *"Oh pourquoi Hanne? Je voudrais faire la connaissance avec votre soeur."* – "Oh why Hanne? I would very much like to meet your sister." It was obvious Hanne didn't want anyone to get to know 'the real' me if she could help it, but she did manage to introduce me to her ex- boyfriend who lived just above her apartment, and suggested he accompany me back to the Okanagan to help me pack.

A gorgeous white Persian cat graced Hanne's apartment and soon, to her amazement, timid 'Snowball' befriended me. To pass the time while Hanne was resting, I read a German novel on the inflated mattress next to her bed, which her boyfriend had set up for me. Speaking of her boyfriend, I asked Hanne why he avoided speaking with me. her reply: "He's very discriminating."

Hanne's last back surgery had not been successful, leaving her in a hospital style bed most of the time. Her medications were delivered on a daily basis because it was not safe to leave her with more than one day's prescription at a time. She warned me about her bad nightmares, for which she had always had to be isolated when hospitalized, lest the whole ward was kept up with her agonized screams. Thankfully, she didn't have any nightmares while I was there. I assumed that Hanne had a religious belief since she had reconverted back to Catholicism, as well as to her maiden name, Fahrmann. When I told her about my basic Christian beliefs, she said, "Oh, it's all made up by men. I don't believe anything anymore."

Hanne was very proud of her brand new Mazda sedan and tried her best to take me on a few outings. She managed, with the aid of heavy pain medication, to take me to West Island Mall. We always had fun shopping together. Actually, shopping was one of the few activities we truly enjoyed together, usually turning it into a frenzied activity, as if looking for an adrenalin fueled fantasy, but Snowball remained calm in the basket of her shopping cart, like a long-haired white puppy with a fancy leash and blanket.

Hanne also managed to drive me across the city for a look at our very first home on rue Casgrain. We looked at each other in disbelief from inside her parked car when we saw the old tenement building, just as we had seen it when we had first arrived in 1956. "It would have been an excellent revenue property," she said, "but Hermann and I talked Mother into selling it when we had to get married, but I must say, Vati really liked you." Oh, my beloved Vati, those uncharted waters once promised a smooth and safe journey. If you only knew.

On the topic of "Rue St. Laurent," I once listened to Stewart McLean on CBC's radio program, "The Vinyl Café," which portrayed the life of the "Anglos" in French Montreal of the 50's. He joked that the English were at that time considered to be living constrained and narrow lives, and that all parts east of Rue St. Laurent, now officially named Boulevard Saint-Laurent, had this forbidding *"je ne sais quoi"* mysterious lack of allure about it. I guess my original perception as a ten-year-old immigrant was not far off the general consensus.

Hanne attempted to observe my personal hygiene habits though I always used her bathroom to change my clothes, but she was determined I was not changing my underwear often enough and she put out a half a dozen of her extras for me. Using some home spun psychology, I saw the connection between her as a seven-year-old expected to attend to six-month-old baby "Emily" and change my stinky cloth diapers all by herself, and if the job hadn't been done, or not done just right, she'd have to face harsh verbal and physical consequences. And that's just my theory.

We viewed several vacant units in her apartment building with my move to Montreal in mind, but I sensed that she would soon need full time professional care, and she was admitted into a care home within a year. It was too late to revive my old dream of some enjoyable retirement years with my sister. The loss of Mother nine years earlier hadn't reunited us, and an opportunity to retire in Mother's spacious home in the Okanagan Valley had created an even wider rift.

I was looking forward to meeting Cameron, Hanne's grandson, whom she had helped raise since he was ten years old when his beautiful mother, Brittney, had passed away at age 32. I always wondered if the comment Brittney's doctor had made regarding her sudden weight gain at age twelve or thirteen, had contributed to her eating disorder, because he had told her that she looked like a pig.

With a little prodding on my behalf, Hanne did finally call Cameron, but I could tell from her subdued tone of voice that she was not exactly encouraging my great nephew, and he and his lovely girlfriend never did come to meet his great aunt Emily.

Many of Hanne's thoughts were centered around Mother's harsh treatment of her when she was just a child. In a soft voice she confided, "Mother was never home, and when she was, she made me work like an adult. I really hated having to be the first one to get out of our warm bed at predawn, and have to run to the farm for our daily milk." That's when it dawned on me that a lot had usually been accomplished before I had ever been woken up, and when I had been, I was usually still half asleep while Mother hurriedly dressed me and gave me my breakfast – usually ersatz coffee with milk, and bread with butter and jam. No wonder Hanne felt I was the favored one. I always got to sleep in! She also confided that her problems were of her own making and that she hated herself for it. It also saddened her to see that I had not lived up to my potential. I was the one that was supposed to "make it" of the three of us. She even admitted she was sorry for my unfortunate marriage to Dale. We agreed that we'd had a few strokes of bad luck. She said that she loved me, that she had always missed me, and that even her Persian cat had been looking for me.

My niece, Brittney, had a successful career as a model. She was a beautiful young woman, gone too soon.

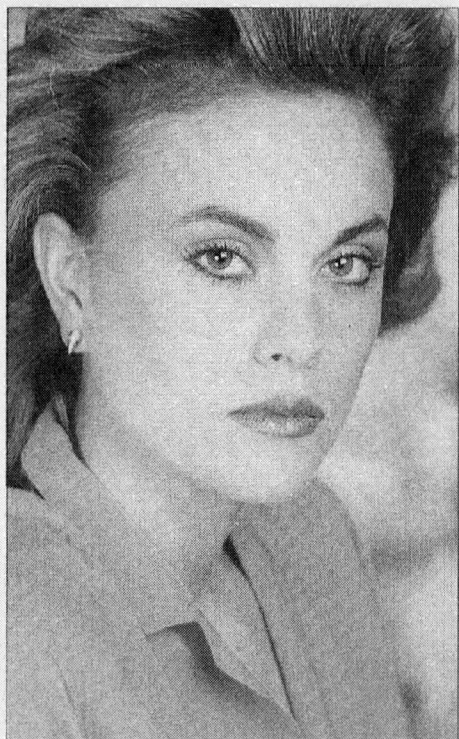

Family portrait:
Hanne with
Brittney, Miles
and Hermann.

Hanne with Snowball,
on my visit with her in
Montreal, 2009.

Distant cousin Guenther
with his Persian cat, on
my visit with him in
Austria, 2005.

Chapter 29

2009: COHABITATION WITH JOHN

Immediately upon my return from Montreal, John handed me an extensive co-habitation agreement drawn up by his daughters and a lawyer – an ex-mayor and old personal friend. He emphasized how costly it had been for him to have it set up, and he had me find an independent lawyer to validate the agreement at my expense ($168.00). The document basically stipulated if things didn't work out with us, he could give me one week's notice and one thousand dollars for relocation expenses. If we remained together until his death, he would leave ten thousand dollars, plus up to six months of occupancy in his condo, at a reduced rate, until I found new accommodations.

I knew that John had already gone through two extensive and expensive divorces, and I understood his need for a prenuptial agreement to protect his assets, but I felt demeaned as the scapegoat, made to pay the price for his previous troubles. So I signed it uncontested and unquestioned on his terms. Besides, I had nothing to lose, or so I thought.

It had finally dawned on me, that John, most likely on the urging of his daughters, had tried to coerce me to move back to Montreal. I'd never imagined that he had an ulterior motive of life without me, when he had so often, verbally and in writing, professed his love for me (as his special angel). Had he honestly told me, in no uncertain terms, that he wanted me to leave for irreconcilable differences or for whatever reason, I would have honored his request, and perhaps even moved to Montreal to be with my sister after all.

I am a natural caregiver, and I had enjoyed tending to John for the most part. Dancing, swimming, and travel had kept him feeling youthful with a partner twenty-one years his junior, but his health deteriorated, and I had turned into a full-time companion, lover, homemaker, and health care provider – while paying for room and board.

He loved to cook Ukrainian style (delicious with plenty of onions and garlic), but he usually left huge messes right after I had done a thorough cleaning, and I did not savor his cooking because I was aware of his unsanitary practices, perhaps due to his limited manual dexterity from rheumatoid arthritis which had severely deformed his hands. I had tried my best to lift him (225 pounds) whenever he fell, changed his bedding due to incontinence, lifted his walker into and out of his vehicle every day, scrubbed him down on his shower seat, chauffeured him to numerous specialists, shopped for groceries, groomed him, did the laundry, mended, massaged, trimmed his hair, helped with his compression stockings, helped with his paper work, and did housekeeping myself when a paid domestic quit due to his abusive language and commandeering ways. His Viagra-induced sexual demands and the pervasive messes he made everywhere, including urinating into my bathroom sink if I wasn't looking, eventually proved to be too much.

I was also plagued with a guilty conscience. Whenever I walked down the hallway, down to the main lobby, and through the parking lot of the building, I was reminded that I was living in sin, when respectable tenants silently passing by me seemed to reciprocate that feeling. But my heavenly father whispered, "Be patient, my dear. You have persevered the best you knew how. But it will take time to guide you back to the path of righteousness. Hang in there. I will deliver you from your tortured soul."

~/~

John agreed to make a kitten my Christmas present to help ease my depression. I let him choose one he took a particular liking to, since it was going to have to cohabit with someone known as not being particularly fond of domestic animals. At the SPCA, John pointed to Griffith, a rather aggressive and not particularly approachable young cat, but Griffith it was if they were going to get along. The cat settled in nicely, and Joe seemed to like him in the beginning, but I could tell that he was uncomfortable with any attention I was giving Griffith. He complained that I enjoyed the cat more than I did him. I'd noticed that John hit him, and I started to groom and play with the cat out of his sight, usually in the bathroom with the door locked. When we went out, Griffith liked to sleep on the seat of John's scooter, parked inside the entrance of the condo. John did not like to find Griffith snoozing there when we came back, and smacked him off hard with his walking stick. Then someone snitched about a pet being kept in the condo. We could not find a home for him and sadly we had to take him back to the SPCA.

Samantha and I had kept in touch, and she temporarily helped preserve my sanity by taking me out on long drives through the Okanagan Valley. She stopped at various vineyards to try and market her beautiful artwork which she had had converted into greeting cards. Every time we spent time together, she was like a soothing balm to my spirits. She also took me for drives for no reason at all, and we had become soul mates. I was like a mother to her and she was like the loving daughter I'd wished I had in Emma. I hadn't heard from Samantha for some time, when she finally called me from Chase, B.C., as a happily married bride.

~/~

John insisted on taking me to the hospital when I exhibited symptoms of depression again. We had been waiting in the emergency ward for several hours when an administrator finally showed up and said, "We have taken a good look into your records, Emily, and we are beginning to see a strong pattern." I thought, "Great! I am about to receive an accurate diagnosis." In the back of my irrational mind I was thinking, "Yes, they have finally determined that conventional treatment over twenty-five years has not worked, and they have decided to send me to my homeland for appropriate treatment." Although I was aware that I was thinking outside of the conventional box, I was still disheartened to hear that my real problem was in finding affordable local housing. I then told the attending psychiatrist on duty that I was homesick, to which he retorted, "That is impossible!" I also told him that I suspected my first husband had exploited my daughter in her teenage years, to which he literally exploded at me and almost shouted, "How do you know that? That's not true!" He dismissed my complaints because they had nothing to do with my current situation, yet I felt they had everything to do with it, psychologically. "What you need is to get good and mad" is all he had to say, and sent us home.

John's chronic back pain and foot problems were becoming unbearable, and he was determined to have it corrected. His specialist warned him of the risks outweighing the benefits considering his multiple health issues, but the specialist finally gave in to John's persistence and agreed to do it. I remember John emphatically insisting, "I want it done, and I trust you 100%." A doctor can do only so much, and unfortunately, the wound wouldn't heal and he had to have further surgery. It took almost five months of hospitalization until he could be released.

During his hospitalization, a nurse stopped me in the hallway and confided, "I have been a nurse for over twenty years, and this is the first time a patient's verbal abuse has brought me to tears." John threatened to sue another nurse because she had asked him to politely say "please" to a request. "I am not in a school to learn manners!" he had yelled. I saw his exasperated general physician walk away from his bedside, saying under her breath, "This man has the mentality of a five-year-old."

One day, John's old friend who had helped draw up our cohabitation agreement nonchalantly walked out of the hospital's front door with a large adjustable shower chair for John's home use after his discharge, and when his three daughters had heard about particularly unacceptable behavior with a hospital employee, they quickly came to his rescue with prolific apologies and flowers. John liked to remind people that he had made a generous donation to the local hospital foundation. I was shocked, insulted, and demeaned when one of his daughters suggested that I had a good excuse to feel free and party while John had been hospitalized since I had been completely dedicated to John throughout his ordeal. He counted on seeing me every day and he let me know if I missed a day or two. Dr. Razl had also encouraged me to visit John every day and to wear makeup and look nice to help lift his spirits, and I myself was utterly lost and lonely.

One night around Christmas time, I had an anxiety attack. I think it was in anticipation of my upcoming responsibilities as his live-in caregiver. I couldn't stop hyperventilating and I called for an ambulance. We happened to be discharged at the same time, early in the New Year, neither feeling very well.

While John's first six months back at home centered on his post-operative care, my own immunity had shut down. I had contracted a fungal infection in my big toe, and an H-Pylori staph infection in my stomach (most likely from the germs of the festering wound in his foot), which took me an equal amount of time to heal with special antibiotics for which I had no coverage. All the while I kept paying John rent, and half of our food bills on the first of every month as was stipulated in the co-habitation agreement. For this he had opened a separate bank account, distinct from his other business accounts, and proudly updated it at his bank every month.

An unexpected call from George, my old landlord who had posted rooms for rent at the shelter and had 'rescued' me from the facility, had called John to see how I was doing. With John's approval, George and his wife took me to A&W for lunch. They didn't think I looked very well.

John's daughters synchronized their visits carefully, so none would get overwhelmed with the tasks at hand, one of which was to prepare paperwork for his bookkeeper in another city. They brought Rescue-Me tincture from a health food store, and wine flowed freely to help keep an even keel on things. I was really impressed with their show of solidarity as sisters and how they handled their father, and I often told them so. But I must have given them the impression I had become lazy and antisocial because I would automatically crash as soon as they arrived for their visits. It was as if my body and soul had finally received permission to rest. However, their visits were not effective breaks for me any longer. The theater and a dinner out on the first night of their arrival just did not cut it anymore, and they must have wondered if I was no longer serving my purpose as a cheap live-in-caregiver. The fact that I was unhappy, I thought irrelevant, even if they thought it was a good reason to leave.

In the summer of 2010, John once more insisted on taking me to the hospital because I had been showing signs of withdrawal again. During my stay there, a cleaning staff employee, of all people, encouraged me to go to the shelter for women, and a big deal had been made over a zip lock bag with excess Citalopram antidepressant pills someone had found in one of my drawers at home. On his morning rounds, my doctor exclaimed, "You've been hoarding a stash of pills!" I explained that over the years, I had been taking only a fraction of my antidepressant prescription medication because I couldn't tolerate the side effects. I hoped to be able to fight the depressions by myself as well, and the excess of pills had accumulated over time. I hadn't had the occasion to find a way to dispose of them responsibly without dealing with the suspicious eyes of a pharmacist. After my discharge, I found telltale signs that my room in John's condo had been thoroughly searched.

Just like the cleaning lady at the hospital, John also pressured me to check myself into the shelter. I telephoned the shelter for no particular emergency, but I was automatically admitted. I was assigned to a cot next to a queen size bed covered with dozens of beautiful stuffed animals. My young roommate said, "I am practicing for an act in an upcoming competition, and I have room in my heart for you, too." I wasn't sure what she meant. I felt some compassion for her because I noticed evidence of bulimia in the bathroom, which brought back memories of the eating disorder I had in my youth. She was away for one night and came back saying, "I really wore him out." I could only try to imagine who he was.

Some days later, I walked out in disbelief when I opened the door to our room, and saw my roommate, unaware of me, rehearsing a sexually explicit act among her little zoo. Stella, a shelter executive I had once admired for surviving marriage to a criminal husband, contacted me within minutes of the encounter and ordered me to pack. "You are leaving! Start packing!" she quipped. In a stupor, I fled into the back yard of the shelter to compose myself, when one of the residents, sitting in the shade of a tree with other victims of abuse, commented, "You've sold your soul to the devil." I have no idea on whose information she had based her conclusion, unless my failure to do my turn at the dishes that night had caused a silent revolution.

I wondered how much longer it would take to endure the madness of this world, and what it would take to redeem myself. I was just barely able to cling to that promise. But God seemed to say, "I give you only as much as you can endure, and I might just find a room for you in the promised kingdom – at least a safe if not ideal oasis from your current turbulence." In the interim, I felt thankful for His gift of a sense of humor, albeit somewhat dry.

While Stella was waiting for me to finish packing my things, my roommate, confidently sitting cross-legged among her little zoo, asked, "Is she going to the psych ward?" Stella ignored her question. I left her the large box of Laura Secord chocolates and a bouquet of flowers which John had sent to our room. Stella then took me to the emergency ward at the hospital. Not one word was exchanged. At hospital admissions, while pointing her chin towards me, Stella told the particular doctor she had requested to see, "This person once was a loyal friend of mine but not anymore. Make sure she sleeps tonight." Heavily sedated, I slept in a crowded hallway for the night, after which I was transferred to the psychiatric ward where I remained for the rest of August. The only meaningful experience on the ward was feeling blissfully mesmerized by a movie called "Heidi" the original. I couldn't tear myself away to get in line for my night time medication, so a nurse brought it to me.

On one of John's visits, a thrilled young patient almost jumped into his arms if his cane and walker hadn't gotten in the way. Instead, she gave him a big hug and cried out, "John, it's so good to see you! I just love you!" At that point I saw visions of him at local night clubs, paying girls to sit on his lap. He had always been a popular patron at nightclubs, with the inside pockets of his dress jacket were stuffed with five dollar bills to amuse himself and his girls.

To pass the time, I attempted to identify other patients' mental issues, I worried over the psych nurses' mental health (they looked far too serious), and after her electroshock treatments, I took an old lady for walks in the fenced-in outdoor patio. I waited for mealtimes, watched smokers line up for their smoke break outdoors, and tried to focus on a book, wondering which of the various psychiatrist on duty would see me for my next consultation, since Dr. Razi had given up hospital visitations a long time ago.

Another doctor from the hospital advised me to move out of John's place as soon as possible and recommended I start my search on the ward's communal land line. I thought it impractical and illogical advice since I had to be discharged to follow though on advertisements and come and go freely.

On our last visit at Dr. Razi's office, John asked the doctor if he had been intimate with me as a patient. I thought I saw lights flashing all over the walls of his office when Dr. Razi proudly nodded in the affirmative, both men beaming at the thought. He then intimated, "I don't think either of you will ever have another relationship again."

While I was busy packing and checking the advertisements at his condo, John had begun to frequented his favorite old hangouts downtown. He was suddenly going out three times a week until the wee hours of the morning and he was obviously getting support and encouragement toward his resolve to evict me.

On one of his late night returns, I woke up in the early morning hours by a bellowing voice, "I want to speak with the supervisor! I am going to report him to the authorities! I am not satisfied with your service! Your taxi driver intentionally overlooked me. He ignored me as I was flagging him down outside the nightclub!" Then I braced myself in anticipation of a confrontation and a blatant demand for sex. It would come easy to him, fully anticipating my refusal and justifying his resolve to evict me all the more. I tensed up and pretended to be sound asleep as he plomped down beside me and heard him say, "I used to feel so sorry for you, but not anymore! Did you find a place yet?" I tensed up and my heart was pounding with anxiety until I felt him leave for the comfort of his own bed. That night I thanked God for John's dependency on the mechanical contraptions he'd had installed for assistance in getting in and out of bed, and the six pillows he needed to support his back, hips, knees and feet.

John had made it a habit, not long after the co-habitation papers had been drawn up, to refer to me as his roommate, rather than as his angel sweetheart. I simply cringed whenever I overheard him emphatically saying to someone in authority, such as to a visiting nurse from Interior Health, "I have a roommate here," while most likely pointing to the door of my claustrophobic, dark, interior room of the condo with no walls or windows to the outside, into which I had withdrawn, except to get something to eat or drink in the kitchen after John had gone to bed. I felt like a hostage in bondage. One night, I fainted while pouring myself a glass of buttermilk. I tried my best to clean up. In the morning he said, "That is a fine mess you made." Yes I had, and this time it was I who had made a mess.

For the first time in my life I had become addicted to a drug. I was addicted to sleeping pills, and I even sneaked some of John's sleeping pills out of his bedroom. Their side effects caused me to start fainting and collapsing. He reported me, and suddenly it felt like an enemy was observing me. Pressure was on to get me out quickly. I had overheard his oldest daughter on the speaker phone accidentally left on, saying, "I think she wants to die." He answered, "Yes, she is disintegrating. I'm giving her the boot." Then he intentionally misplaced his newly prescribed sleeping pills to further his cause.

The co-habitation agreement clearly stated that all John had to do was give one week's notice. My dignity had already been violated. Griffith, my cat, was gone, and there was not much left to live for. Family was unavailable, and I had forgotten to pray, but I think God was with me all along and he knew that justice would prevail, even if He had to watch me hit rock bottom, so I could be healed with His love.

When I had used up my regular monthly supply of sleeping pills within one week, I asked Dr. Razi for another prescription, and he complied. My overdose came with that extra month's supply. I was very well aware these pills were over and above my usual dose, but I am not sure if the doctor was keeping track. A year earlier, I had shown him a suicide note which he took lightly, almost as if amused. Ah well, he was putting in time for retirement, while I was just another patient he'd gotten tired of, just like he did of my Mother back in the early eighties.

I swallowed the whole contents of the prescription medication, and paramedics showed up almost instantaneously and took me out in stretcher. I wondered, "How did anyone see? Had there been a secret video camera installed somewhere in my room?" My door had been shut tight.

I expected my stomach to be pumped and medication administered to counteract the horrible side effects of my overdose, and I asked a nurse for something to calm my nerves for severe withdrawal symptoms, but I was told, "NO! You overdosed!" as if punished and blacklisted by the hospital.

Overnight, someone had placed a white laundry bag on the floor of my locker with my favorite summer dress inside. The dress had been all ripped up, and as I was being wheeled over to the psych ward via a lengthy maze of hallways, I noticed that someone had dropped a prayer rosary on top of my belongings, as if to say, "You'd better start praying, Emily!" This time I felt totally abandoned by my Father in heaven, and undermined by the establishment as well, but deep down inside I knew I would get through this ordeal as well.

Then, in an interview, which I assumed confidential, I happened to call John a "dirty old man" and that did it! The irritated old-school shrink had heard about it. He had already made derogatory and discouraging comments in the past such as, "Your life is shattered," "You've come from the school of hard knocks," "You are nothing but an unpaid prostitute for John," "You made your bed, now lie in it," "You'll never be in another relationship again." He clearly empathized with John because I had referred to him as a "dirty old man." On John's next visit to the hospital, he said "Emily, I once felt so sorry for you, but not anymore." At that point I felt like Satan and his demons, depraved and cruel enemies of mankind who have contributed so much to the suffering on earth, had really gained a foothold. I felt condemned to hell. All the heavenly and earthly powers that be had suddenly came down on me like a doomsday prophecy and threatened to disintegrate me right there and then.

Another doctor expressed doubt that I had actually overdosed on sleeping pills and he made me feel obligated to admit to something I didn't do, rather to something I did do. He kept asking if I really did do it. I kept nodding and saying "Yes." I believe that this was an attempt to keep Dr. Razi's "slight" oversight off the record, but it is a good thing that my former pharmacy has kept my records.

It seems I was acceptable as John's lowly servant on condition I played my part well in the eyes of his daughters, of society and even of the psychiatrists. I have frustrated more than one psychiatrist, but I had always known there was only one place I could find real justice, true love and unbiased compassion, one place where I would be understood as the whole person I was created to be. The Great Creator's grace and his wonderful sense of humor made me almost chuckle at the folly of it all.

~/~

After my discharge, I continued transporting John to his various specialists with his truck, since he had lost his driver's license, but soon he had me take it to the shopping center's parking lot every day with "For Sale" signs in its windows, when ordinary advertising hadn't caught any buyers. There was no local demand for a gas guzzling truck of its size in the Okanagan, even with all its bells and whistles, so he had it shipped to one of his daughters, and then we used my car and taxi service. It pains me to admit that I still submitted to his sexual demands because I thought the rest of my stay would turn into an unbearable nightmare, nothing short of finding myself barefoot and desperate in the streets, and ending up in the shelter or psych ward again, if I didn't co-operate right to the end.

Our cat, Griffith.

Chapter 30

2010: SEPARATION FROM JOHN

John had repeatedly assured me that he would help me with a down payment if I was to find an exceptionally good deal on a mobile home, and I assured him that I didn't mind at all if the title were to remain in his name. He asked his realtor, Duncan, to show me some low priced mobile homes, but none was cheap enough, and I would have had to settle for a real dump to satisfy John's greed for good deals, so I rented a semi-basement apartment I could afford on my disability pension income. I purchased the vacating tenant's furnishings and I made do with immediate necessities she so generously set up for me. God had also sent me a few "angels" to look out for me and elevate my spirits during this transition. Some even brought me hot meals.

Shortly after my move, John and his daughter came by with pizza and a new microwave oven as a housewarming gift, and while John kept me busy in conversation, his daughter inspected every nook and cranny of my apartment. I almost felt guilty for having brought a few staples with me to help tide me over, such as toilet paper and some groceries I had already paid for. She commented, "You know, with you and my dad, it really was never meant to be." As a strict vegetarian, she then did some yoga on my living room floor, while John and I had our pizza. I eventually asked his daughter if she and her sisters had kept the brand-new pine bedroom set with the new mattress set I had purchased for two thousand dollars, but had left behind because there was no room in either of my two storage lockers. She bluntly answered, "No, we got rid of it."

The clause in our co-habitation agreement, which stated he would issue $1,000 towards moving expenses had been forgotten because the agreement stipulated a ten-day notice, in writing, in order to validate the contract. Therefore my claim was deemed invalid by the sisters. I was too weak, physically and mentally, to take on the task of unloading my storage locker at that time. I had developed osteoporosis and arthritis. I also have Raynaud's Syndrome. In layman's terms, it is the malfunctioning of one's internal thermostat, where the parasympathetic nervous system over-reacts when the body gets chilled, turning hands and feet white and blue. It can be quite painful and gangrenous if not treated immediately. I felt strong enough to take on the huge task by September of the following year. The grand grand total for my monthly storage fees had amounted to roughly $15,000 (a healthy down payment for an acceptable mobile home I had admired a year earlier.)

I decided to drop into Dr. Razi's office with a little present and say "hello" as a peace-making gesture. Dr. Razi had, after all, given me some acceptable advice over the years with much needed fatherly comments such as, "Use your head, not your heart." and "Nice women always recover." He had also given me few fashion tips, and this time, all he had to say, "A very gracious gesture from you." and graciously showed me the exit door. As an afterthought, I thought I had always gone out of my way to be as pleasant as possible with my psychiatrist, out of respect for his position and age, but I recalled already having been shown the door when a complaint over my situation John had not gone over very well with him, and he had gotten out of his chair and pointed the door to me, saying "You are not yourself. See you next time."

~/~

Five years' worth of wood particles from a nearby saw mill had seeped through the roll-up doors and into my storage lockers, and dust had caked the surfaces of all boxes and plastic bins, not to mention pervasive mice nests. Some days I managed to move two carloads full of everything that could possibly fit into my car. Then one third of its contents went to the Salvation Army, and one third went to the dump, and everything else had to be washed down in the bathtub of my apartment. It took exactly three months of daily sorting, repacking and cleaning, until the lockers were completely empty. All the while I felt like I was under observation as I was going through my daily drudgery. I had a nightmare about it on November 29th, 2010, when I woke up to a dream I called "My Storage Locker": I had been crying and frantically searching for the keys to my storage locker. I searched in a train, I searched on a bus and in desperation I contacted the police. All of a sudden I had turned into a frail old woman, with emaciated arms and legs flailing about in wild abandon, trying to fend off the heavy boxes that were pummeling on top of me, and rolling down a steep cliff along with my battered body. I woke up in a state of sheer panic.

~/~

John kept showing up with his scooter, uninvited, from all the way across town, even on the coldest winter days. I had allowed him inside several times, until he pressured me to move back with him. He had never given up on the idea of cohabiting again, and on the very same conditions as before. Love letters, flowers and professionally laminated poems kept coming, and I started to refuse them. He had also said, "No one will ever love you more than I do." His words were touching and perhaps true, but when I reminded him that he had kicked me out, he protested, "I never did such a thing!" I was very angry by then, and repeatedly declined fancy dinner invitations whenever his daughters came into town. I once heard an expression to the effect, "Never underestimate the ire of a scorned woman." Had it not been for my faith, I might have resorted to more devious means.

But, neighbors who saw this poor, old, ailing and freezing gentleman waiting at the door, and even knocking on my street level windows, seemed ever so sorry for him – an old man who had once taken a poor waif into his abode and even on trips overseas. And now she was turning him away, freezing cold with pizza and flowers in the basket of his scooter. "How is this mean, thankless, heartless bitch named Emily, in apartment #4, capable of abusing such a nice old man?" is what must have gone through their minds, while I endured intentional heavy stomping from the tenant above, whom I had seen communicating with John from his scooter up to his balcony. The stomping eventually subsided after several complaints to the landlord.

Recently, some of the tenants look at me with a friendly new curiosity, but my reputation as John's ex-partner still tends to haunt me. I seem to wear a label saying, "Warning: Fallen woman, undeserving and outcast." Mercifully, God has allowed some fading of that label, because it is written, "In the image of God we are made," not in the image of man-made labels.

I have striven to reclaim as much of my former being as possible. The year after John had evicted me, I turned sixty-five and my Alberta Pension from the University of Calgary had kicked in, offsetting the disability pension income I had received for twenty-four years, and on that income I was able to maintain my car and my colorfully decorated apartment.

For a while though, it seemed like I had nothing left to live for but for old memories, photos, and a broken heart, but one year after John and I had broken up, I decided to contact Stuart, my old high school sweetheart from Montreal. I discovered that he had been recently widowed from his lovely wife Lisa after a happy marriage of over thirty years, and like a ray of sunshine from Edmonton, mutual old memories suddenly sprung to life, and we didn't know that we were about to embark on brand new journey of the re-discovery of our intertwined lives.

~/~

Meantime, in the spring of 2012, my experience with gallbladder surgery had not been the best; I had been carted off into the operating theater in an awful hurry, like cattle for the slaughtering house. I'd never had such poor treatment prior to any of my previous surgeries, and I expected to see the same anesthesiologist I had had my preoperative consultation with. Instead, I looked up into the face of a strange substitute who had the demeanor of a mean butcher. Moreover, I do not take surgeries very well. I hemorrhage, and for the second time in my life, I required a blood transfusion. Nasty stuff, but lifesaving nevertheless. I felt blacklisted at the hospital once more, and John was genuinely upset that he hadn't been informed about it.

I was able to resume my usual activities within a few weeks, and I became one of the first volunteers with a home care program which connected me with Joan, a senior and former ballroom dancer, in need of a volunteer to take her out to dances and help her overcome the loss of her husband. At one of the dances, John observed us and my friends across the dance floor all evening long. When I had introduced Joan on our way out, he said, "I could use you as a volunteer too, you know." His taxi was waiting outside. Watching him go home alone was a very sad moment. That night he called to say, "Emily, I need you." Feeling bitter and still very angry, I suggested he call an ambulance not knowing that just three days later, I would be called to his deathbed. I don't know if he heard me, being on life support, but I tried to be as graceful as possible. I comforted him with the hope of an afterlife. I was tearful. My words were heartfelt. I could easily have opted for some resentful ones, and I didn't. He may have told his daughters something to the effect, "I am dying, and don't you give that bitch a penny!" What had happened to the European prince and princess? Had they gone to war? Our predecessors had been at war with each other, and I couldn't help but sense a hint of discrimination or retribution for what Hitler had done to his East European country. The following morning, one of his daughters interrogated me on the telephone as to when I had received the call to see him, by which nurse, where and what time I saw him, and what was said. I was the last person to see him.

Over a twelve year period, I had lavished John's daughters with praises and admiration for their strong sisterly bond, and their ability to handle their father diplomatically. But this time I had lost some respect.

~/~

Six months after John's passing, I managed to attend his memorial service held at his favorite night club, having seen his obituary in a local newspaper. Dozens of images projected on an overhead screen, covering his life up to 2000 were commented on, except there were no slides to depict the last twelve years of his life. Our relationship during that time had been conspicuously eliminated, perhaps at the last minute at my unexpected appearance. So, some of the great times he had had on our travels overseas, which had been once-in-a-lifetime highlights of both of our lives, were not acknowledged. I was too numbed and shocked to get up and share my memories of John, including praise for having given me the nicest surprise party in his mansion on the hill for my 56th, and my only birthday party ever. I recognized Justin, a mutual friend of John I hadn't seen for a long time, and I joined him at his table. He blatantly asked, "Did John leave you anything?" I hesitated, refocused, and responded, "No, nothing." Justin was shocked and said, "But I know you did so much for him." No one else present befriended me.

Two years later at a volunteer luncheon, John's ex-realtor, Duncan, commented that he had been extremely disappointed in John, not only as his personal real estate agent, but by the way I had been treated. I told him that John's daughters had dropped off several boxes filled with every single photo we had ever collected, as if wanting, behind seemingly genuine big smiles, to eliminated all evidence of my association with their father and purge me out of their lives permanently.

Had I been a nasty, greedy, selfish bitch? Or could it be simply a bruised ego? I could be wrong, but I personally think that there was some fear of legal action for sexual misconduct, violation of human rights, or worse. Or had I been just another tramp in his life? Did I have a bad reputation by association? A dog will get patted when his trusted master has died. Some will die along with his master, and the insults and rejections I experienced nearly devastated me as well, but I had a friend in my savior Jesus, and I had a very special friend to lean on – my high school sweetheart, Stuart, who plays a prominent role in my life.

I came across a quote by the Archbishop of Canterbury: "Who knows whether in retirement I shall be tempted to the last infirmity of mind, which is to write a book." I had to laugh. Seriously, I hear it takes courage to candidly reveal your life to the world. It's scary! But WW II flying ace Eddie Rickenbacher knew that "Courage is doing what you are afraid to do. There can be no courage unless you're scared."

"Start by doing what is necessary;
then do what's possible;
and suddenly you are doing the impossible."
– Saint Francis of Assisi

Emily the pirate, at a seniors' dance with a broken arm; Halloween, 2014.

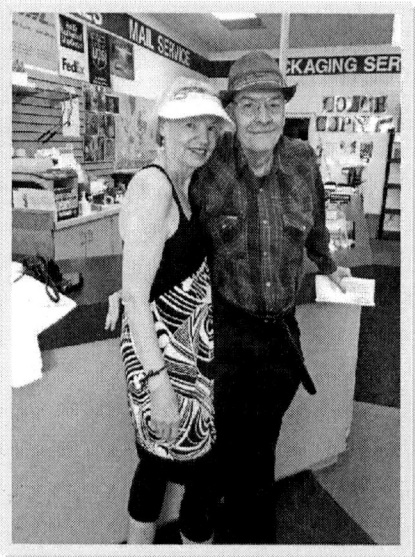

Emily (69) reunited with her high school sweetheart Stuart (71); Edmonton, Alberta, 2015.

Chapter 31

2012: RAYS OF SUNSHINE: SHANE, STUART, SAMANTHA, JOAN
My last connection with Shane had been at Mother's funeral fifteen years earlier when his father had retired to Mexico, and I FINALLY had an opportunity to see my son on a one-on-one basis again. He had been living with his father for around 25 years, and had started a business of his own. In April of 2014, I took the Greyhound bus to Vancouver Island.

Shane and I were naturally overjoyed to see each other. He looked great, now a tall and well-built man, and I found him still as easy going as he had always been. He thought me smaller than he had remembered me. We had an invigorating walk from my motel, and along the pier, to his vintage antique shop. Since his partner was away, he managed the shop on his own, and we mostly ate and visited there. We got along splendidly, as usual. When we reminisced about the past, he confessed, "Dad was obsessed with Emma, and he never did anything with me when I was a boy. It was you, Mom, who always played with me, trying to compensate for it. One of my best memories is when you and I went for a drive to a Kananaskis Country tree farm in search for the perfect Christmas tree. I took advantage of Dad financially to support my drug addiction, but I am clean now and supporting myself."

When I asked him how his father had been occupying himself in his retirement, he answered, "Oh, he's still a creature of habit. He helps me collect antiques and he also likes to hack computers." While I had an arduous overnight bus trip back to my Okanagan home, with a five hour (1am to 5am) lay over on a hard bench in the Vancouver bus terminal, I rejoiced and gave thanks for having my son in my life again, and I hoped that the reunion might spark a reconciliation with his sister Emma as well. However, whatever had transpired between us had soon spread, and severely upset everyone except myself.

My friend Samantha, with whom I had crossed paths when we were both homeless, had kept me updated on her new life in Chase, B.C., as a newly married wife. She had visited me in the Okanagan regularly, but the best news was when she and her husband moved back home to the Valley. They have since hosted an art exhibition of both their works at a local art gallery, and we eventually intend to celebrate our literary and artistic merits with a trip to Austria and Italy to admire some of the old masters, and to give thanks for a total remission from Samantha's chemotherapy for cancer. I pray that she will continue to be a ray of sunshine for me for a very long time.

Meanwhile, since our first reconnection in 2011, Stuart and I had been catching up via lengthy telephone conversations with all that had transpired over the past 48 years. He had been extremely busy as a historian, writing and publishing articles on biblical prophecy. He and his wife had enjoyed road trips through almost all of the 50 states of America, yet he is still wishing I had said "yes" to his proposal of some fifty years ago, and I kind of regretted not having taken the risk.

Unfortunately, Stuart's present health due to COPD has not permitted him to leave his home for extended periods of time, but when he confided, "You always had the best accent in the world," it felt like nine warm rays of sunshine, instantly compensating for the relentless teasing I had endured for rolling my r's throughout high school. I soon dug out my original manuscript, and with Stuart's encouragement and support, I proceeded to catch up on the previous seven years (of my life).

But, after all these years, plans with Stuart were still going "flat." In September of 2014, two days before my scheduled bus departure for Edmonton, I took a horrific fall while hiking down a steep cliff and fractured my humerus and rotator cuff. I had to wonder if it was God or the Devil intervening so often? But by June of the following year, after extensive home care and physiotherapy, I was finally able to make that long-overdue visit with Stuart a reality, and we finally saw each other in person as we are now, not through rose-colored glasses as we were in the prime of our youthful lives. We didn't faint of shock from our aged appearance. Otherwise, nothing had changed, and he hoped marriage was still in the cards. This has not come as a surprise to our friends and old acquaintances, since they had come to the conclusion that Stuart and I had developed common 'mental health' issues. He baptized me in the waters of a community swimming pool with permission of an elder from the head office of his ecclesia in Ontario. I am certain that the ceremony reconfirmed some skeptics' notion that we are both insane indeed. The irony is almost comical considering we took an IQ test recently, both resulting in the 140's range. Perhaps there is a grain of truth in the saying, "There is a fine line between genius and insanity."

Stuart has recently jogged a special memory in my brain. Ahh, now I remember. We were senior high school students when he took me to Toronto to meet his favorite aunt. Oh, how we so effortlessly moved across the dance floor in the Emperor Franz Joseph Stube. Everyone stepped aside to watch us do the Viennese Waltz, and I was terribly embarrassed for taking up their space while he swirled me around. We used to dance the night away, and we could possibly have danced into the sunset for the rest of our lives, but we have had five years of stimulating conversation over the telephone, reconnecting us to our youthful times, and sadly also to missed opportunities. He has been a steady vessel of encouragement, meaning, and support, and I have tried to reciprocate in kind, by helping him give up the hope that the past could have been different and let go of the past we thought we had wanted.

In Stuart's ardent letter, he uses some of the romantic German words I had taught him in our college years, when not too busy translating his German historical manuscripts into English, and I see not only a man who has been devoted to me, but for the first

time of my life, I have come to know what trusting a man unconditionally feels like:

February 26, 2016

Mein dearest Liebchen Emily,

*This is probably the sappiest letter you have ever received, but
considering how gorgeous you are, both physically and mentally,
and how many men have been hopelessly in love with you over your
lifetime. Anyway, I keep looking at the photograph of you on the
chesterfield with your niece and nephew. It is in my mind constantly,
and realize with the deepest regret possible, what I may have lost. I
would have sought to spare you the nastiness of this present world,
but through circumstances beyond our control, was not able to. A
song from the fifties "My Heart Aches for You" is constantly running
through my mind. It is not just that I wish we could be together now,
but that we could have been together for the past 50 years, again
with regard to circumstances beyond our control. You know that if
possible, I would have given my life to save Lisa, but the 'till death
do us part' prevented me from so doing. This condition now applies
in my mind to our relationship, and there is nothing you can do or
say that will prevent me from doing anything in my power from saving your life now or for eternity, as you have sought out on your
own through Baptism into the body of Christ. I love you more than I
could possibly imagine in every way possible. I thought the light had
gone out of my life when Lisa died, but you have restored it simply
by being in my life again as you were 50 years ago. Ich alles Liebe
Dich meine Liebchen.*

Aufwidersehne mit Liebe, Stuart!

I also give tribute to my good friend Joan, an extra special ray of
sunshine from the Okanagan Valley. She is a beautiful 93 year-old-
lady I have come to respect and love as an example of unwavering
strength and courage since I had met her as a visiting volunteer,
searching for new interests after my break-up with John. Her keen
interest in my story has fueled my desire to keep at it until satisfactory for publishing, and so far she is my biggest fan. Joan has

filled an empty void inside of me since Mother's passing, and I wouldn't want to trade that feeling of unconditional love and support for all the world. I am welcome to join in on her retirement center's activities, special events, and entertainment, a peaceful and safe haven to escape to, observe older seniors, and ponder on the assisted living options I will eventually have to consider.

With my dear friend, Joan, 2003.

Chapter 32

2014: AFTERTHOUGHTS
Children, if they are going to thrive, have an intrinsic need to see their parents in a happy and committed relationship, and I remember how intensely I had desired the same between my mother and any one of her partners. Emma's spirits had no doubt lifted with my glowing accounts of John. I seemed happy and my depression had lifted, and we proceeded to exchange many letters, parcels and family memorabilia until, unfortunately, my life had derailed once more, creating yet another rift. Disheartened with me, she no doubt continued to idolize her 'soft spoken' father, and continue to depend on him for support. After all, he had surely convinced her by saying, "You don't want to turn out like your mother."

"Yesterday is gone and its tale is told.
Today new seeds are growing."
– Rumi

My sister Hannelore resided in a care home for approximately three years after our last get-together in Montreal. Prior to her passing in December of 2014, she had suffered with multiple complications, including Parkinson's disease. Several meaningful conversations over the telephone enabled us to have a satisfying closure to our relationship. I could not fly to Montreal for her funeral since I was still requiring physiotherapy for my fractured arm, while I had also been reluctant to meet estranged family members under those circumstances, though some might beg to differ on that theory. Regretfully, for the same reason, I hadn't flown back to Montreal for Brittney's funeral either. I hope that one day, Hanne's grandson Cameron, and my nephew Miles, including their respective families, will want to meet me of their own volition, perhaps upon having read my memoir, making our long absence a truly rewarding win-win situation.

In one of our last conversations, Hannelore suggested I take a paternity test to verify, once and for all, if we had the same father, but for me the proof lies in a recent photo of my forty-three-year-old son, which shows a strong resemblance to our father. Grandfather and grandson, father and daughter bloodlines established without a doubt. I need not search any further. May my dear sister rest in peace in the arms of her Savior!

~/~

I had not been on speaking terms with my ex-husband Dale (who had retired to Mexico near his cousin Kevin) since our acrimonious divorce of twenty-eight years, but he had heard that I had broken my arm, and gave me an unexpected telephone call, saying, "One can't make up for lost time, but I still love you, and the door is always open to you." He then added in an incredulous tone of voice, "You know, your sister actually had the nerve to accuse me, as her brother-in-law, of not having done enough for her. Also, she never had anything good to say about you either, Emily. She even tried to hurt me by insinuating that you'd had a long term intimate relationship with Hermann. Did you know that he has passed away?"

This time I didn't get any of Dale's usual glowing reports regarding Emma and Shane, except to say that Shane's addiction had cost him over half a million dollars over the years, and that Emma and her partner, Qiáng, were having financial difficulties (possibly due to the downturn of Alberta's oil industry). I could hear repressed tears in his voice, but it would have been futile to remind him how he had originally ignored my concerns about the future of our children. He didn't like it that I had conscientiously controlled any emotion in my voice, expressed neither regret nor anger, or that I did not shower him with any friendly familiarity he may have hoped for, and I am sure that he had resigned himself of any hope for a reunion at that point, because I intentionally gave him the impression I was no longer the vibrant woman he once knew. His final reminder, "You were really lively, you know," I interpreted as a weak attempt to put me down, because deep-down he had found pleasure from my misfortunes.

Then he filled me in on the latest news on his side of the family (as if I were interested), and for one fleeting moment I entertained thoughts of a reconciliation, if only for our adult children's sakes. But reality quickly told me that he had undermined and sabo-taged my credibility, and manipulated the children and the system against me, and that he would never change his 'sanctimonious attitude', a phrase my original lawyer had used to describe him. The damage had been done, and there was no point in reminding him that he once said, "You are smarter than I am." and that he had taken my money to purchase an antique car, the funds I had put aside out of my earnings for private or even boarding school, with the intent of straightening the children's lives for healthier and happier pathways.

~/~

Regardless of my heartbreaks and losses, long-dormant seeds have been kissed by the sun, have sprouted, and are bursting into bloom. My season of darkness and uncertainty has passed. The butterfly is out of its cocoon! Old passions are resurfacing. I have freedom and time to finish my memoir with the support of an Okanagan writers' association. I am practicing yoga. I am learning a new instrument through the local ukulele club, I am finding my singing voice, and I am volunteering for seniors. I have found a wonderful circle of friends who are great support network, as well as exceptionally kind and friendly neighbors, Helen and Hubert, Barbara and James. The best part of it all is knowing that God is blessing me because I am giving Him the credit for his mercy, and as long as I continue to rely on Him, I shall remain out of harm's way.

My self-image has changed from timid victim to humble victor, scarred and weary, yes, and heavy-hearted at times, but all is truly well with my soul. I no longer need to escape my demons by compulsively moving around on that self-prescribed prescription called "The Geographic Cure," though I admit, the constraints of living in a chilly north facing, semi-basement apartment without a balcony, next to a busy street, poses a challenge at times, while at the same time, a blessing in disguise, providing a safe, quiet, and isolating shelter, fertile only for reminiscence, focusing on my inner world, doing my penance, writing, and praying for dreams to come true. Oh, Canada, where dreams come true!

My intent is not to point fingers or badmouth. I might even have incriminated myself, as was insinuated by a casual friend who happened to be a retired psychologist wanting me to join him in his retirement to Mexico, which I was not prepared to do so shortly after my fiasco with John. (I assumed that the psychologist had followed through on his plan on his own, until I heard that he had made it as far as Abbottsford, BC to be near his sister.) I have done my best to reveal my experiences honestly and by lending transparency to my life.

It would be easy to label me as unstable and lacking good judgment, given the pathways I have often chosen in those 'uncharted waters' of mine, and I take full responsibility for having placed my trust and hopes into the hands of some professionals and other mortals, but who were some to tell me I couldn't go back to my homeland, that I'd do better by returning to my husband, that I was responsible for losing my job at the U. of C., asking me if I was sorry for my actions, telling me I made my bed and had to lie in it, telling me I'll never find another relationship, and telling me that I am damaged goods?

I must admit I have a tendency to beat myself up for my depressions and for some of my bad judgment calls, and wonder if if they caused me to harbor a negative and excessively cautious attitude. The following quote by Rumi may have a grain of truth to it, but I still find it somewhat unfair, unsettling, and hard to digest:

Your depression is connected to your insolence
and refusal to praise.

– Rumi

I wish to bring to the helm the life-long struggles of the sixteen post-World War II era immigrants, as depicted in Ursula Hegi's book, *Tearing the Silence: On Being German in America*. I wish to shed light on women's as well as men's issues, the ramifications of sexual abuse, the causes and treatments of depression, and of the old system's woeful lack of understanding of mental health issues. Above all, I need to express my undying love and appreciation to my Almighty Creator for his grace, which surpasses all of humanity's comprehension, and I consider my ability to continue with my memoir as a gift from a Higher Source, through my faith in the promises of God that, if I endured and learned from my ordeals, he would would make my redemption possible in a most wonderful way. It says in Ruth 2:12: "The Lord recompense thy work, and a full reward be given thee of the Lord God of Israel, under whose wings thou art come to trust."

I am happy to say that my faith in mental health care has been restored through a supportive, kind, attentive, and non-judgmental geriatric psychiatrist who is new to the Okanagan valley; and for eighteen years, I have also enjoyed the excellent care of a wonderful family physician who demonstrated the patience of 'Job' by seeing me for too-many-to-mention minor physical ailment, when all I really needed were kind and calming words of acknowledgment.

I cannot imagine my progress without my special friends and soul mates, Samantha, my telephone buddy Lorraine, with the counsel of Sally at the grief center, whose incredible spiritual enlightenment showed me how to rediscover my childhood through her inspirational tapes and books. She likened me as a spiritual hero and reminded me that dandelions grow through cement cracks. I am grateful for the wonderful mentoring from Kate at the local victim care society. Last but not least, I thank all of my great friends: Joan, Luisa, Ella, Ellen, Ruth, Maureen, Pauleen, Patricia and Cathy. Last, but certainly not least, I thank the staff at the home volunteer program, who have blessed me with their enlightened, educated, sympathetic and respectful support. To protect innocent reputations and avoid some potential unhappy reactions, I have chosen to use nicknames for those mentioned in my memoir, but to each one of you who has been a friend and caretaker, you know who you are, and I thank you with all my heart.

I have had my trials and tribulations, and I have dealt with them the best way I knew how. Every time I felt slighted and felt disappointment, I gave thanks for the freedom to cross over to the sunny side, knowing my Creator would be there for me, and though I have prayed for reconciliation with Emma and Shane, as well as with extended family, and if showing them my home country is not in God's plan, and if my days here on earth are limited, I hope to have fulfilled my purposed on this earth, and hopefully go to the promised land for a joyous reunion.

"You pay God a compliment
by asking great things of him."
– St. Teresa of Avila

And there are higher powers. I say that because a recent Facebook blog by my son states that he has completed a successful stay at a Buddhist temple and has made an oath to abstain from any harmful substances, and that he believes in the holy. Shane had also been approached by a Hindu fortune teller in Thailand who told him that his body has traveled the world, but that his heart was with a lady named Emily. He said, "Your mother's name is Emily, no?" Hope does spring eternal.

~/~

God has endowed me with an appreciation for all of his gifts: creative hands, keen eyesight, boundless physical energy, an appreciation for music, and food for body, mind and soul. He is guiding me in the building and trusting of new relationships. He is giving me the much needed exuberance needed in old age to transcend regrets, fears, and doubts of the past. He also breathes faith into my soul. It says in the Bible, 365 times, "Do not be afraid," once for each day of the year. My physical endowments will decline, but I shall not be afraid, and I give thanks for the hope of reconciliation with those I may have inadvertently hurt.

~/~

A Final Tribute To Vati, Otto Protzki, Our Canadian Sponsor: *"Be thankful, for Vati Otto Protzki gave us a home in Canada. Always honor him!"* Those words were Mother's mantra every time she reminded us of his good deeds, and I will always honor him, for his intentions were pure. Had he been healthier and lived longer, he might have helped us avoid some painful stumbling blocks as new immigrants, and he would have helped us maintain the family solidarity he would have liked us to have. He had stated, "Ten horses won't ever lure Emily and Hannelore back to Austria." He had intended for all three of us to sail smoothly in 'calm waters' for the rest of our lives, of that I am sure, and for that I will always honor my Vati, Otto Protzki. He may not have been aware that he was a Godly man as a self-proclaimed agnostic, having accepted Jesus Christ on his deathbed, nevertheless.

Chapter 33

2015: OKANAGAN VALLEY; RECONCILIATION AT MOTHER'S GRAVE SITE

It has been an unusually long summer in the Okanagan Valley. Leaves are turning again, and temperatures are cooling to a comfortable level. Appetites are stimulated for homemade stew and apple pie, wardrobes are changing, and friendships are renewing, and as I watch children playing, my thoughts are turned to Thanksgiving, and visions of sunny snow-capped mountains in the distance.

The weather is perfect for bicycling this time of the year, not too hot, not too cold. The biking trail is lined with vineyards, heavily laden with white and purple grapes, ready for picking. But I must attend to Mother, because last night, in a dream, I was standing by her grave site, trying to communicate something to her.

Mother's grave is located on a slight incline, several rows up from a curb overlooking Okanagan Lake. It is inscribed as, "Margarete del Fabrosi: in Loving Memory, 1915-1997." I am attempting to say something, but nothing is coming forth. I cannot conjure up any feelings and I cannot find my voice. So I take out my notepad, sit down on the grass, and begin to write:

Hello Mutti; It's been eighteen years since you were laid to rest here. Eleven years ago, on October 18th, 2004, I had mentioned to you that I had started writing my life's story, which I have re-read, re-written, and re-edited many times since then. I am now working on its last chapter. Though the analyzing of my past has helped me gain a better perspective on life, as well a keen awareness of my mortality, I am a bit hesitant to carry on with my story because I have read a quote that suggests each day one dwells on the past will bring you closer to meeting your maker. A bit scary, but if that is the case, so be it! But that is why I am here today, for inspiration to carry on with my project.

At the beginning of the memoir, if you remember, I mentioned how German gatherings had affected me, and I just wanted to let you know I wasn't particularly conscious of Father's uniform, nor what the badges on it meant when I had proudly produced his picture to my friends. I was pleased that I had a picture of my father at all. I never told you that they attempted to enlighten me on the meaning of the badges. They said, "Your father was in the DAK Elite Unit in the *Wehrmacht a*rmy, and he carried the *Eisen Kreuz* – iron cross for valor under fire," insinuating that Father was a true Nazi. When I asked them to refrain from offering unsolicited data on my distanced father, the response was, "We are sorry to have touched a raw nerve, but this kind of thing is absolutely fascinating."

Mother, you had numerous encounters over the Nazi subject, and I understand that it even ruffled a few feathers of some *backfisch* – teens back in the day, when their only source of knowledge was from biased post-war High School history books, to find gratification by throwing salt into an old wound. I say, "Good for you, Mother" for having confronted those who insisted that the suffering of survivors, including war widows and their children, was justified, just because they happened to live under a certain regime.

You told me that Father was employed in the rationing of goods in war-time Europe. You will understand that imagining him on the battlefront, or working in a concentration camp would have exacerbated my sense of guilt, though you might say, "Forget the nonsense. Don't concern yourself over those matters." But how can I forget the racial slur that Judge Janazcek had dropped at my divorce hearing in 1995? I am telling you now what he dared announce before I could leave my stand. His last words to me from his bench were, "Did you know your relatives in Austria were Nazi conspirators?" I was too stunned to react, but I am sure you, Mother, would have given him an earful. You would have found out who was behind it, and if it was my ex-husband Dale, it would prove that we had a deceptive opponent in our family all along, and if Stuart had known about it, he would have made sure to have Judge Janezcek disbarred permanently for prejudice with malice. Have you heard that Pierre Elliott Trudeau's son Justin Trudeau is now Prime Minister of Canada, and that he has given a speech in the wake of a terrorist attack on a Muslim Mosque in Quebec City in which he emphasized Canada being a welcoming country to immigrants of all nationalities? So you see, it is getting better. I even heard someone on television say, "Canada, where dreams come true. Isn't that encouraging?"

The post-war ravages and your divorce from father while pregnant with me had overwhelmed both you and your first born Hanne, and I understand the circumstances around the time of my birth. I want you to know that sometimes I have wished you had not given me life, but you refused to do it because of your faith, and deep down inside, you must have known that God had planned a special gift as a consolation prize to comfort your agonized soul.

It is only now that I have seen one of Hitler's blitzkrieg invasion at its worst in the movie "The Zookeeper's Wife", that I am beginning to truly appreciate what you must have gone through, if only an inkling of the graphic atrocities depicted in that film. I walked out of the theater with my heart beating too fast and my blood pressure risen, deeply saddened with the defilement man is capable of committing against mankind. I could not sleep well that night and I was reduced to a zombie-like pace throughout the following day. I vouch never to watch another war movie for a long time, if ever, and I give thanks for every day of peace we enjoy in this great country of ours called Canada.

But I also need you to know that I was jealous of you despite your hardships because you lived in your native country, you had your language, and your culture for forty-one years, without major uprooting. I picture you as a young girl frolicking among young goats in peaceful pastures, and later, as a teenager, reveling in the Tyrolean Alps, removed from the hustle and bustle of city life, secure in the safety of tranquil convent life set in the splendor of God's creation. You had contact with family members whom I never had the opportunity to get to know due to the war and the disgrace of divorcing while you carried me in your womb. I am not criticizing, I am not blaming, and may God forgive me, but I feel cheated.

To tell you the truth, given the chance to start all over, exactly as my life has evolved, I would not opt for that deeply confusing path again. I'd prefer to remain as a fleeting twinkle in my earthly father's eyes, and grant my Father in heaven permission to use my soul for another purpose. Please don't be upset, because I know you loved me very much, and you tried to protect me from the harsh realities of life. You tried your best in every possible way, and you would be pleased to know that God may have created me specifically for one purpose, possibly to write this testimony and be witness to my Creator.

Mother, I understand why you could not support me when I had lost my job, my marriage, and my children. You had suffered the same losses too, and you could not bear the thought of your own children going through the same trials. Nevertheless, your condemning words and rejection hit me like a doomsday prophecy with no one left to save me (in my uncharted waters) as depicted in Isaiah 47:8-15, in which I thought that an angry God was venting his displeasure directly at me.

The prophet wrote: *And now hear this, you pleasure-given woman, the one sitting in security, the one saying in her heart: "I am, and there is nobody else. I shall not sit as a widow, and I shall not know the loss of children." But to you, these two things will come suddenly, in one day: loss of children and widowhood. In their complete measure they must come upon you... And you kept trusting in your badness... there will suddenly come a ruin that you are not accustomed to know... with whom you have toiled with your charmers from your youth. They will actually wander, each one to his own region. There will be no one to save you.*

However, since my heavenly Father is gracious and merciful, I decided to take his words as a strong warning and alter my ways, because I don't want to wake up one day and say to myself, "I am truly condemned. It was all in vain." Even King David, who had heroically killed the enemy giant Goliath, needed to seek divine intervention partly due to his turbulent personal life. Psalms 26:2 – *"Examine me, O LORD, and prove me, try my reins and my heart."*

And then I found solace in Jeremiah 29:11–13, *For I myself well know the thoughts that I am thinking toward you, thoughts of peace, and not of calamity, to give you a future and a hope. And you will certainly call me, and come and pray to me, and I will listen to you. And you will actually seek me and find me, for you will search for me with all your heart. And I will let myself be found by you.*

I believe that a merciful God has helped me unload my burdens in order to ground me in something bigger than just the sum of my worldly experiences, and I believe in his preordained and masterfully composed future for every human being. Whether Buddhist, Christian, Hindu, Islamic, Jain, of Jewish faith, Muslim, Sikh, or Shinto, I believe the human race yearns to have one Almighty God only. I was raised Christian, so my source of reference is from my Christian perspective, but I respect other religions. God has many names with basically the same meaning, i.e. the creator, all powerful and mighty, full of mercy. Had I been born Muslim, I would worship God in the name of Allah, had I been born a Witness, I would worship God in the name of Jehovah, and so on. But this is where confusion over some 6,000 languages and more than 4,000 religions call for a need for one pure language as promised in Zephania 3:9.

~/~

Mother, I take much comfort from the encouragement and reviews I have received on my memoir so far, but you may not approve of our lives being exposed to the world this way. My intent, however, is to shed light on the reasons for human suffering, to facilitate understanding and forgiveness in families such as ours, and to find comfort in knowing that in the Promised Kingdom, all sadness will go away, all tears will be dried up, and all things will be forgotten. As Jesus promised, the day will come when all those who are in God's memory will hear Christ's voice, come out of the grave, and open their eyes to a beautiful and peaceful new world. – John 5:28, 29.

> *Hope springs eternal in the human breast;*
> *Man never is, but always to be blessed:*
> *The soul, uneasy and confined from home,*
> *Rests and expatiates in a life to come.*
> – Alexander Pope, An Essay on Man

Mutti, I wonder what it's like in heaven? Are you happy? Have you found loved ones? Have you seen Hanne, Hermann and Brittney? Is your beloved cousin Kaethe there? Are you praying for Emma and Shane? Are you waiting for the rest of us? Are you looking down for us? Have you been busy rescuing orphaned angels?

Why!
Once lush orchards, now concrete!
Engines echoing off the bluffs
Exhaust seeping through the screens
Claustrophobic trap, it seems. Why?

Happy laughter of little ones
Etched only in memory,
Where have all the flowers gone
Plucked away so cruelly. Why?

Pretty once, all wrinkled now
Deep lines etched in grief
It shows, it shows
God only knows. Why?

Old dreams shattered, like the
Austro-Hungarian Empire, battered!
I walked through the fire
And am charred by its mire. Why?

With a difficult journey ahead
In this world of disarray
Mankind has been misled
And *really* we *all* know why.

My poem reflects the general condition of the world as it is now, from my point of view (literally). Its sentiment may be of some comfort to you, since you have already departed from this world.

~/~

Did you know I need my computer in order to find my daily bearings? I click on "Uncharted Waters" first thing, and only have to read a few random lines to find myself instantly grounded and deeply connected to my "insane" existence (as some have labeled it), and realize that I had quite a life? But you'd be aghast to know that I work in my pajamas until noon.

I leave the cemetery with a mellow, bittersweet feeling, but this time I hear, *"Emily, du hast wirklich etwas gemacht aus Dir"* - "Emily, you really have made something out of yourself. I am glad you have broken the silence. You have done well, my dear, even you work in your pajamas."

~/~

P.S. I am still hoping to learn about an elusive piece of informati Mother had once attempted, but could not bring herself to press, obviously wanting to share a particularly difficult tim her life, *"Sitz Dich hin, Emily. Ich muss Dir etwas sagen. Wann noch nicht im Bilde warst..."* - "Sit down Emily. I have somet to tell you. A long time ago, when you weren't in the picture born yet) ..."

Mother never managed to complete the sentence.